S0-BCA-802

FOR ORGANS, PIANOS & ELECTRONIC KEYBOARDS

E-Z PLAY TODAY

88

THE BEATLES GREATEST

ISBN 0-634-09324-X

HAL•LEONARD® CORPORATION

7777 W. BLUEMOUND RD. P.O. BOX 13819 MILWAUKEE, WI 53213

Visit Hal Leonard Online at
www.halleonard.com

CONTENTS

Across the Universe

Registration 8
Rhythm: Rock

Words and Music by John Lennon
and Paul McCartney

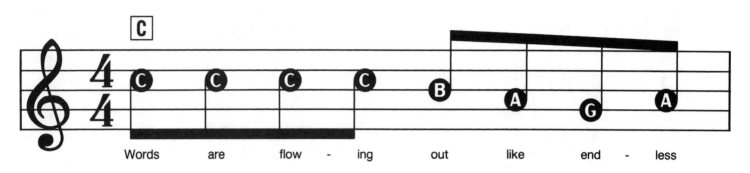

Words are flow - ing out like end - less

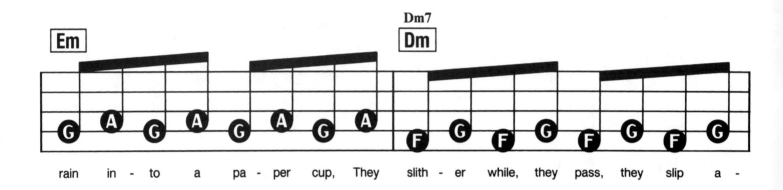

rain in - to a pa - per cup, They slith - er while, they pass, they slip a -

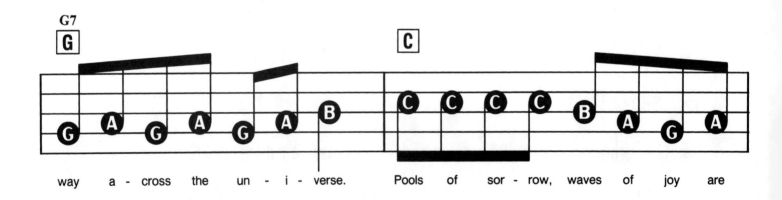

way a - cross the un - i - verse. Pools of sor - row, waves of joy are

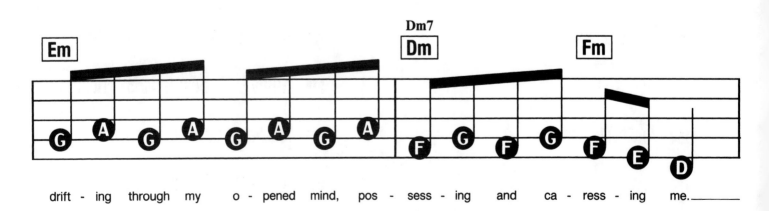

drift - ing through my o - pened mind, pos - sess - ing and ca - ress - ing me.____

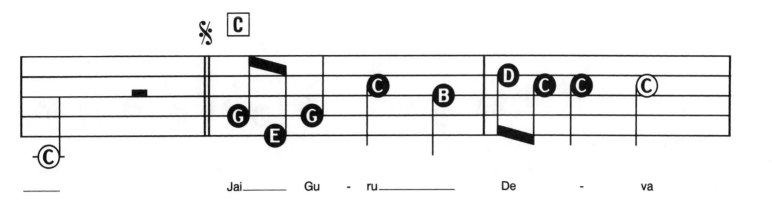

Jai_____ Gu - ru_____ De - va

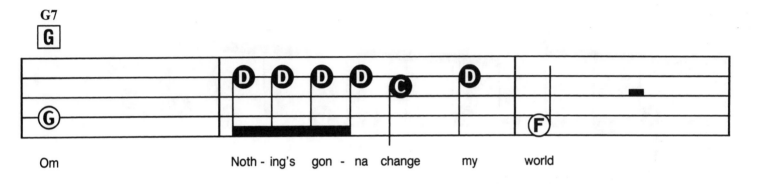

Om   Noth - ing's gon - na change   my   world

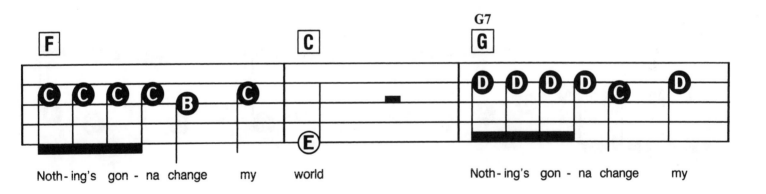

Noth - ing's gon - na change my   world   Noth - ing's gon - na change   my

To Coda 1

To Coda 2

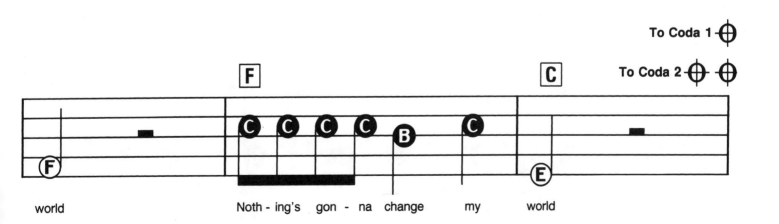

world   Noth - ing's gon - na change   my   world

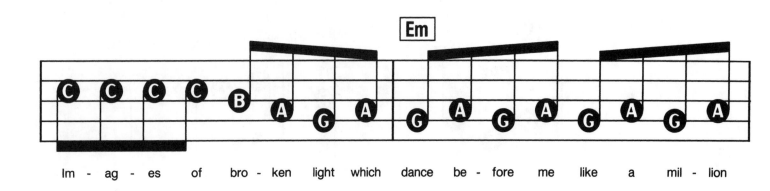

Im - ag - es   of   bro - ken   light   which   dance   be - fore   me   like   a   mil - lion

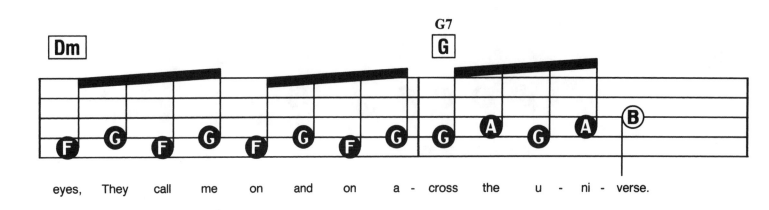

eyes,   They   call   me   on   and   on   a - cross   the   u - ni - verse.

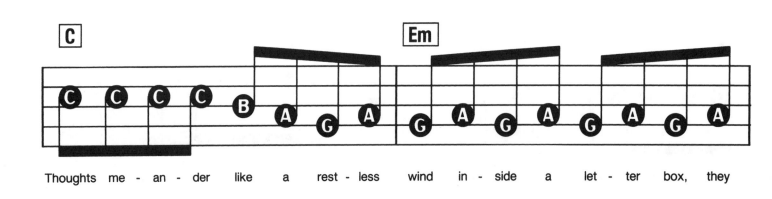

Thoughts   me - an - der   like   a   rest - less   wind   in - side   a   let - ter   box,   they

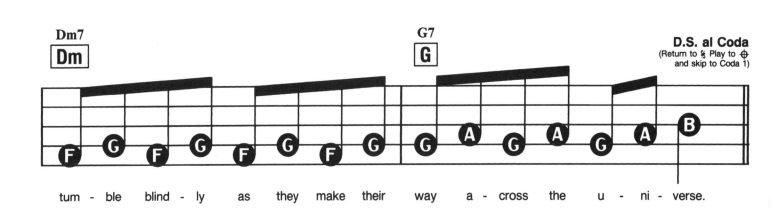

tum - ble   blind - ly   as   they   make   their   way   a - cross   the   u - ni - verse.

CODA 1

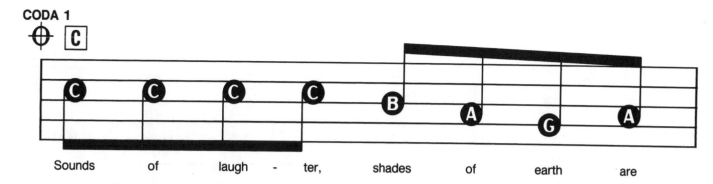

Sounds of laugh - ter, shades of earth are

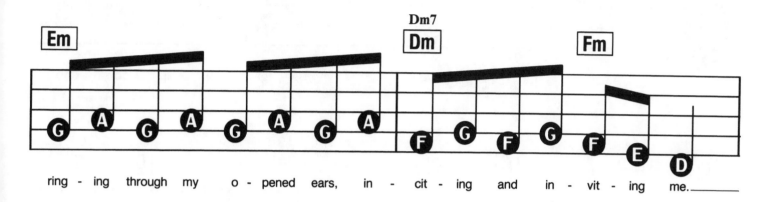

ring - ing through my o - pened ears, in - cit - ing and in - vit - ing me.____

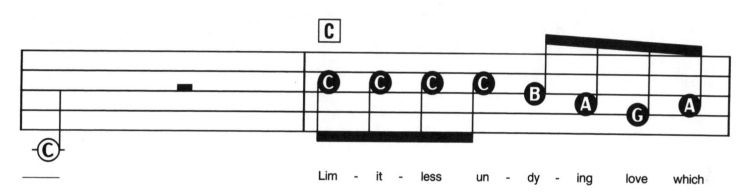

Lim - it - less un - dy - ing love which

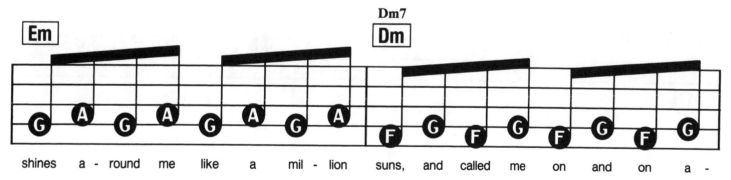

shines a - round me like a mil - lion suns, and called me on and on a -

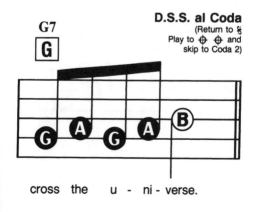

cross the u - ni - verse.

D.S.S. al Coda
(Return to ⅀
Play to ⊕ ⊕ and
skip to Coda 2)

CODA 2

Repeat and Fade

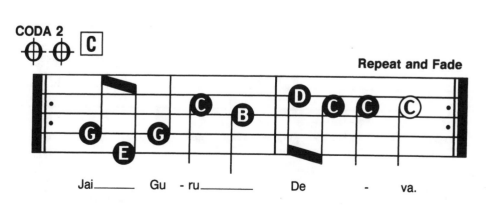

Jai____ Gu - ru____ De - va.

Ain't She Sweet

Registration 3
Rhythm: Fox Trot or Swing

Words by Jack Yellen
Music by Milton Ager

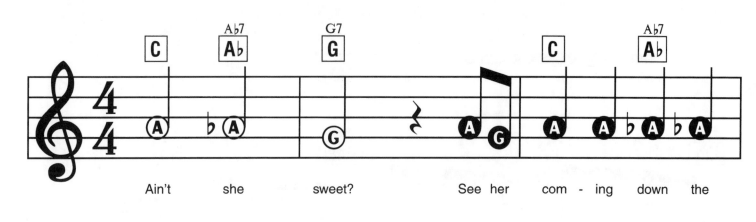

Ain't she sweet? See her com - ing down the

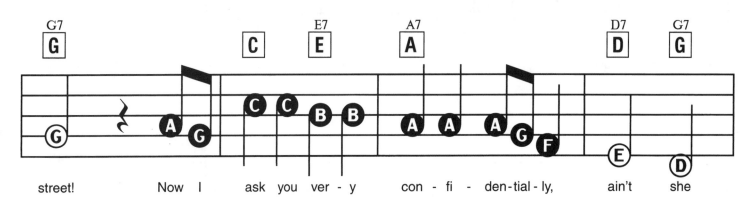

street! Now I ask you ver - y con - fi - den - tial - ly, ain't she

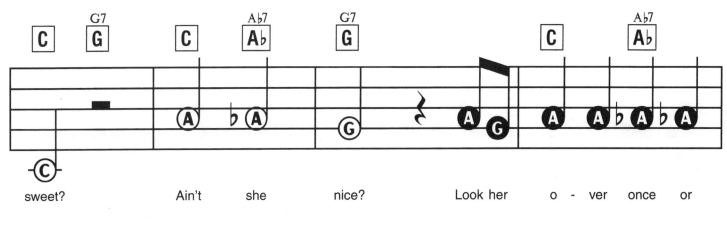

sweet? Ain't she nice? Look her o - ver once or

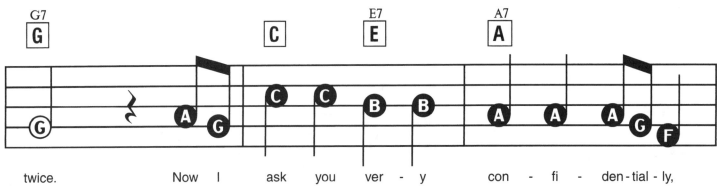

twice. Now I ask you ver - y con - fi - den - tial - ly,

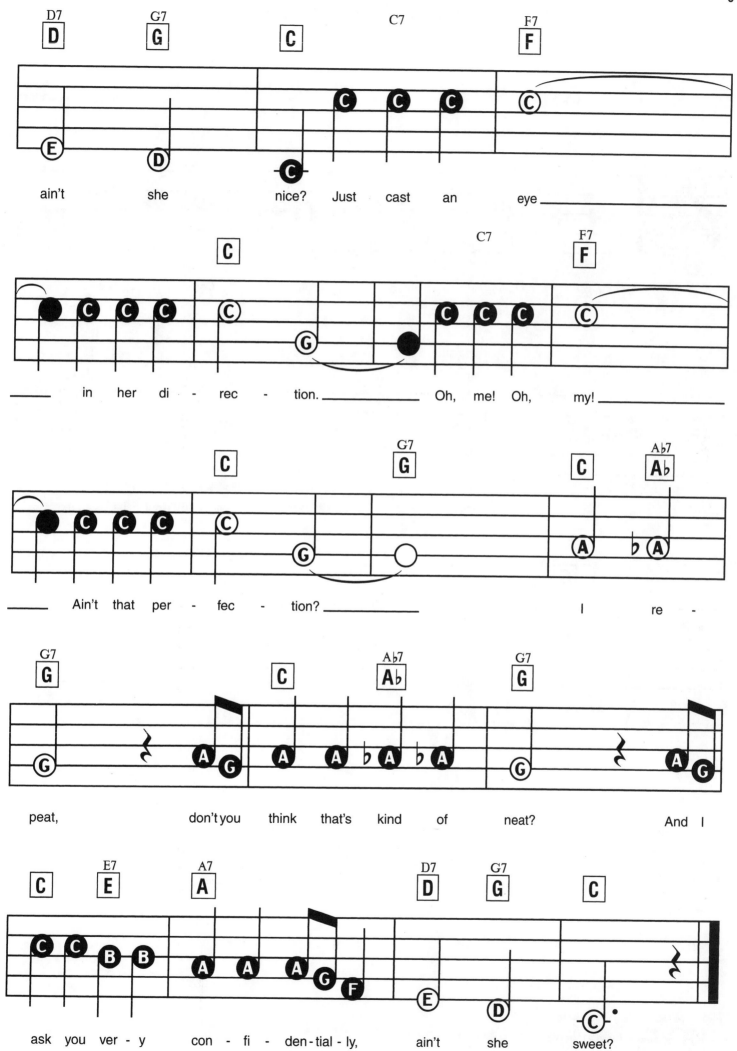

All Together Now

Registration 7
Rhythm: Shuffle or Rock

Words and Music by John Lennon
and Paul McCartney

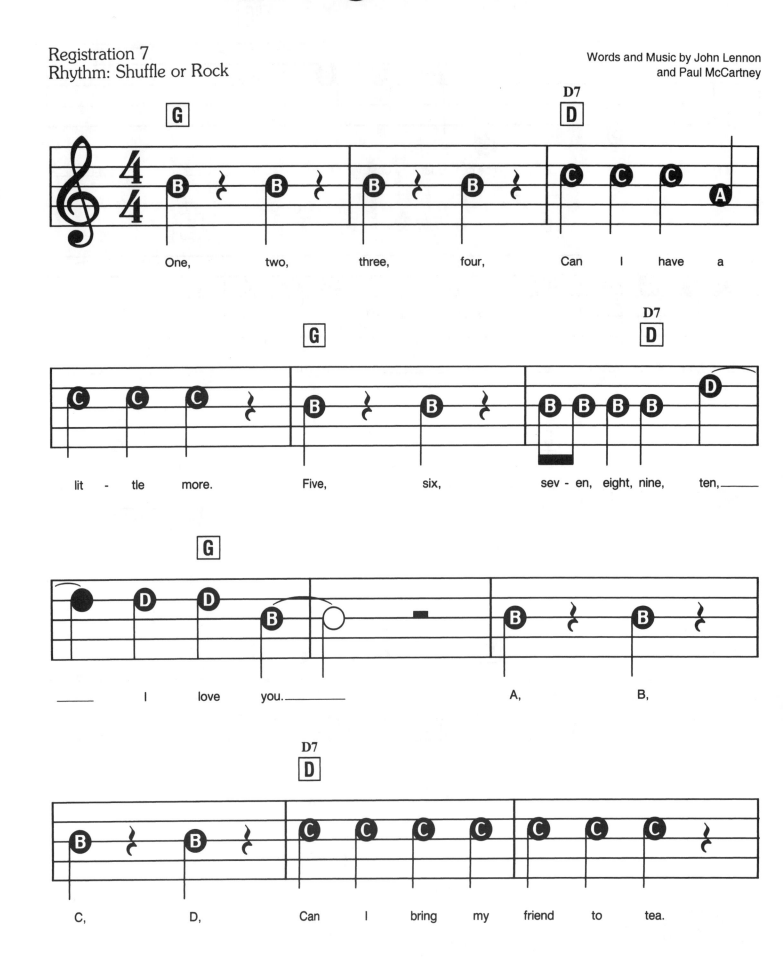

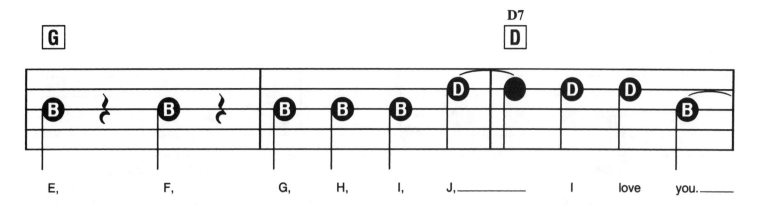

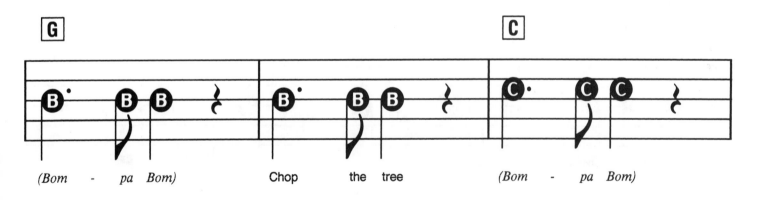

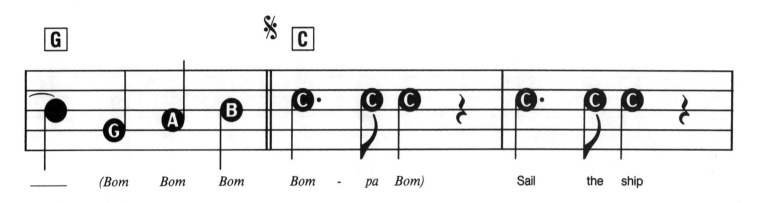

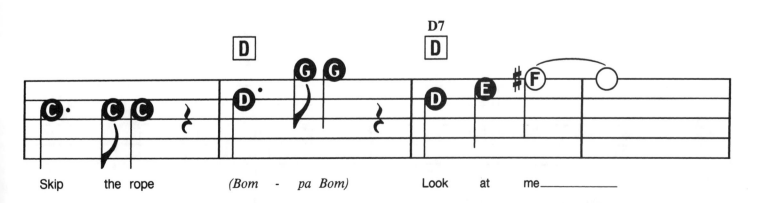

12

To Coda ⊕ G

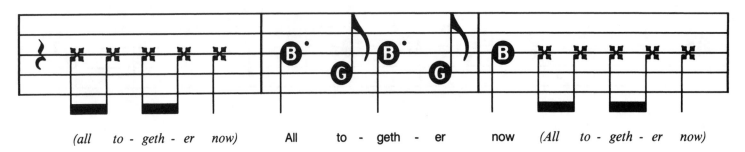

(all to - geth - er now)   All   to - geth - er   now   (All to - geth - er now)

D7
D

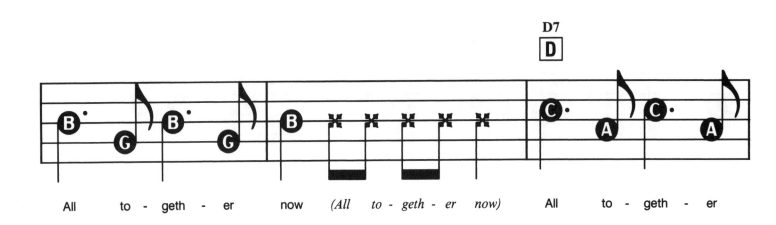

All   to - geth - er   now   (All to - geth - er now)   All   to - geth - er

G

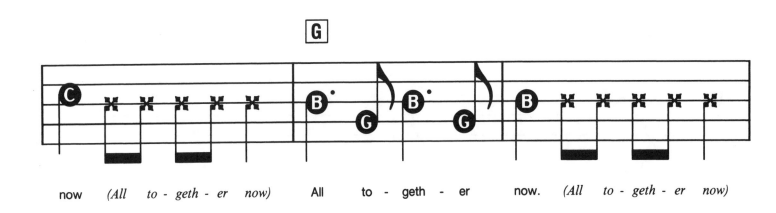

now   (All to - geth - er now)   All   to - geth - er   now.   (All to - geth - er now)

D7
D

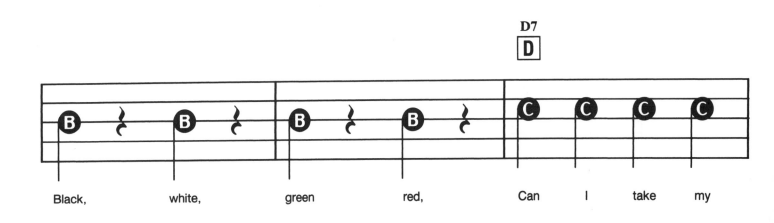

Black,   white,   green   red,   Can   I   take   my

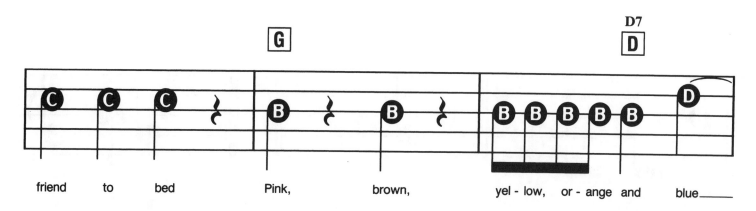

friend   to   bed   Pink,   brown,   yel - low,   or - ange and   blue_____

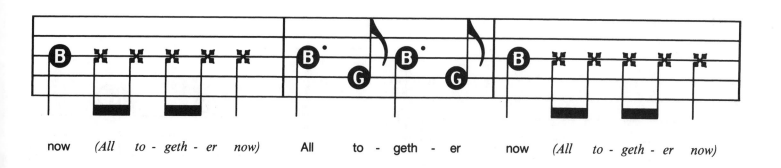

_____   I   love   you._____   (All   to - geth - er   now)   All   to - geth - er

now   (All   to - geth - er   now)   All   to - geth - er   now   (All   to - geth - er   now)

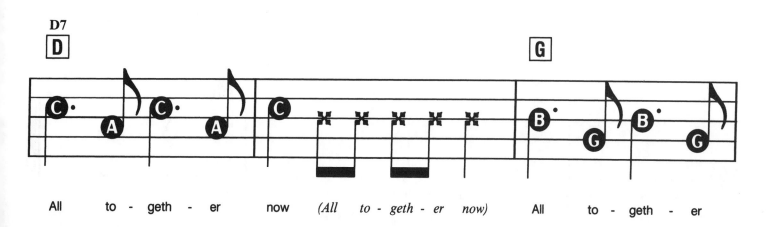

All   to - geth - er   now   (All - to - geth - er   now)   All   to - geth - er

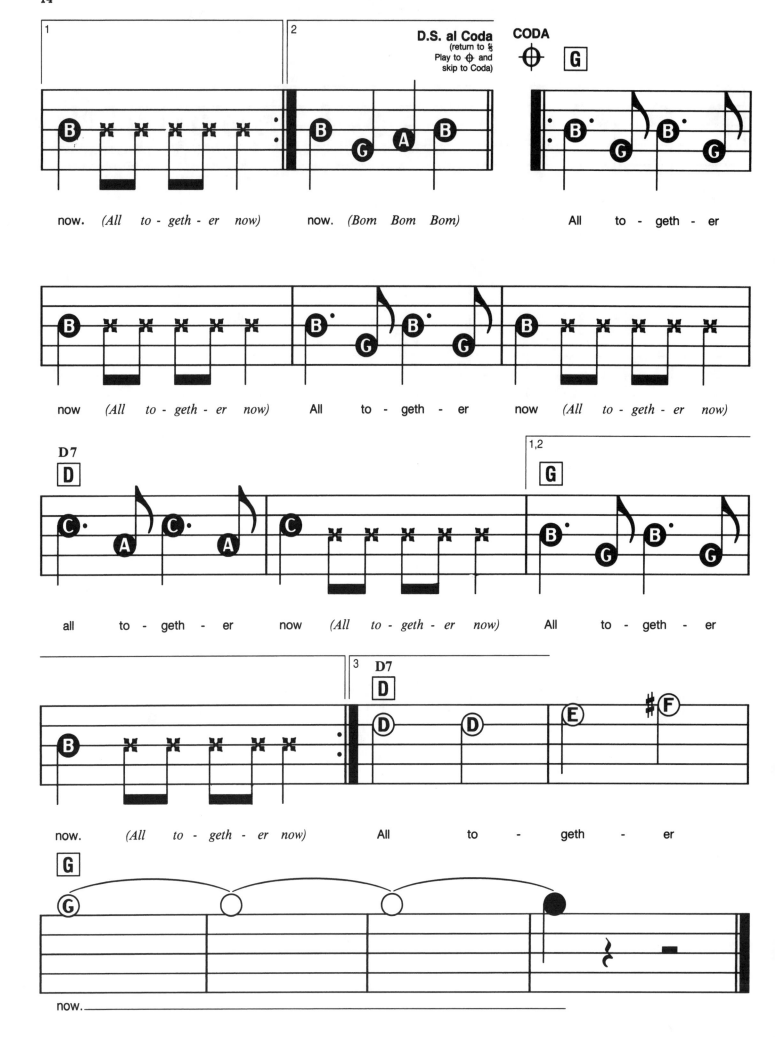

All You Need Is Love

Registration 5
Rhythm: Shuffle or Swing

Words and Music by John Lennon
and Paul McCartney

16

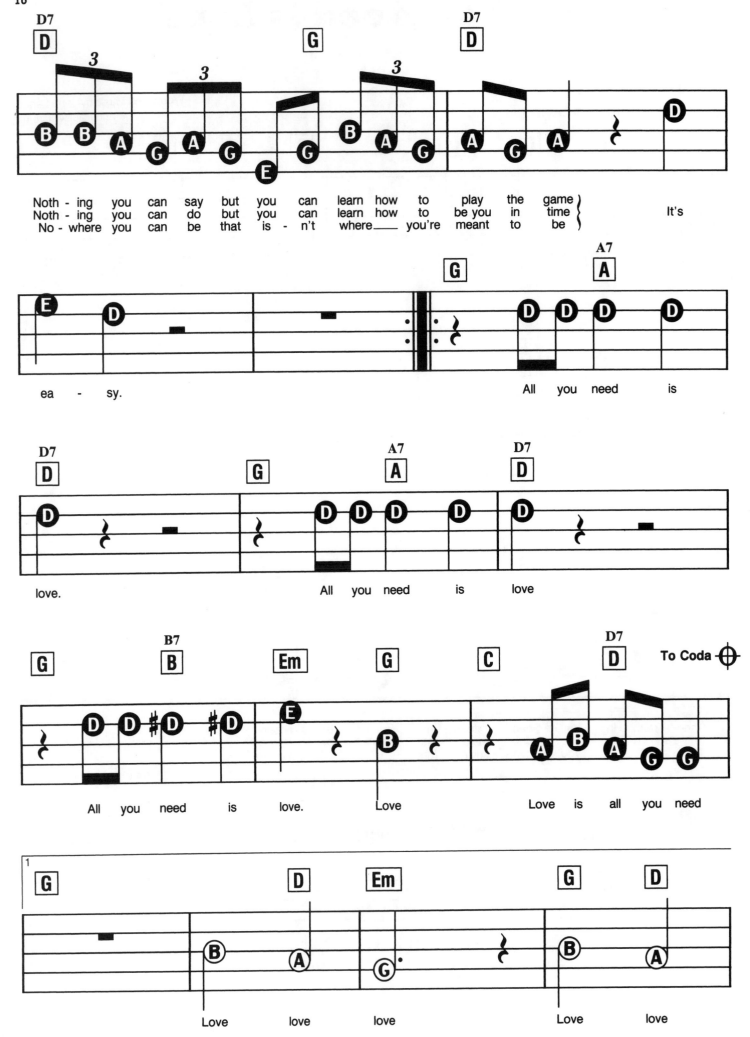

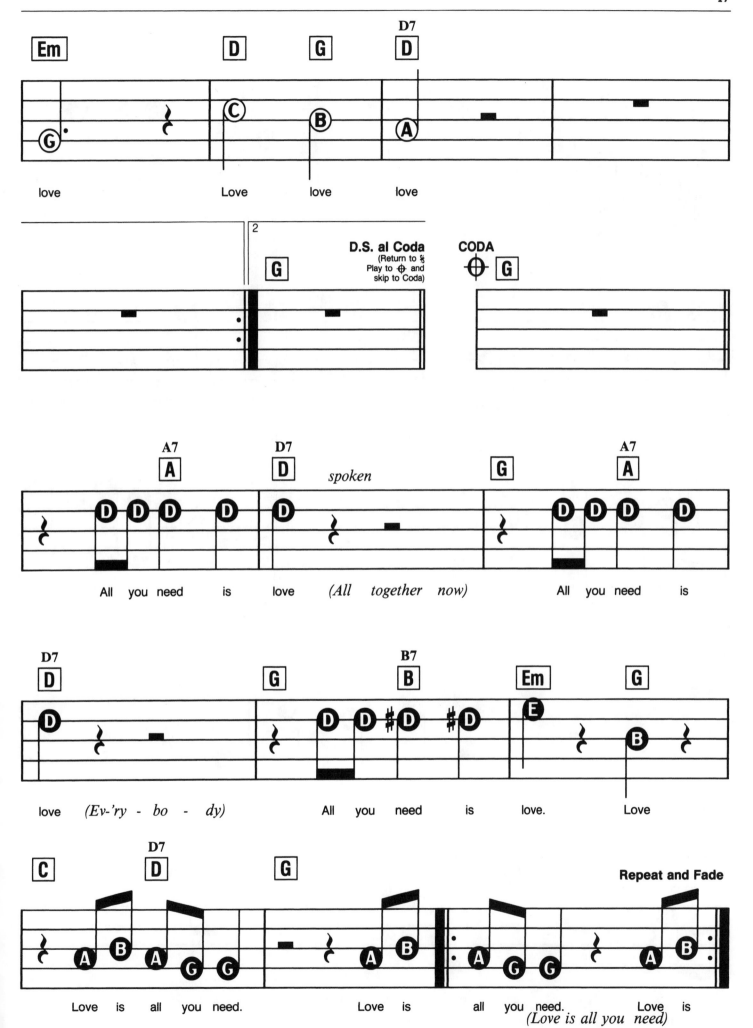

Baby You're a Rich Man

Registration 4
Rhythm: Rock

Words and Music by John Lennon
and Paul McCartney

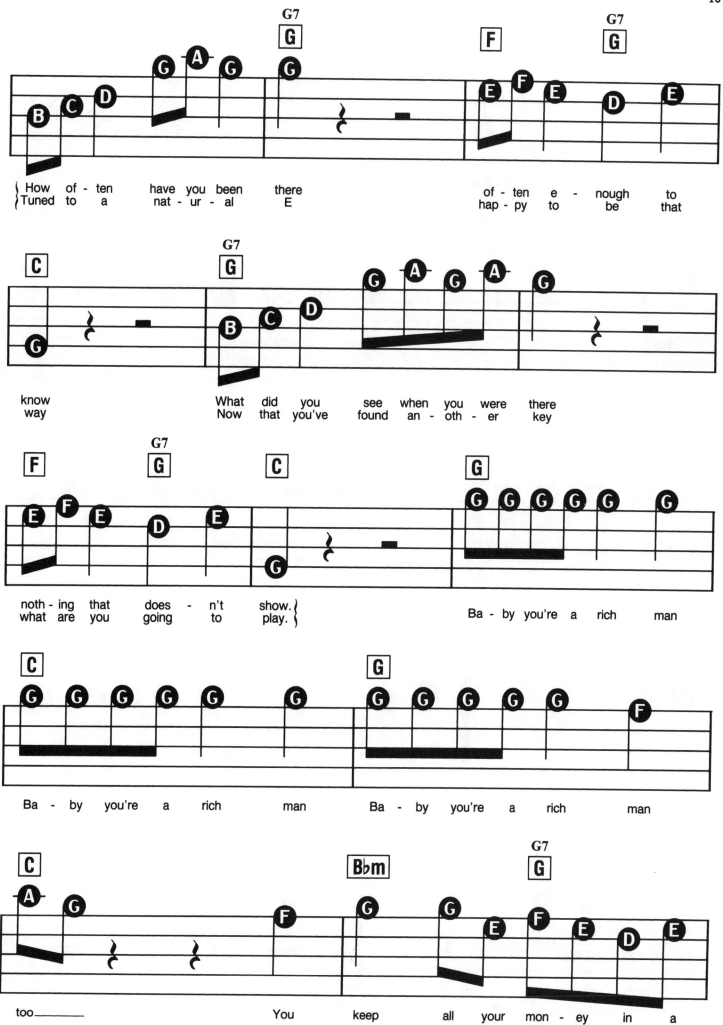

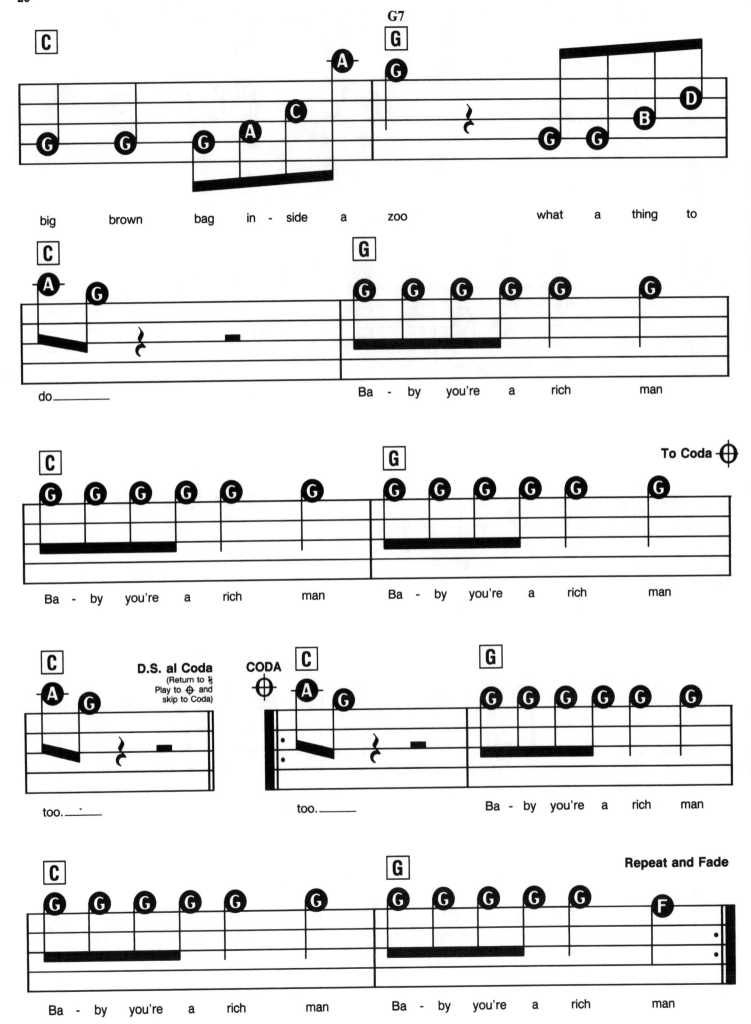

The Ballad of John and Yoko

Registration 5
Rhythm: Rock

Words and Music by John Lennon
and Paul McCartney

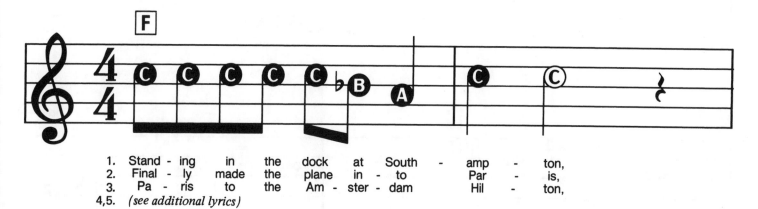

1. Stand - ing in the dock at South - amp - ton,
2. Final - ly made the plane in - to Par - is,
3. Pa - ris to the Am - ster - dam Hil - ton,
4,5. *(see additional lyrics)*

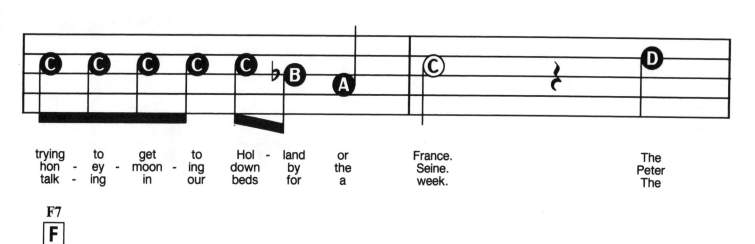

trying to get to Hol - land or France. The
hon - ey - moon - ing down by the Seine. Peter
talk - ing in our beds for a week. The

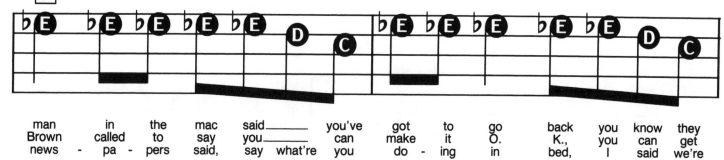

man in the mac said_____ you've got to go back you know they
Brown called to say you_____ can make it O. K., you can get
news - pa - pers said, say what're you do - ing in bed, I said we're

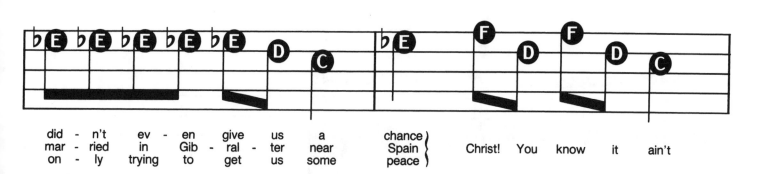

did - n't ev - en give us a chance)
mar - ried in Gib - ral - ter near Spain } Christ! You know it ain't
on - ly trying to get us some peace)

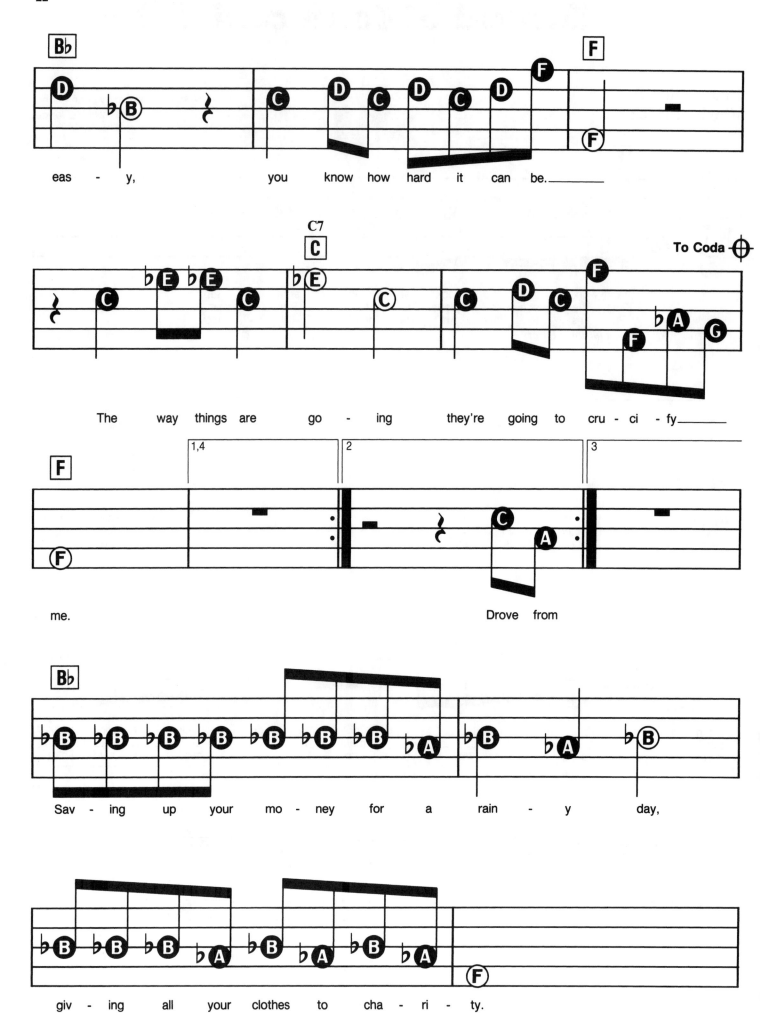

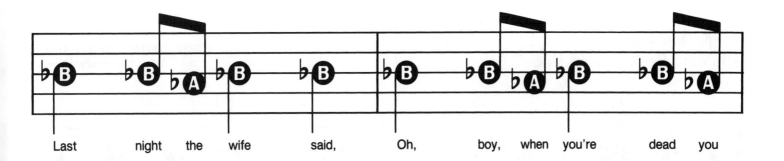

Last night the wife said, Oh, boy, when you're dead you

C7

D.C. al Coda
(Return to beginning [4th verse]
Play to ⊕ and skip to Coda)

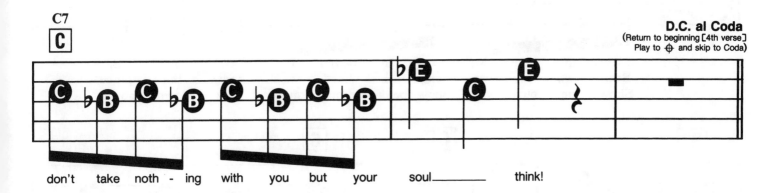

don't take noth - ing with you but your soul___ think!

CODA

C7

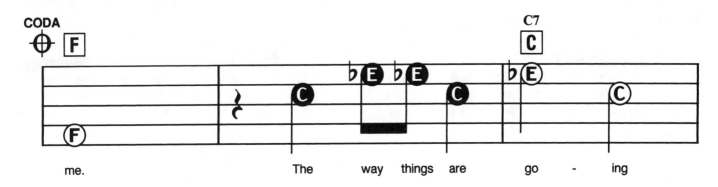

me.   The way things are go - ing

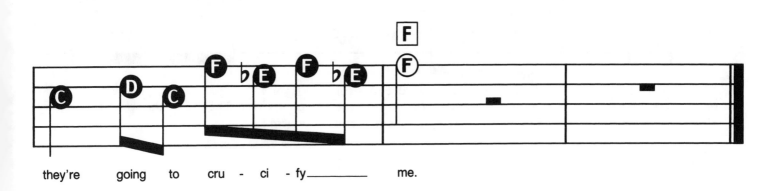

they're going to cru - ci - fy___ me.

4. Made a lightning trip to Vienna,
Eating chocolate cake in a bag.
The newspapers said she's gone to his head,
They look just like two Gurus in drag.

5. Caught the early plane back to London,
Fifty acorns tied in a sack.
The men from the press said we wish you success,
It's good to have the both of you back.

Back in the U.S.S.R.

Registration 4
Rhythm: Rock or Jazz Rock

Words and Music by John Lennon
and Paul McCartney

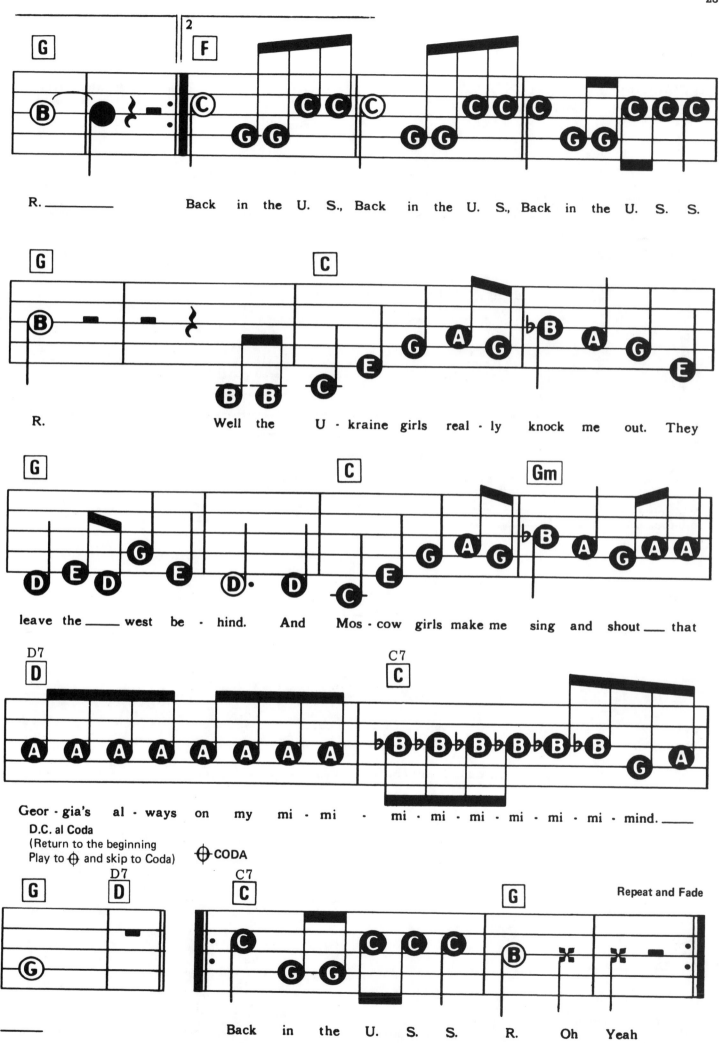

Because

Registration 1
Rhythm: Rock or Jazz Rock

Words and Music by John Lennon
and Paul McCartney

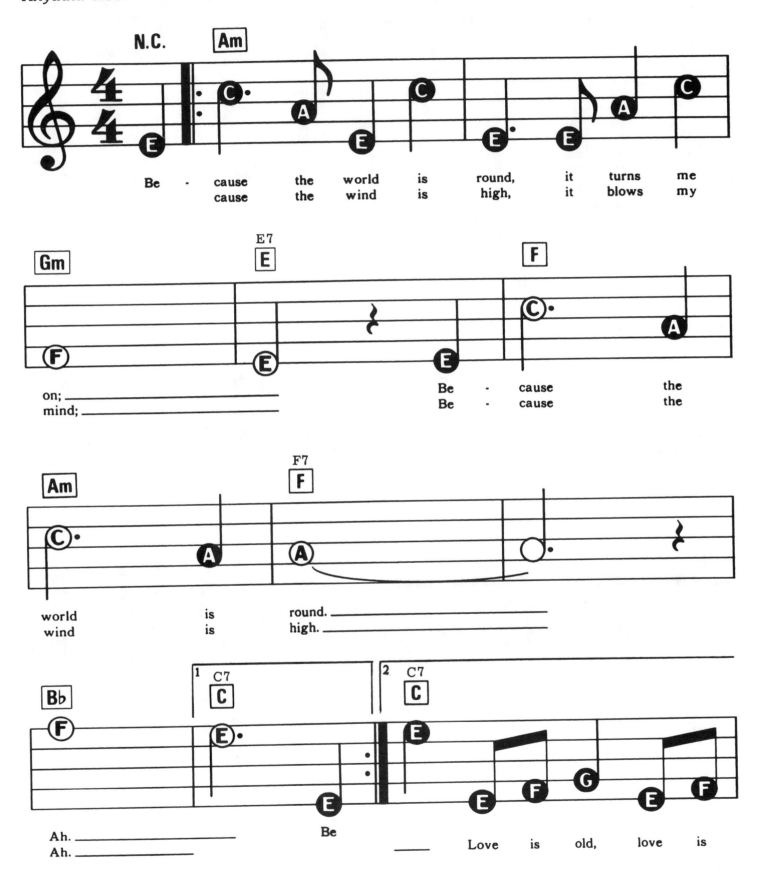

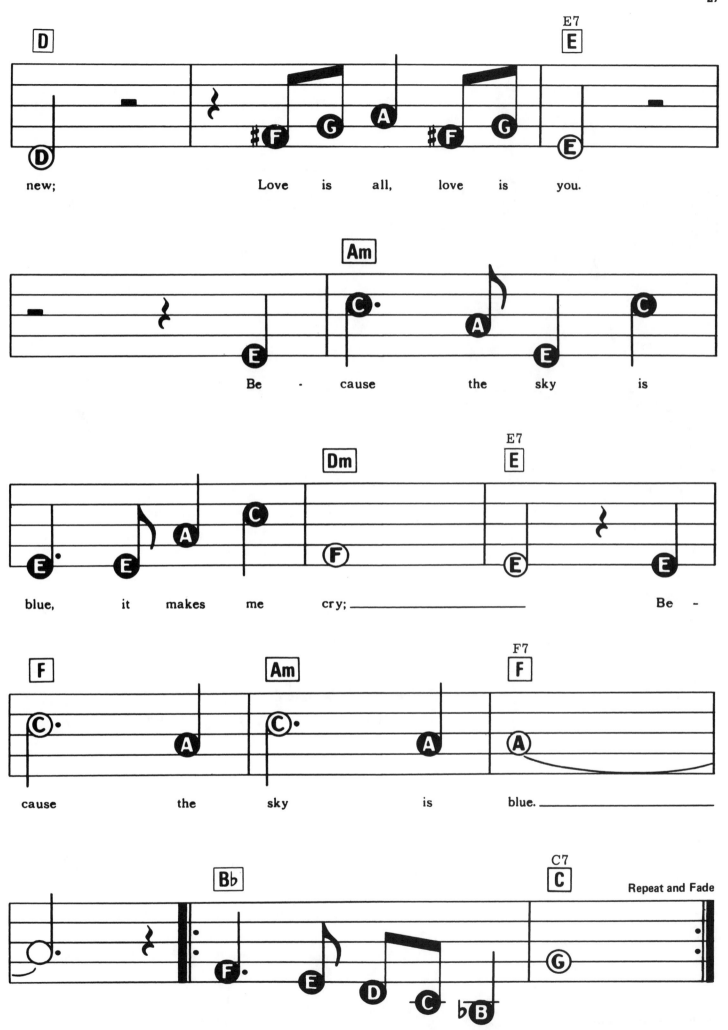

Birthday

Registration 2
Rhythm: Rock

Words and Music by John Lennon
and Paul McCartney

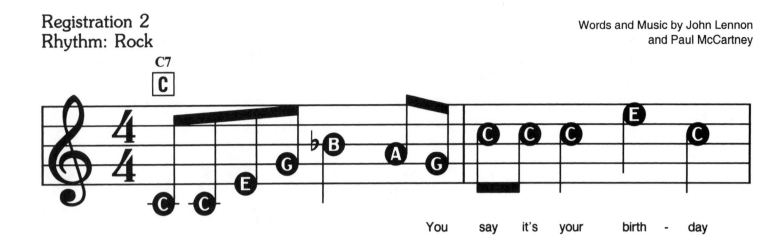

You say it's your birth - day

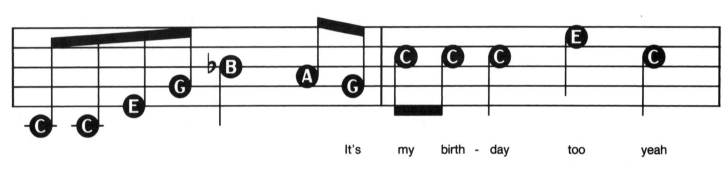

It's my birth - day too yeah

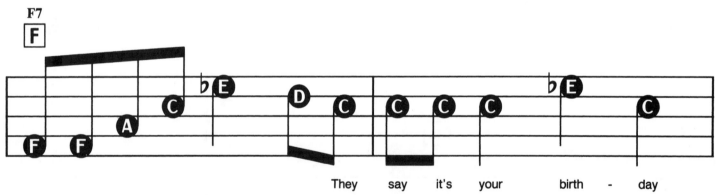

They say it's your birth - day

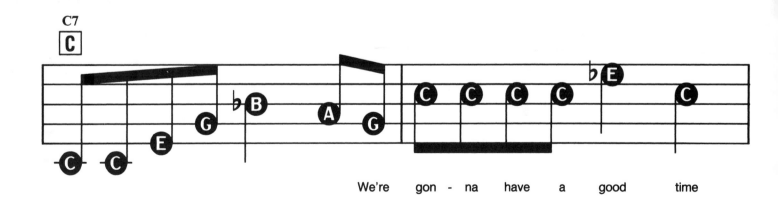

We're gon - na have a good time

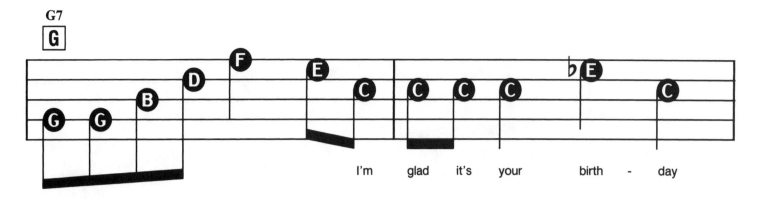

I'm glad it's your birth - day

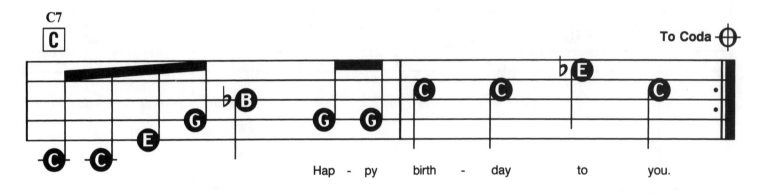

To Coda ⊕

Hap - py birth - day to you.

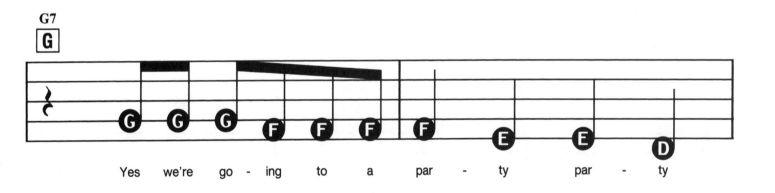

Yes we're go - ing to a par - ty par - ty

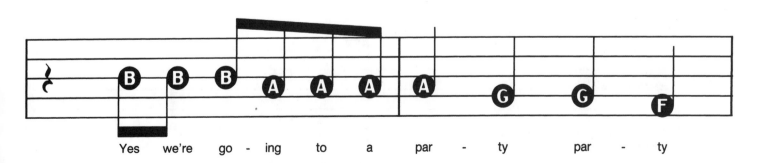

Yes we're go - ing to a par - ty par - ty

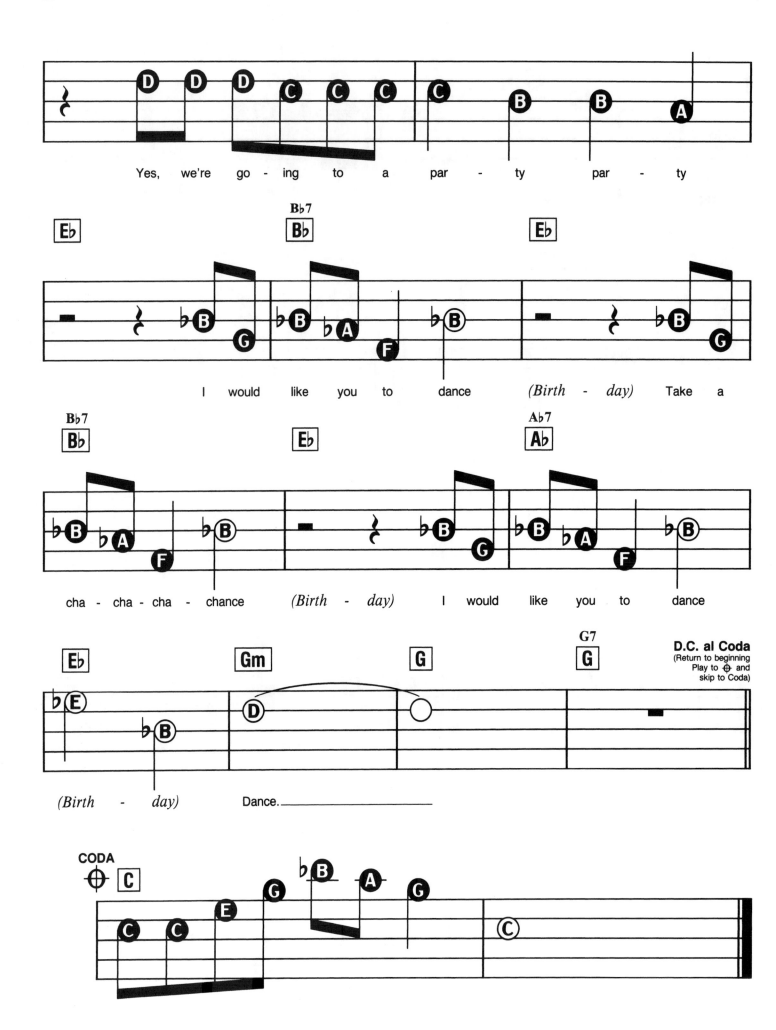

30

Don't Let Me Down

Registration 2
Rhythm: Rock

Words and Music by John Lennon
and Paul McCartney

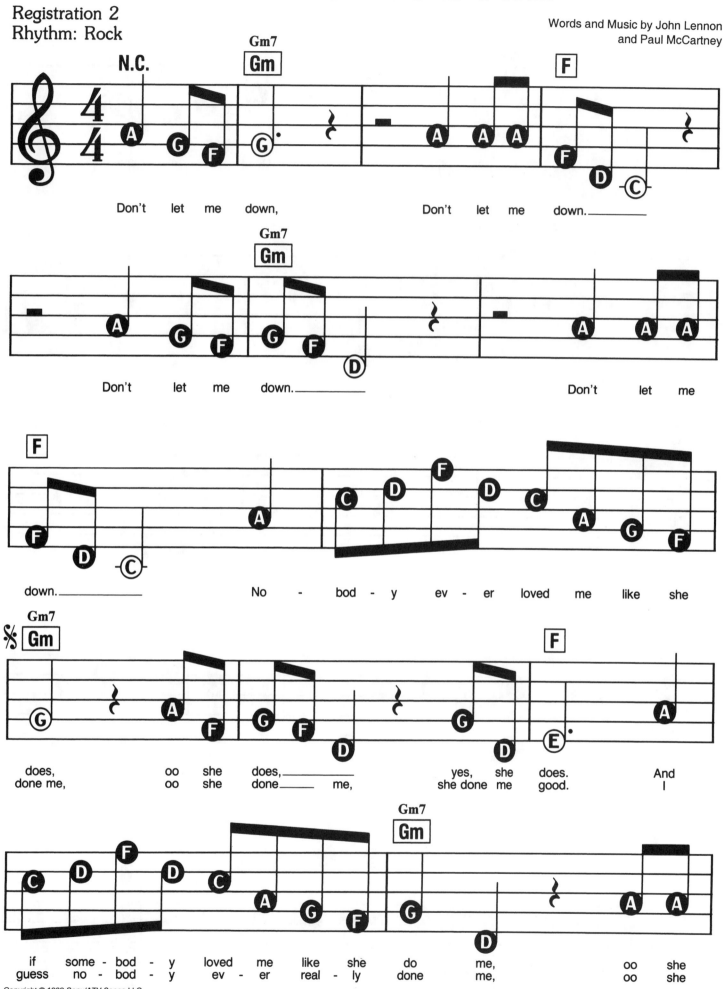

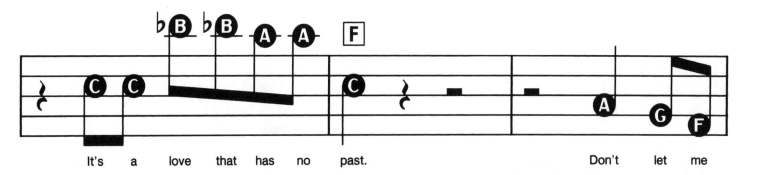

It's a love that has no past. Don't let me

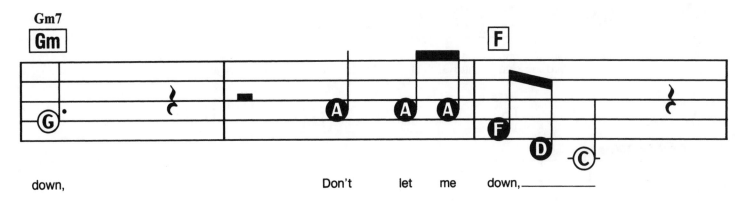

down, Don't let me down,_____

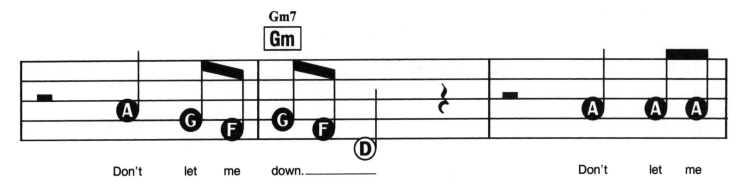

Don't let me down._____ Don't let me

D.S. al Coda
(Return to 𝄋
Play to ⊕ and
skip to Coda)

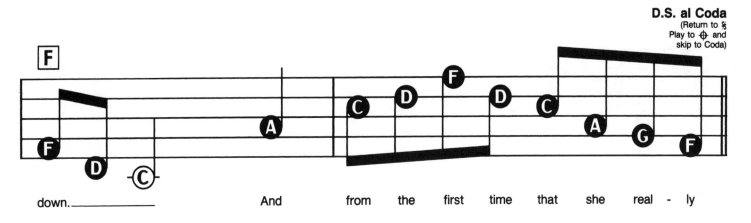

down._____ And from the first time that she real - ly

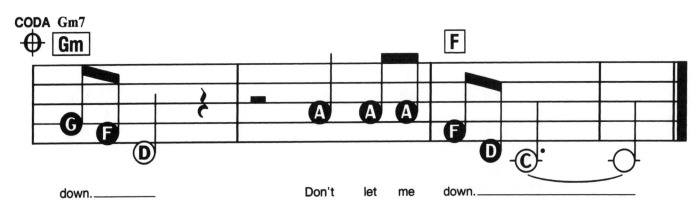

down._____ Don't let me down._____

Blackbird

Registration 8
Rhythm: Rock

Words and Music by John Lennon
and Paul McCartney

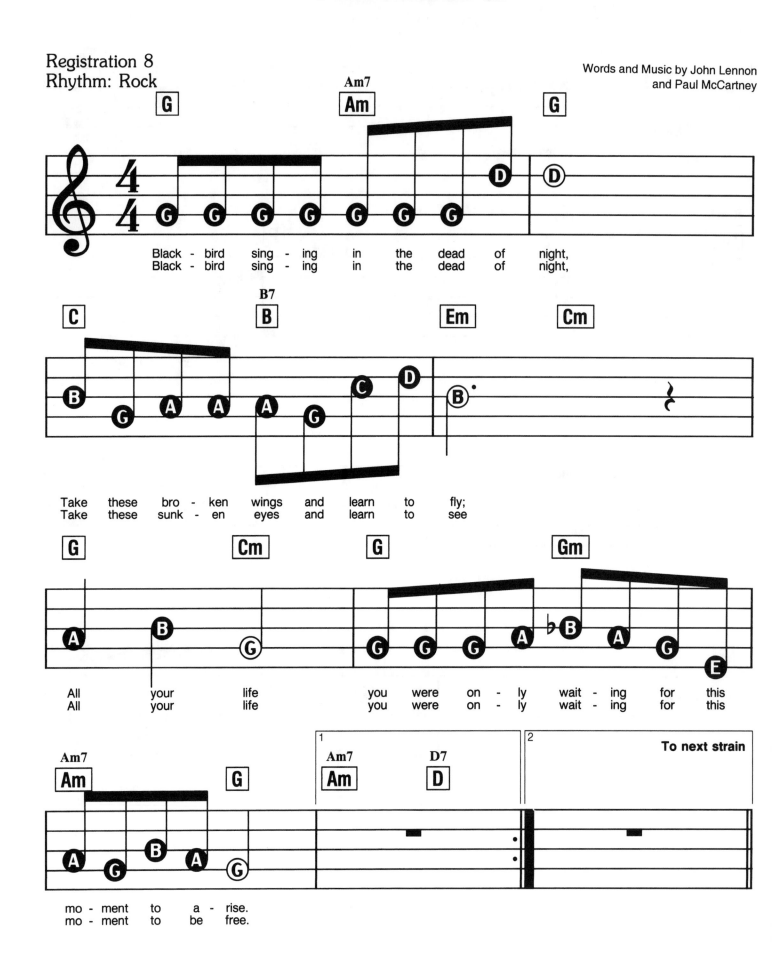

Black - bird sing - ing in the dead of night,
Black - bird sing - ing in the dead of night,

Take these bro - ken wings and learn to fly;
Take these sunk - en eyes and learn to see

All your life you were on - ly wait - ing for this
All your life you were on - ly wait - ing for this

mo - ment to a - rise.
mo - ment to be free.

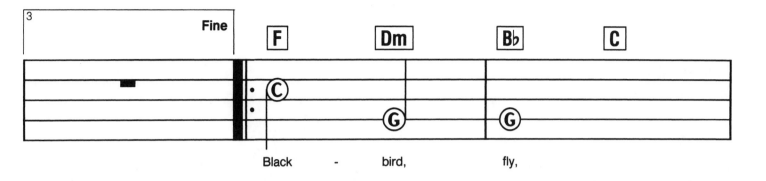

Black - bird, fly,

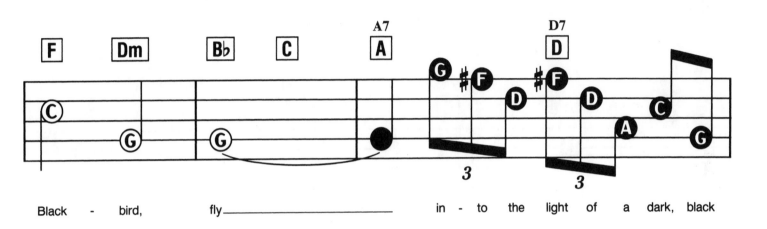

Black - bird, fly_____ in - to the light of a dark, black

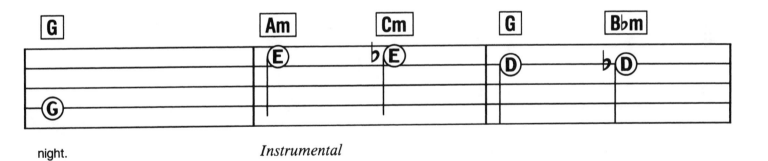

night.   *Instrumental*

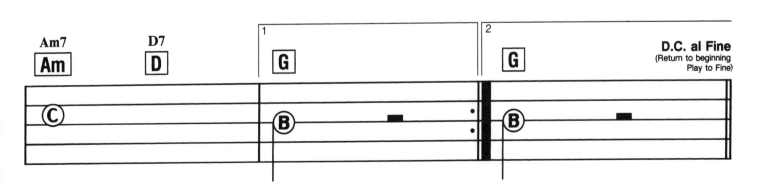

D.C. al Fine
(Return to beginning
Play to Fine)

Carry That Weight

Registration 1
Rhythm: Rock

Words and Music by John Lennon
and Paul McCartney

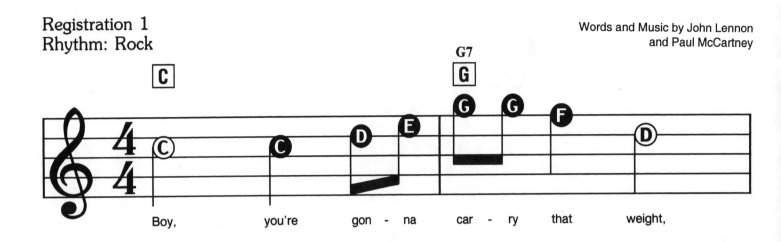

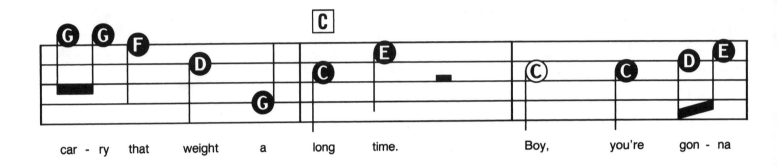

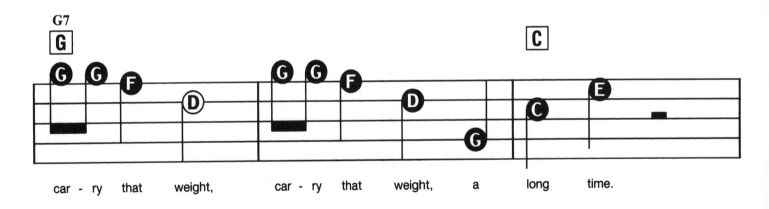

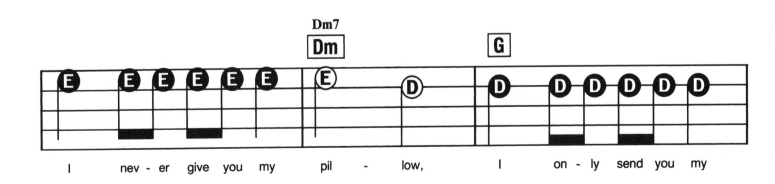

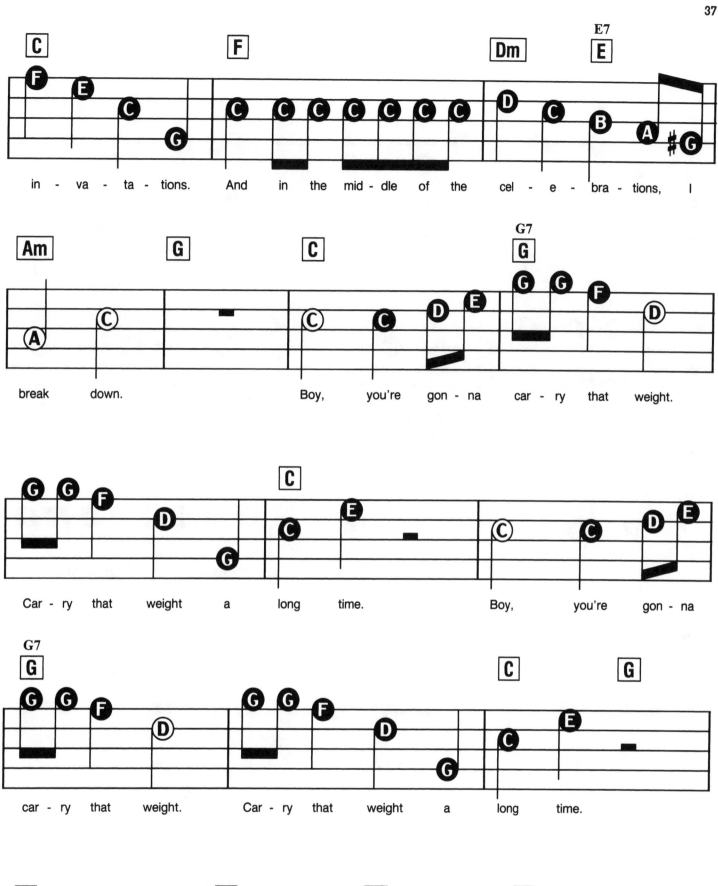

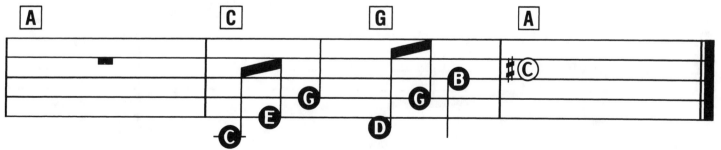

Come Together

Registration 2
Rhythm: Rock

Words and Music by John Lennon
and Paul McCartney

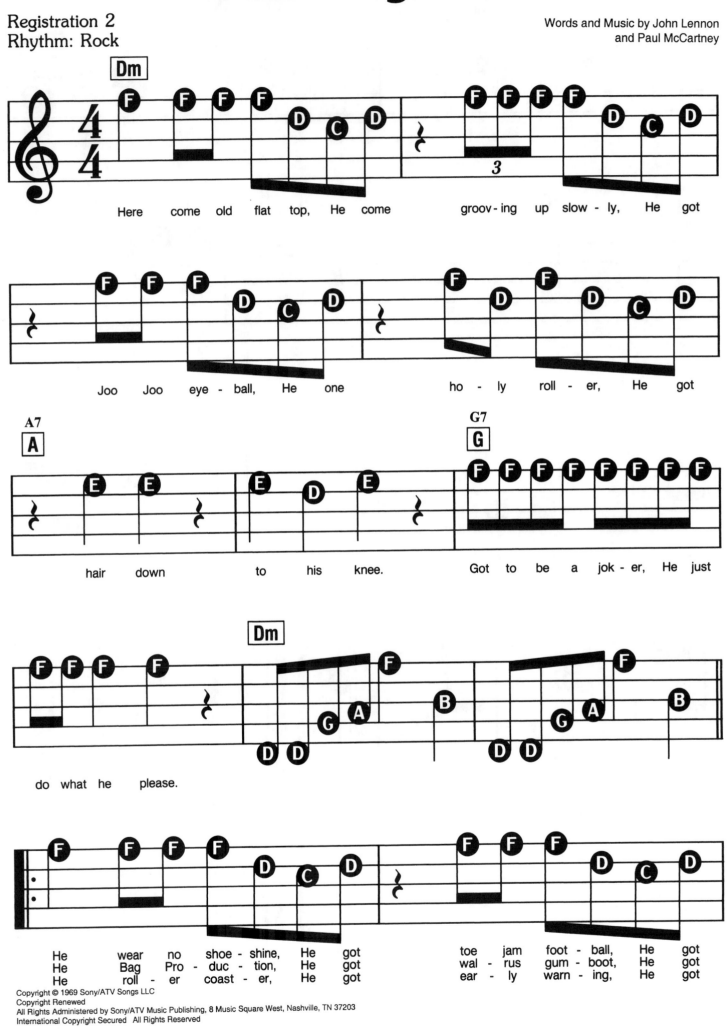

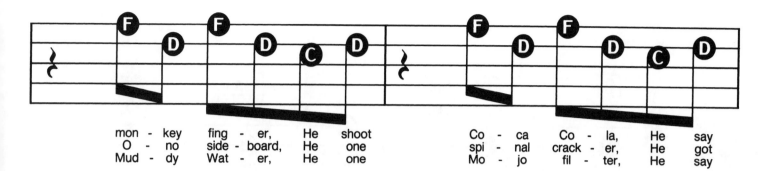

mon - key fing - er, He shoot
O - no side - board, He one
Mud - dy Wat - er, He one

Co - ca Co - la, He say
spi - nal crack - er, He say got
Mo - jo fil - ter, He say

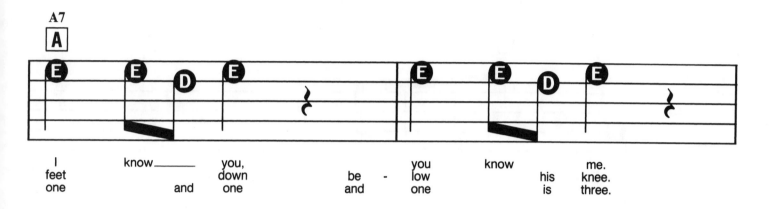

A7

I know_____ you, you know me.
feet one down be - low his knee.
one and one and one is three.

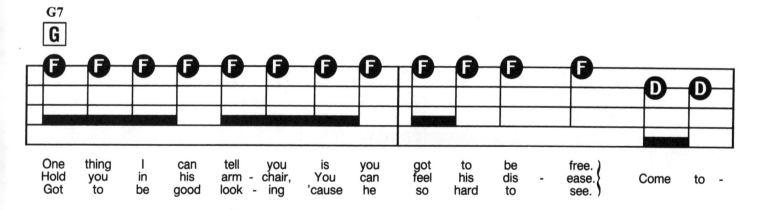

G7

One thing I can tell you is you got to be free.
Hold you in his arm - chair, You can feel his dis - ease.
Got to be good look - ing 'cause he so hard to see.

Come to -

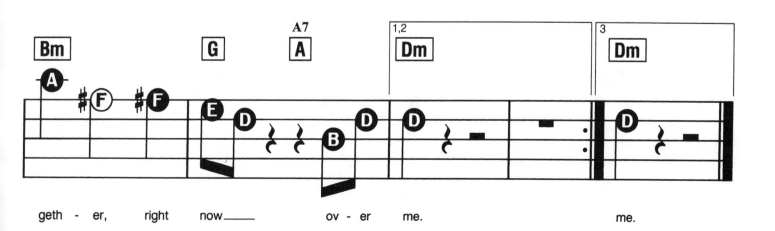

Bm **G** **A7** **A** **1,2 Dm** **3 Dm**

geth - er, right now_____ ov - er me.

me.

A Day in the Life

Registration 2
Rhythm: Rock

Words and Music by John Lennon
and Paul McCartney

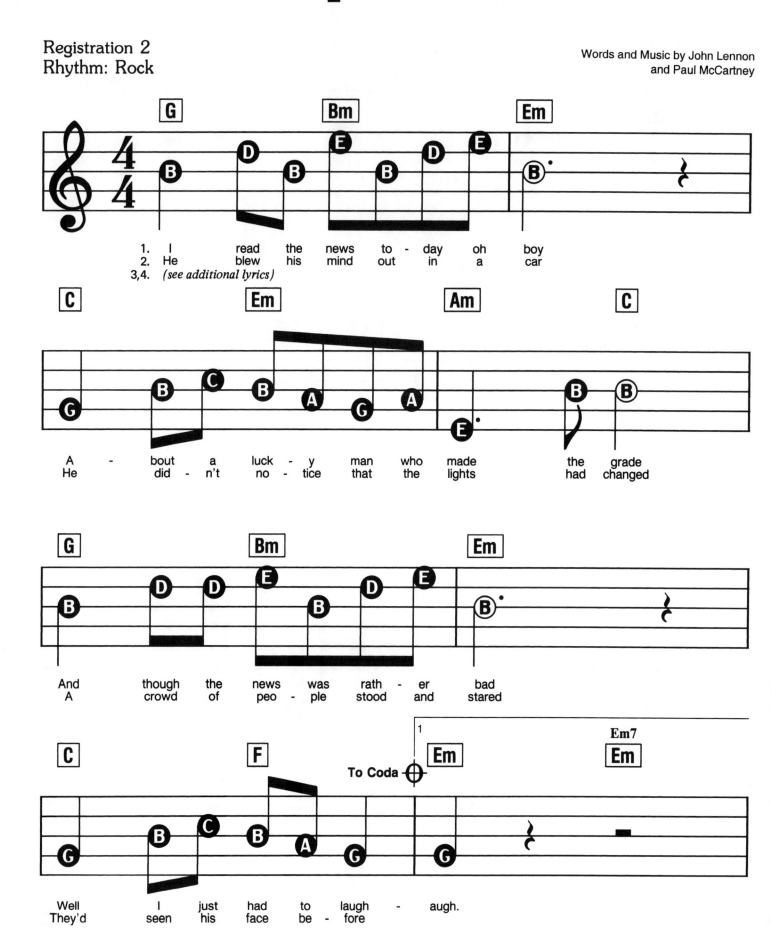

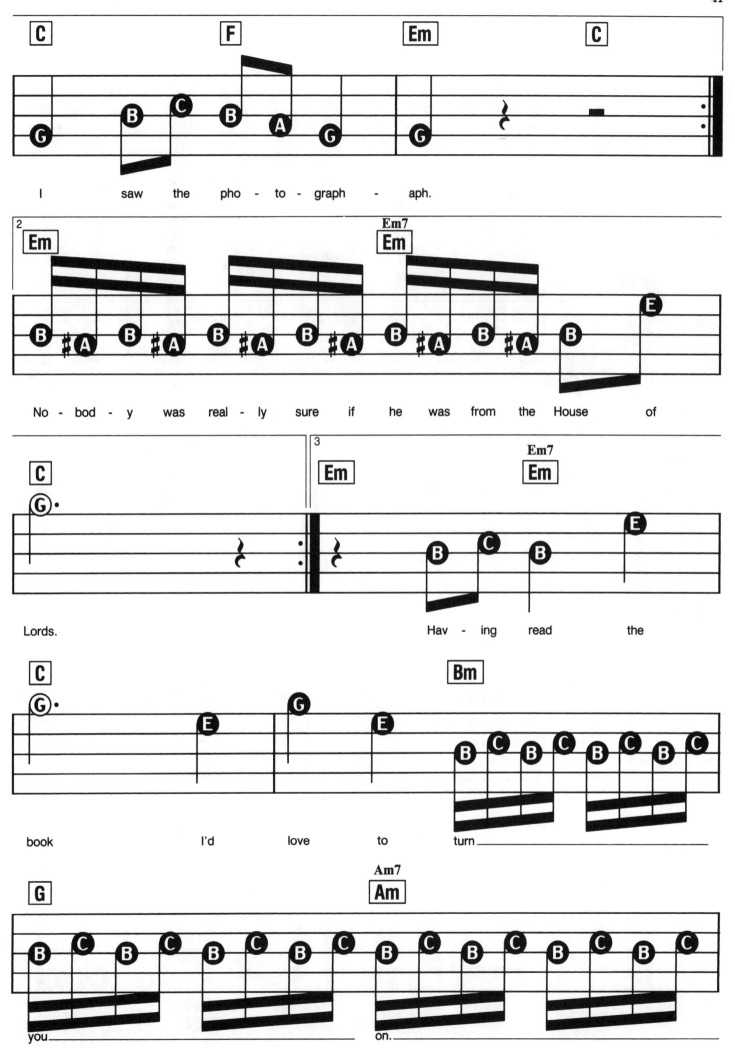

42

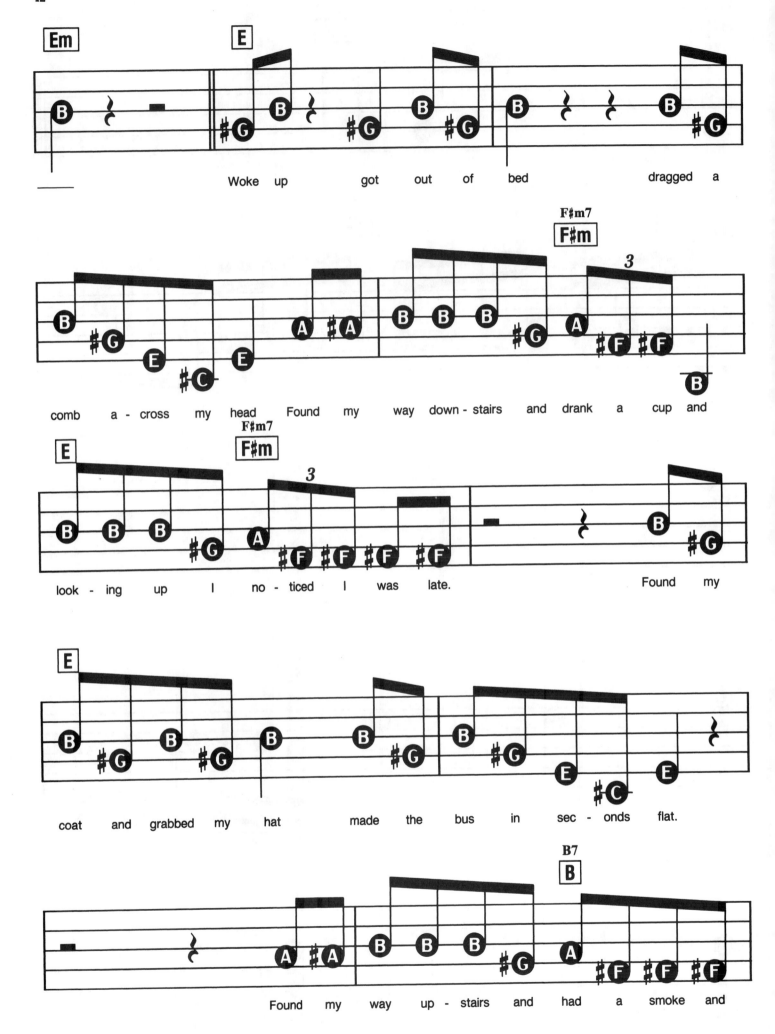

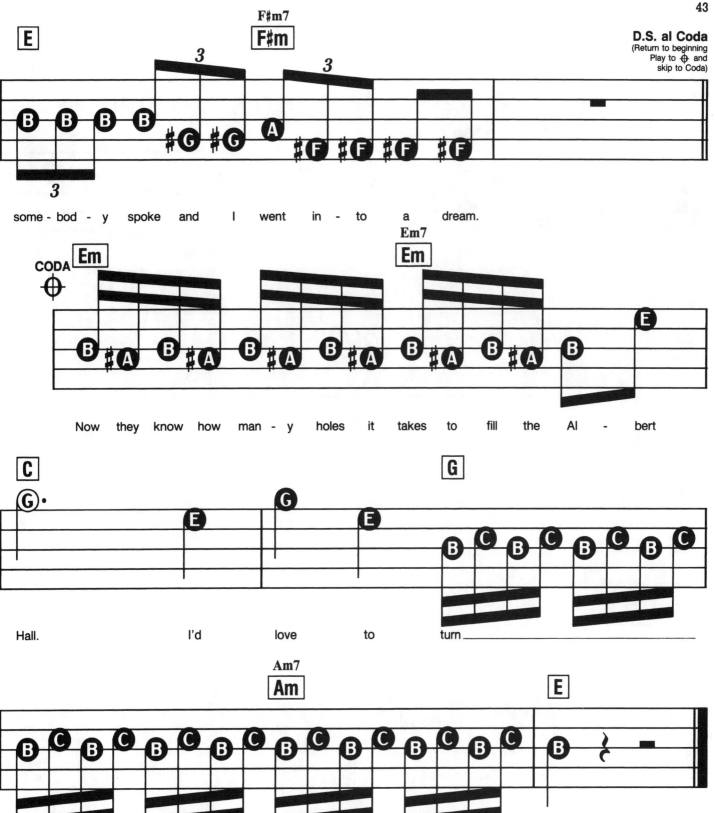

3. I saw a film today oh boy
The English army had just won the war
A crowd of people turned away
But I just had to look

4. I heard the news today oh boy
Four thousand holes in Blackburn Lancashire
And though the holes were rather small
They had to count them all

Dear Prudence

Registration 1
Rhythm: Rock

Words and Music by John Lennon
and Paul McCartney

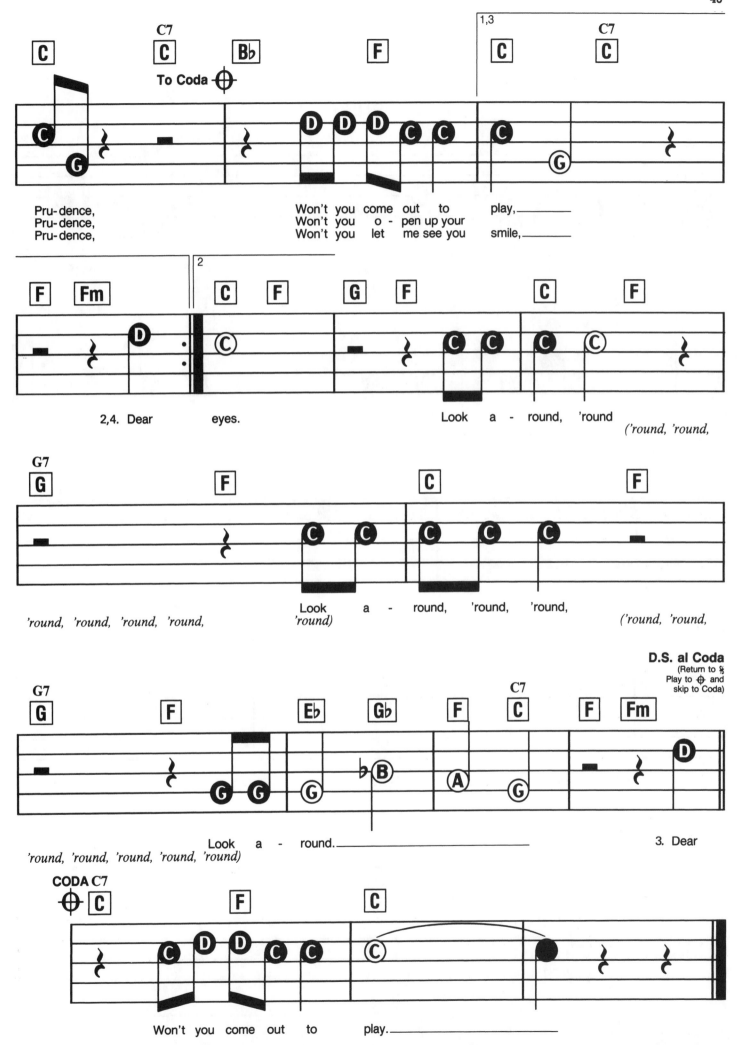

The End

Registration 4
Rhythm: 8 Beat or Rock

Words and Music by John Lennon
and Paul McCartney

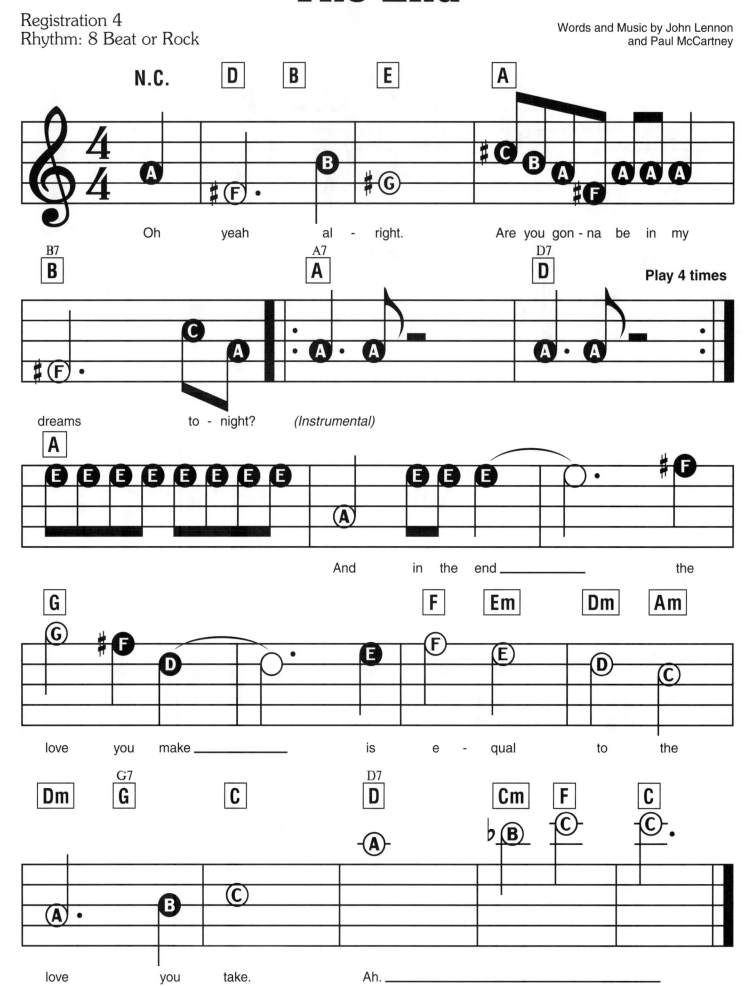

Fixing a Hole

Registration 2
Rhythm: Rock or Jazz Rock

Words and Music by John Lennon
and Paul McCartney

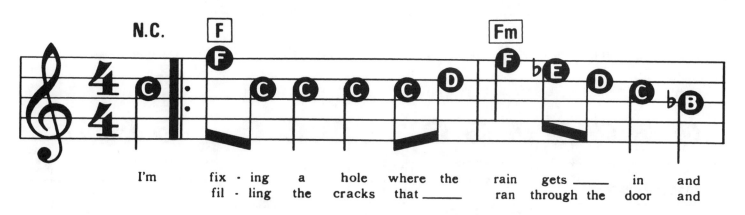

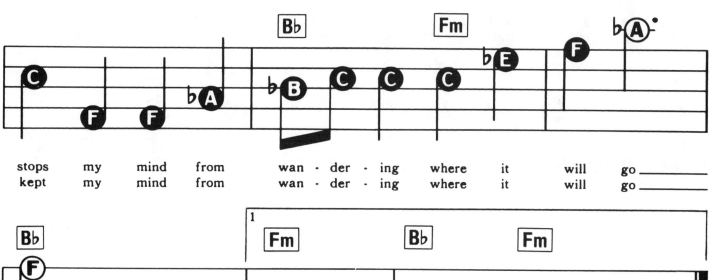

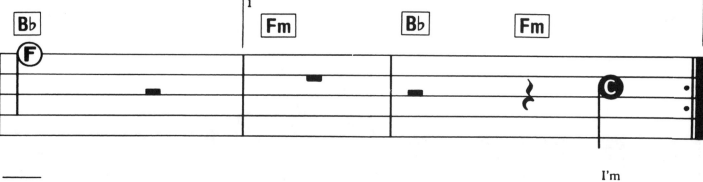

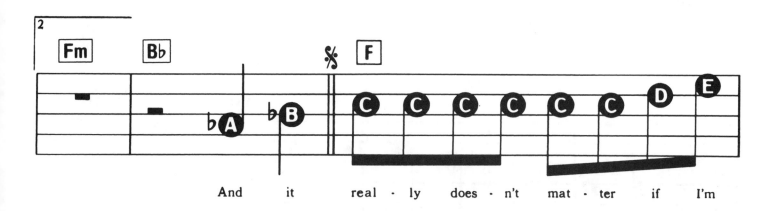

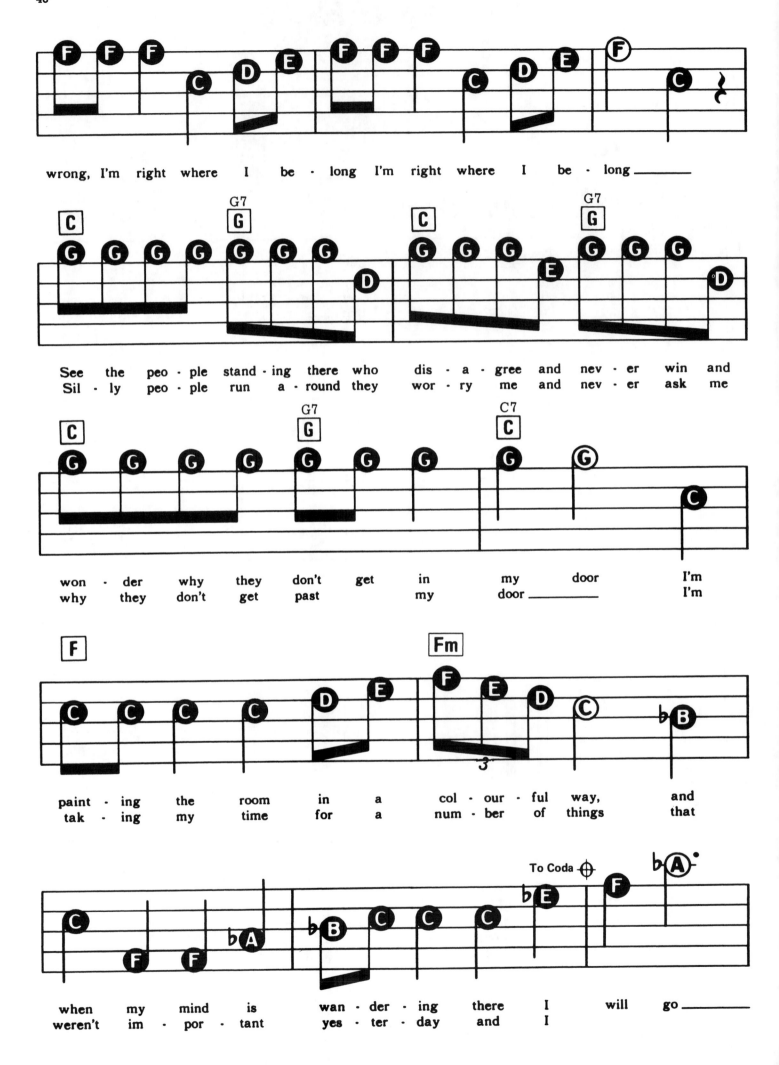

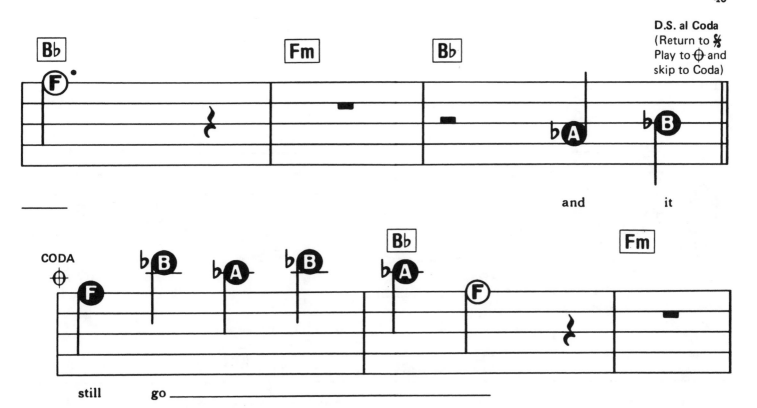

D.S. al Coda
(Return to 𝄋
Play to ⊕ and
skip to Coda)

and   it

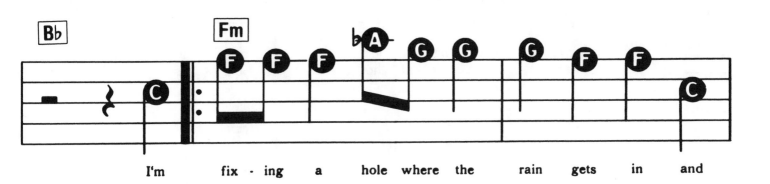

still   go _____

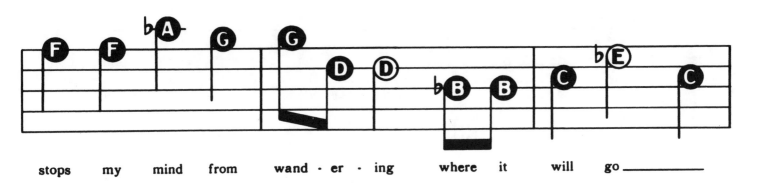

I'm   fix - ing   a   hole where the   rain   gets   in   and

stops   my   mind   from   wand - er - ing   where   it   will   go _____

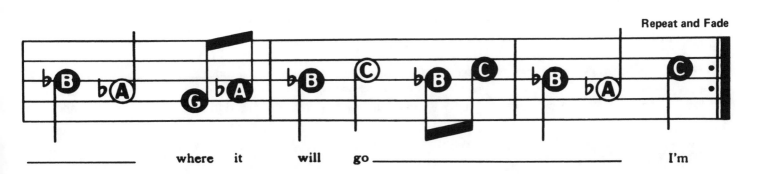

Repeat and Fade

_____   where   it   will   go _____   I'm

The Fool on the Hill

Registration 1
Rhythm: Rock or Bossa Nova

Words and Music by John Lennon
and Paul McCartney

1. Day af - ter day, _____ a - lone on a hill, _____
2. Well on his way, _____ his head in a cloud, _____
3. *Instrumental*

_____ the man with the fool - ish grin is keep - ing
_____ the man of a thou - sand voic - es talk - ing

per - fect - ly still. _____ But no - bod - y wants to
per - fect - ly loud. _____ But no - bod - y ev - er
Instrumental ends No - bod - y seems to

know him, they can see that he's just a fool, _____ and
hears him, or the sound he ap - pears to make, _____ and
like him, they can tell what he wants to do, _____ and

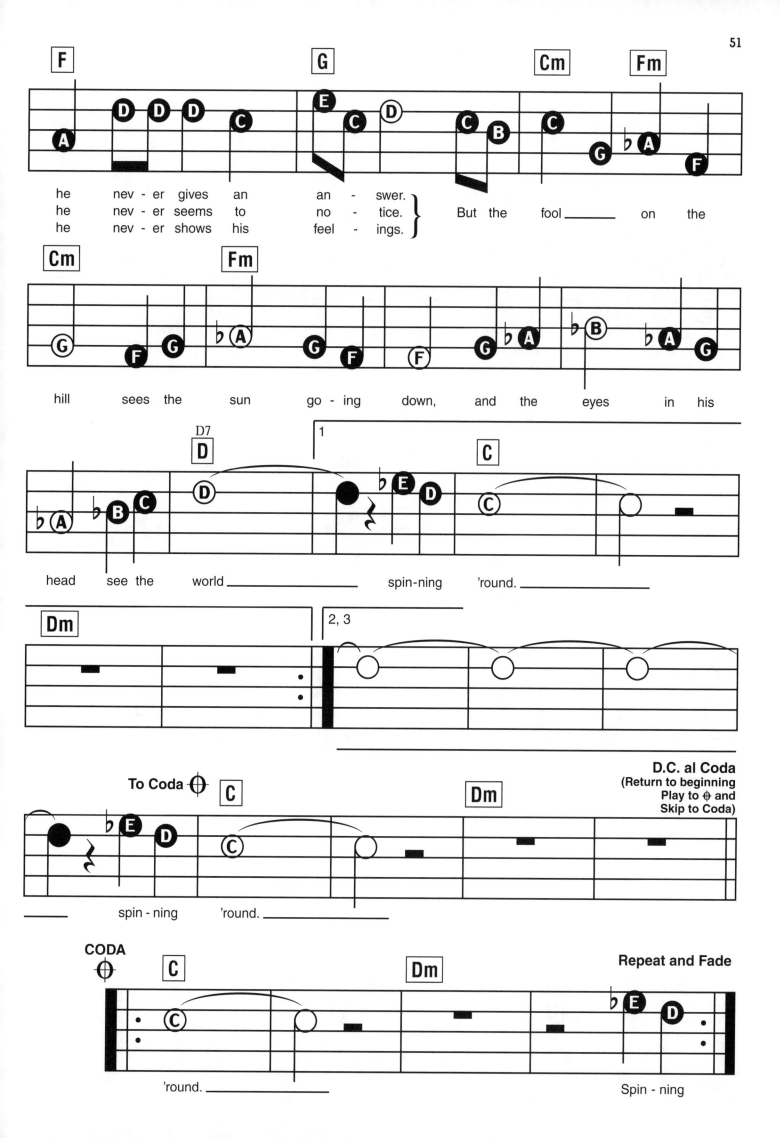

For You Blue

Registration 8
Rhythm: Swing

Words and Music by
George Harrison

Free as a Bird

Registration 8
Rhythm: Rock

Words and Music by John Lennon, Paul McCartney, George Harrison and Ringo Starr

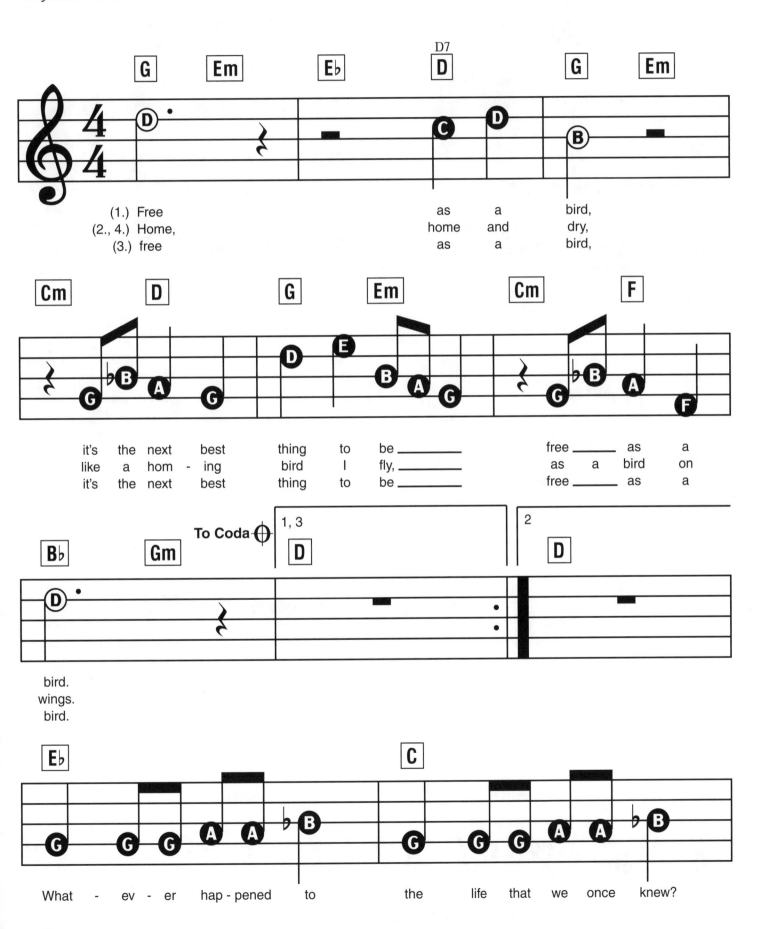

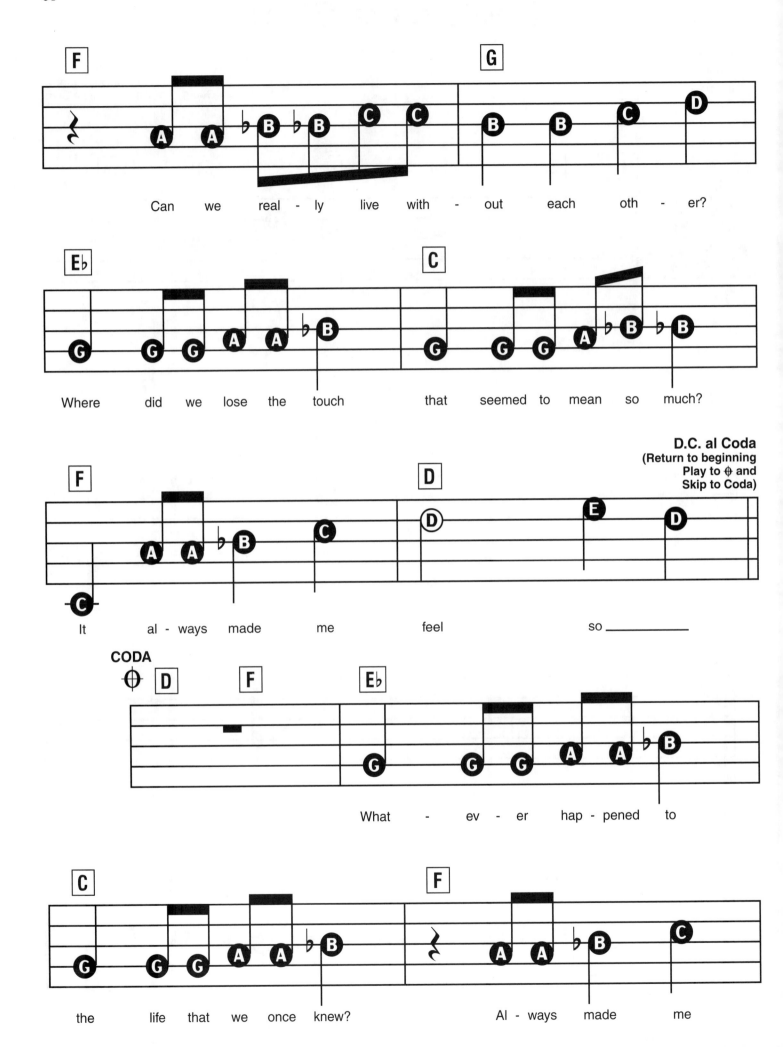

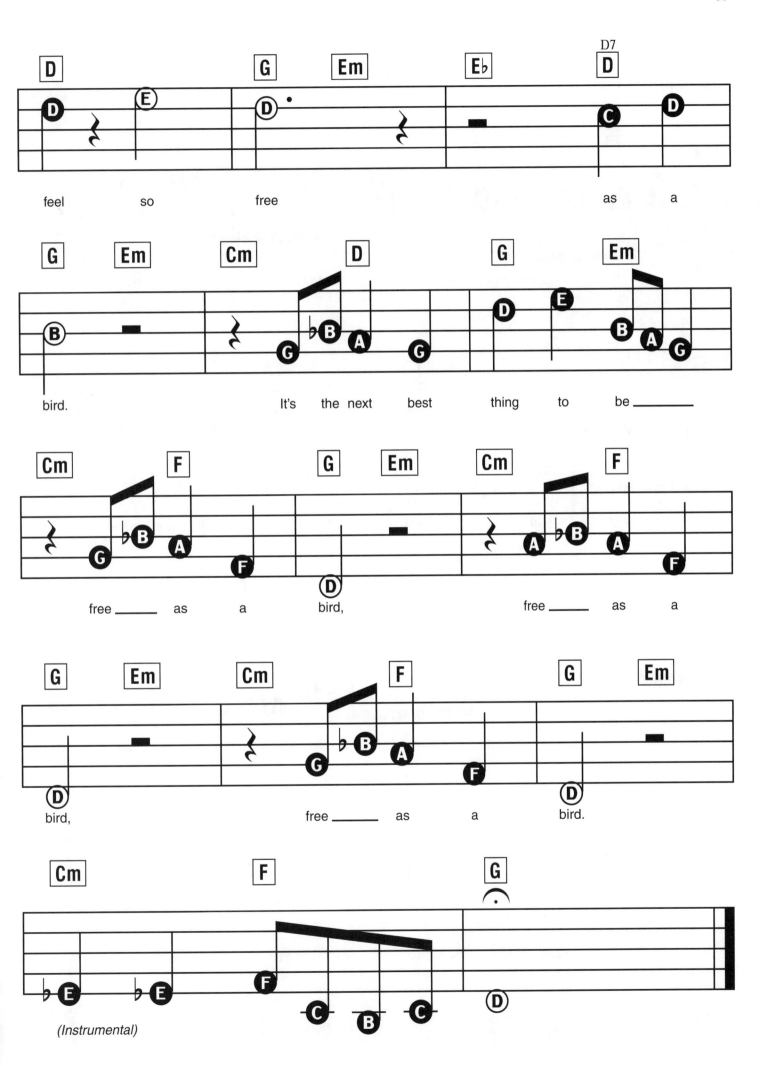

Get Back

Registration 8
Rhythm: Rock

Words and Music by John Lennon
and Paul McCartney

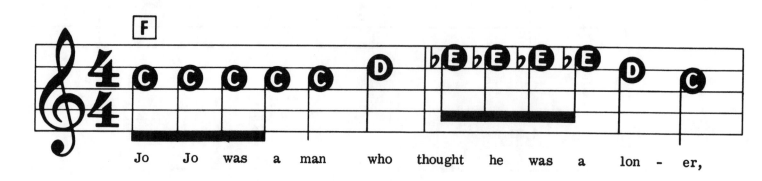

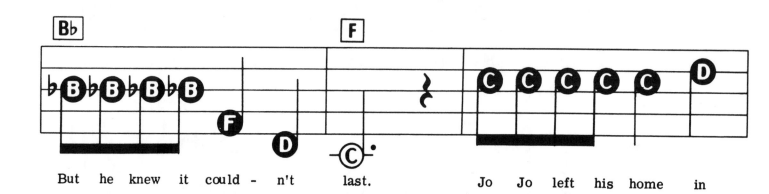

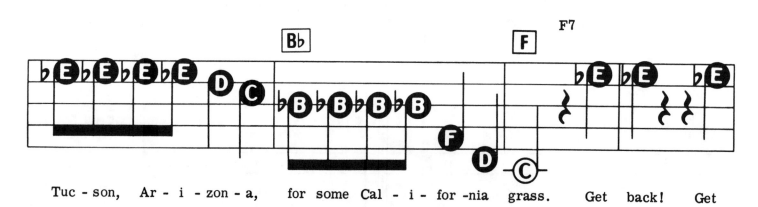

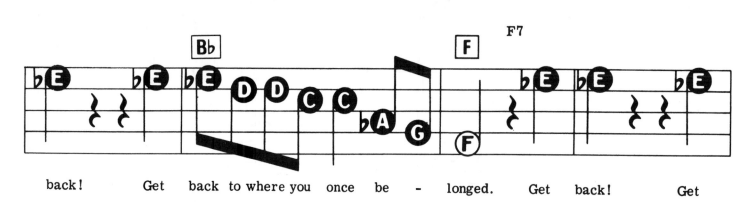

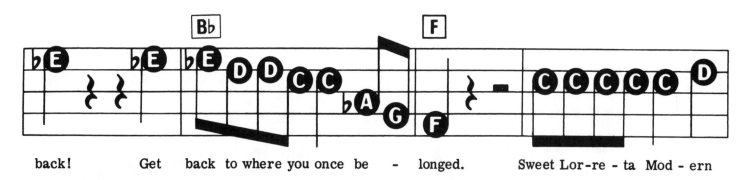

back! Get back to where you once be - longed. Sweet Lor-re - ta Mod-ern

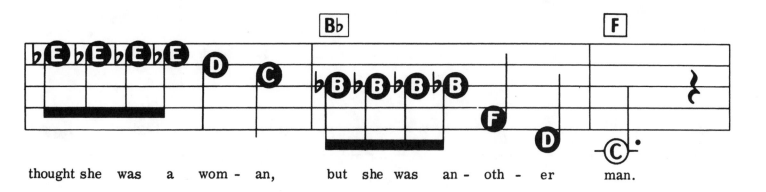

thought she was a wom - an, but she was an - oth - er man.

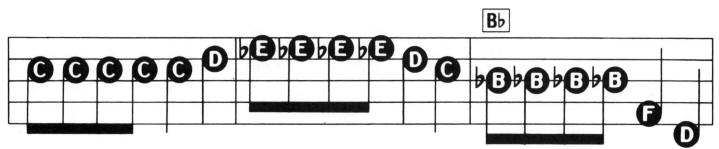

All the girls a-round her say she's got it com - ing, But, she gets it while she

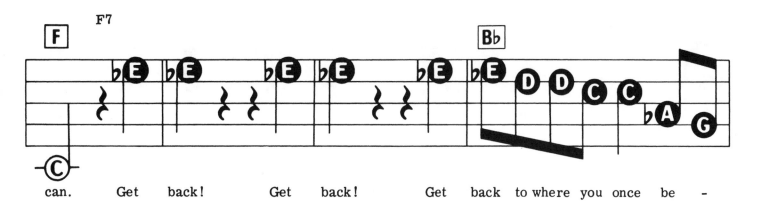

can. Get back! Get back! Get back to where you once be -

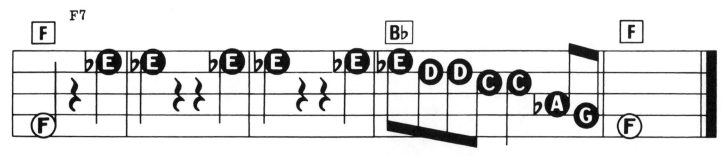

longed. Get back! Get back! Get back to where you once be - longed.

Getting Better

Registration 4
Rhythm: Rock

Words and Music by John Lennon
and Paul McCartney

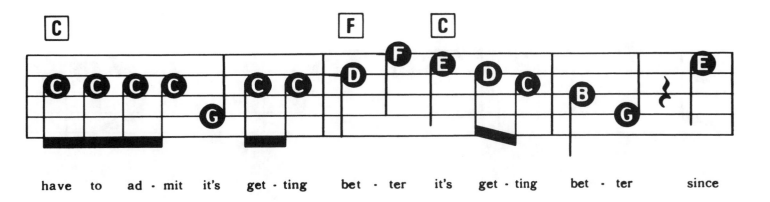

have to ad · mit it's get · ting bet · ter it's get · ting bet · ter since

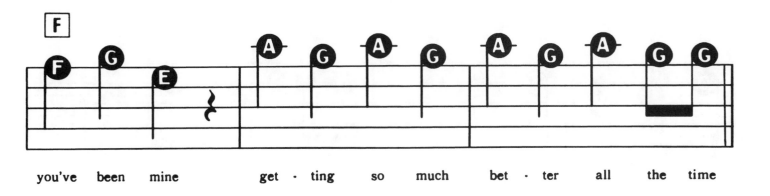

you've been mine get · ting so much bet · ter all the time

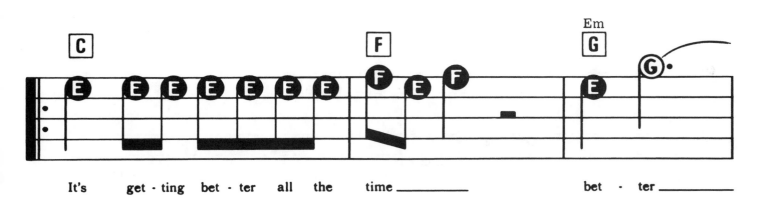

It's get · ting bet · ter all the time _____ bet · ter _____

To Coda ⊕

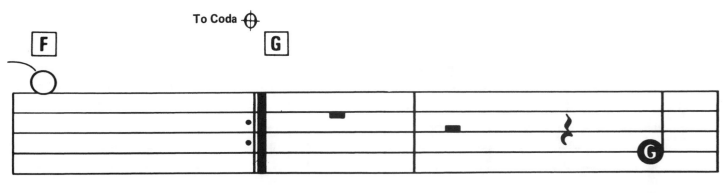

_____ I

60

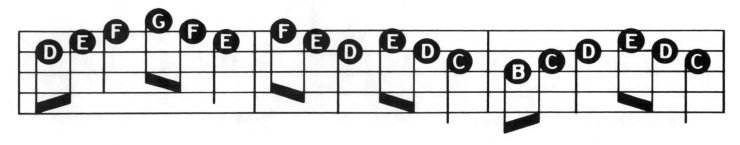

used to be cruel to my wom‑an I beat her and kept her a‑part from the

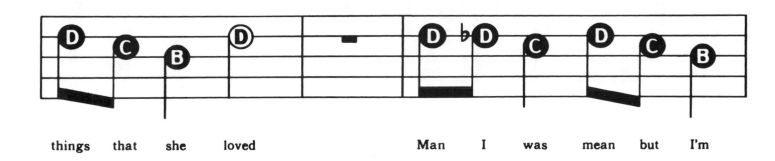

things that she loved Man I was mean but I'm

D.S. al Coda
(Return to 𝄋
Play to ⊕ and skip to Coda)

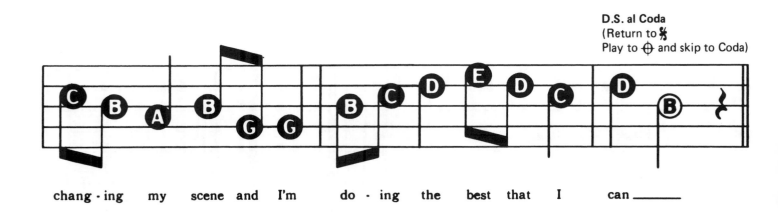

chang‑ing my scene and I'm do‑ing the best that I can_____

CODA ⊕ F C Repeat and Fade

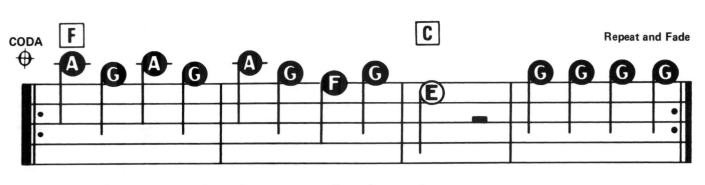

get‑ting so much bet‑ter all the time.

Honey Pie

Registration 1
Rhythm: Rock

Words and Music by John Lennon
and Paul McCartney

Hon - ey Pie, You are mak - ing me cra - zy.
Hon - ey Pie, My po - si - tion is tra - gic.

I'm in love, but I'm la - zy So won't you please come ____
Come and show me the ma - gic

home.
Oh of your Hol - ly - wood

song.
You be - came a
Will the wind that

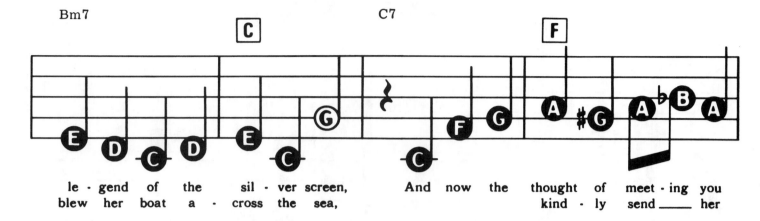

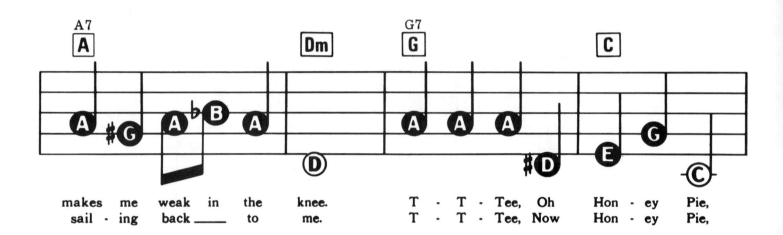

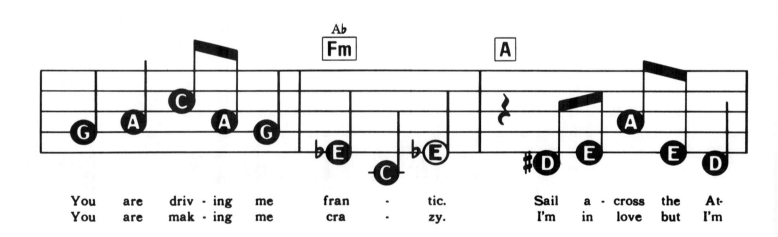

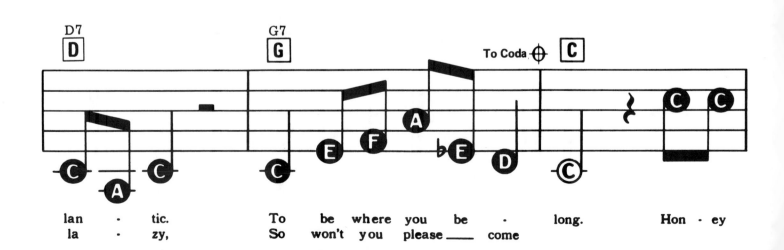

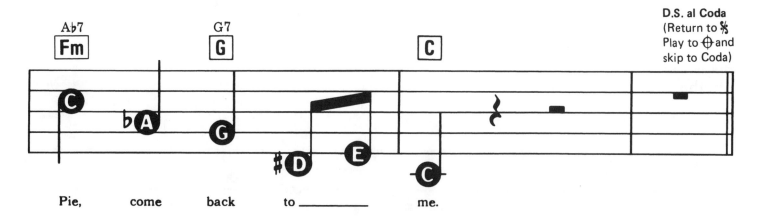

Pie,   come   back   to _____ me.

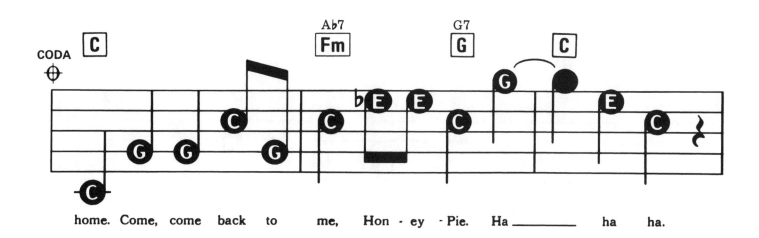

home. Come, come back   to   me,   Hon · ey - Pie. Ha _____ ha ha.

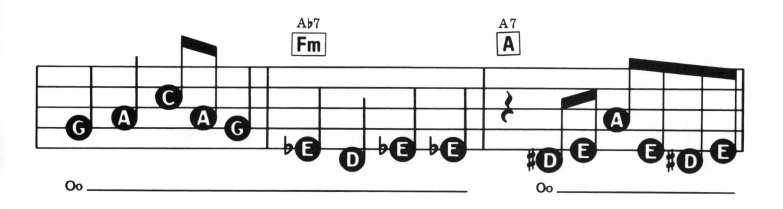

Oo _____   Oo _____

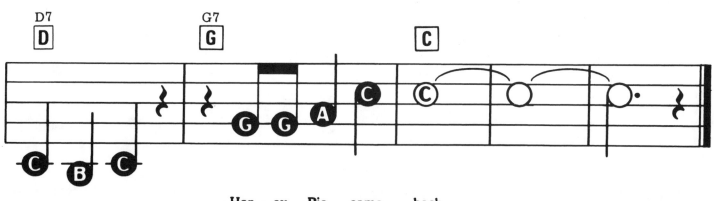

_____   Hon · ey Pie,   come   back. _____

Golden Slumbers

Registration 1
Rhythm: Rock or Jazz Rock

Words and Music by John Lennon
and Paul McCartney

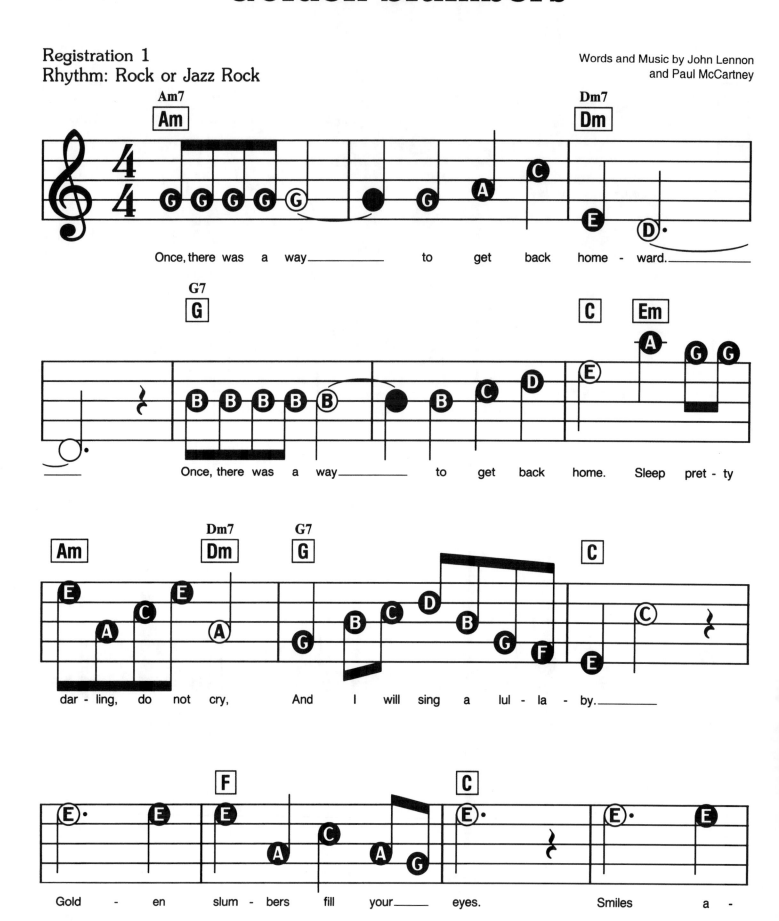

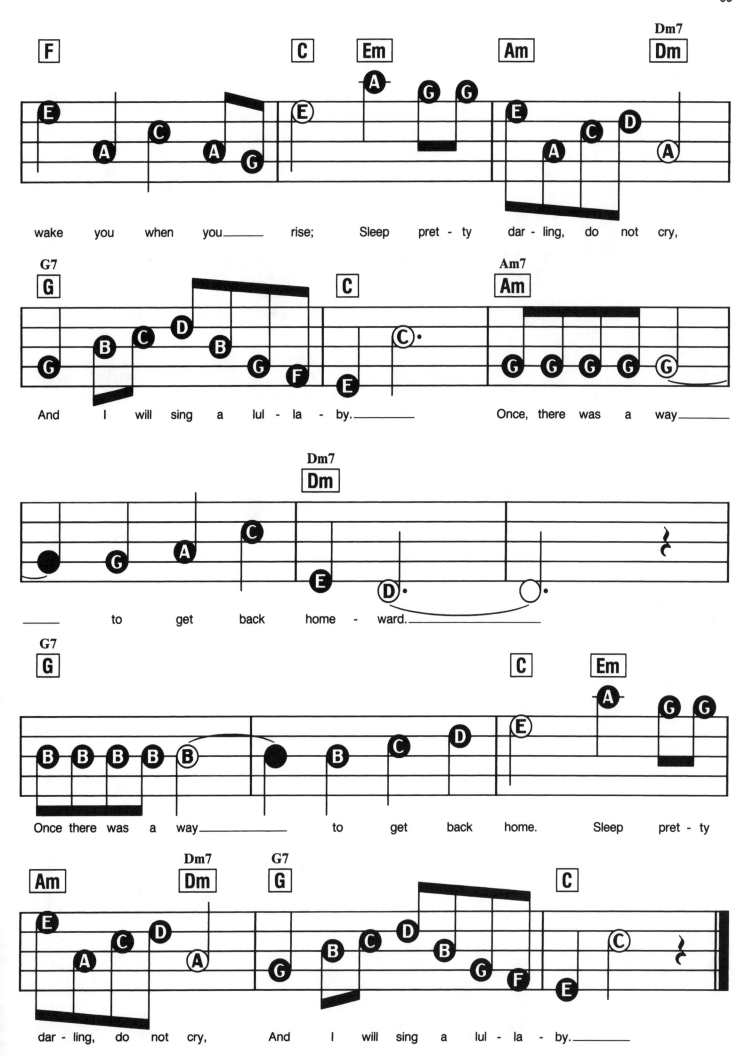

Good Night

Registration 3
Rhythm: Ballad

Words and Music by John Lennon
and Paul McCartney

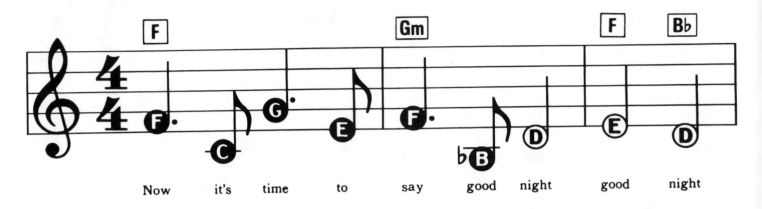

Now it's time to say good night good night

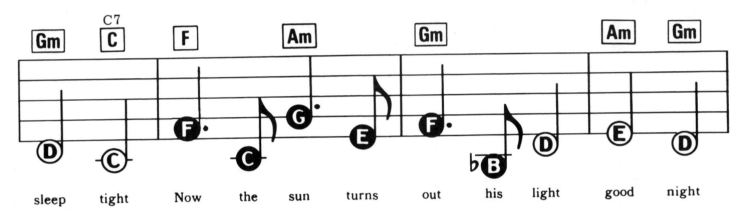

sleep tight Now the sun turns out his light good night

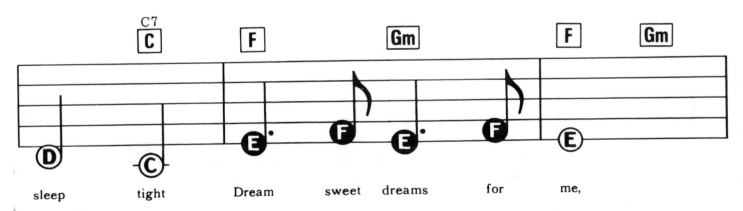

sleep tight Dream sweet dreams for me,

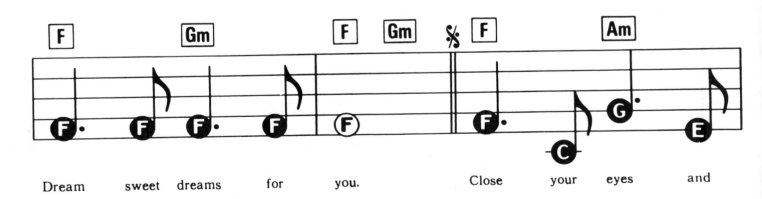

Dream sweet dreams for you. Close your eyes and

67

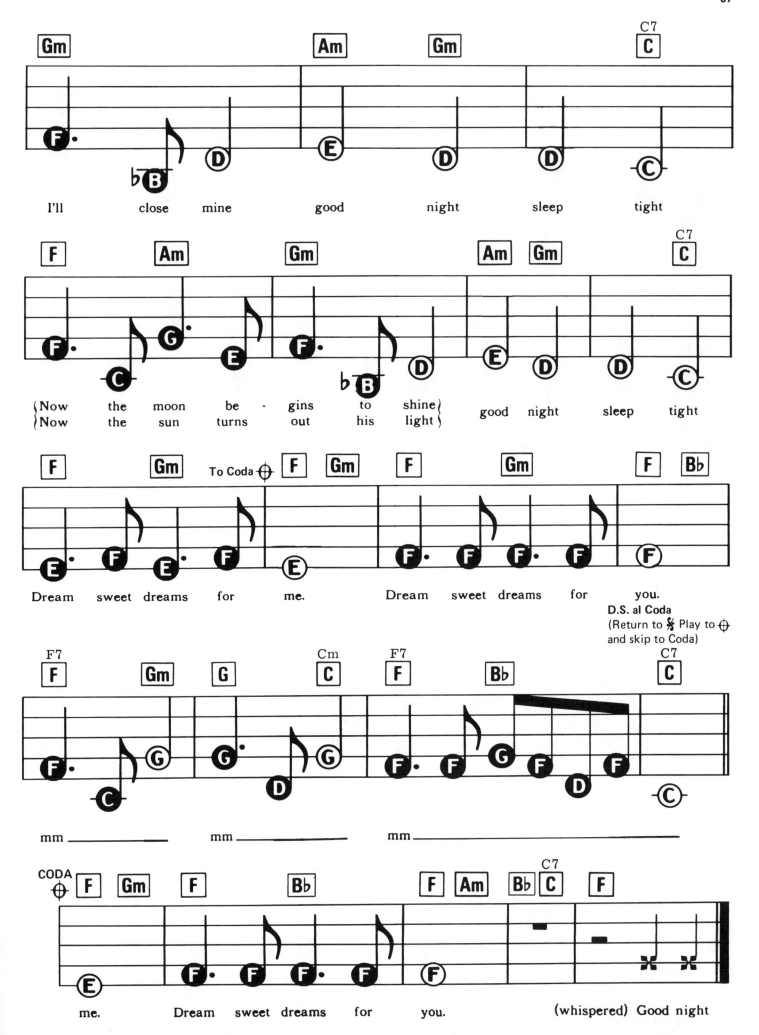

Hello, Goodbye

Registration 3
Rhythm: Rock or Latin Rock

Words and Music by John Lennon
and Paul McCartney

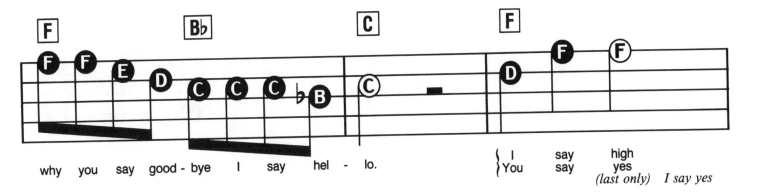

why you say good-bye I say hel - lo.

{ I say high
{ You say yes
(last only) I say yes

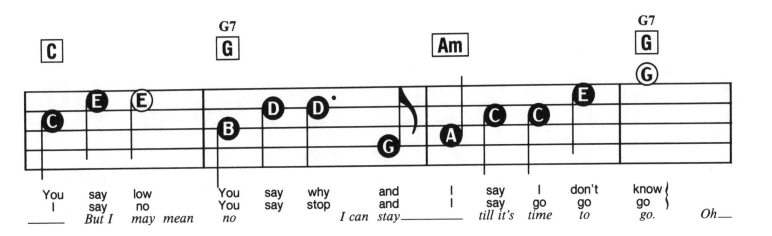

You say low   You say why and   I say I don't know }
I say no   You say stop and   I say I go go }
But I may mean no   I can stay   till it's time to go. Oh—

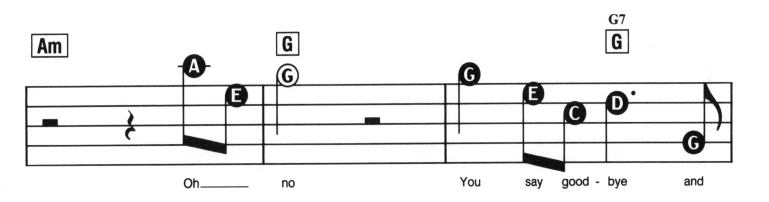

Oh_____ no   You say good - bye and

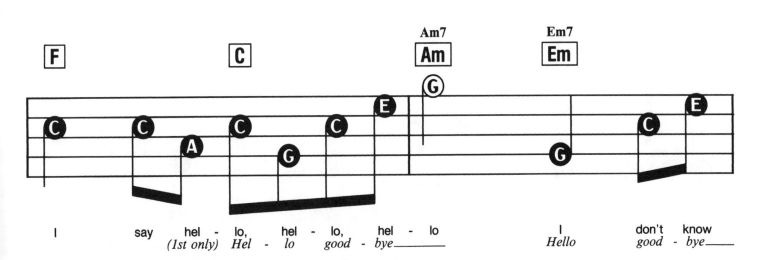

I   say hel - lo, hel - lo, hel - lo   I   don't know
(1st only) Hel - lo good - bye_____   Hello good - bye_____

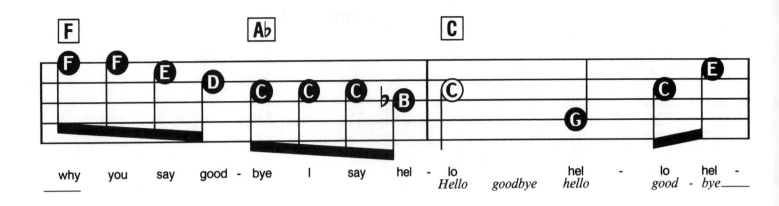

why you say good - bye I say hel - lo *Hello goodbye hello good - bye*___

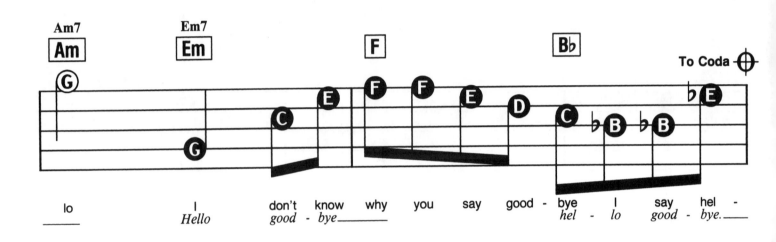

lo___ I don't know why you say good - bye I say hel - *Hello good - bye*___ *hel - lo good - bye.*___

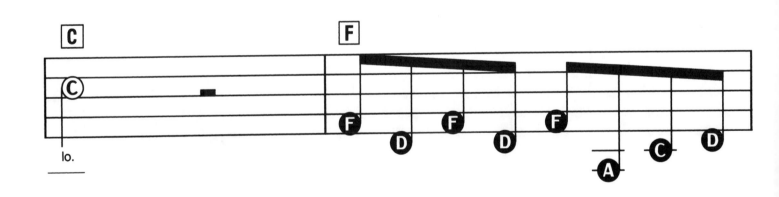

lo.___

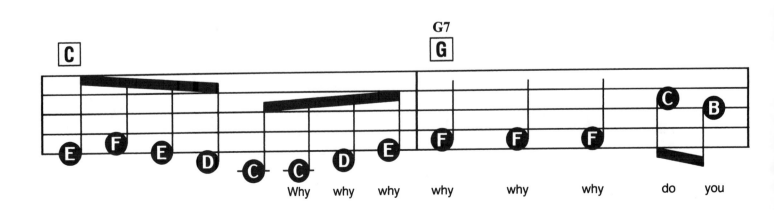

Why why why why why why do you

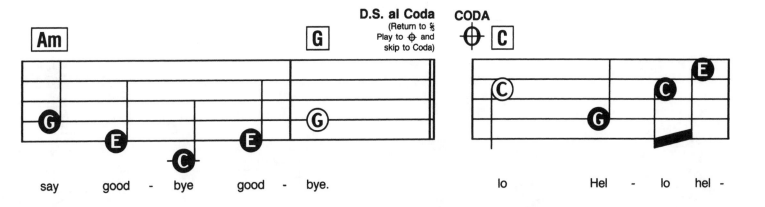

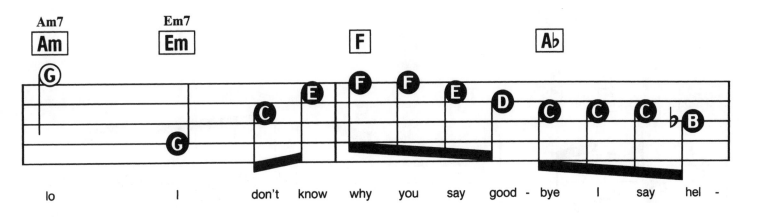

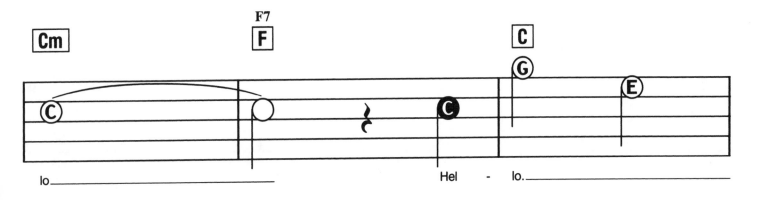

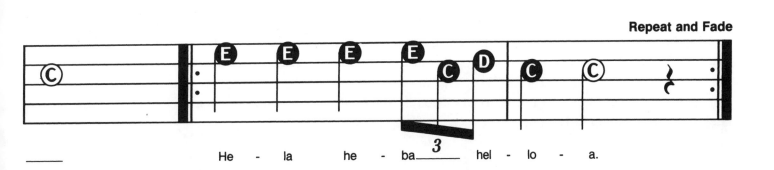

Hello Little Girl

Registration 8
Rhythm: 8 Beat

Words and Music by John Lennon
and Paul McCartney

73

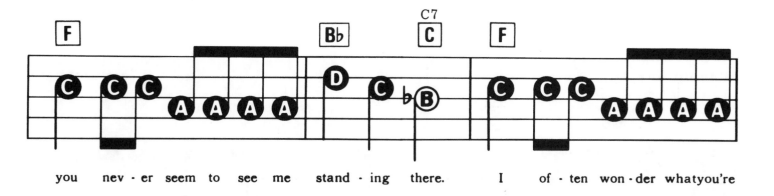

you nev·er seem to see me stand·ing there. I of·ten won·der whatyou're

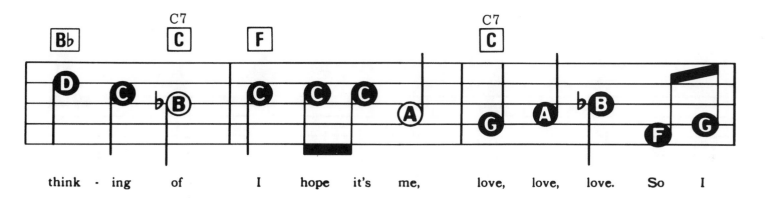

think·ing of I hope it's me, love, love, love. So I

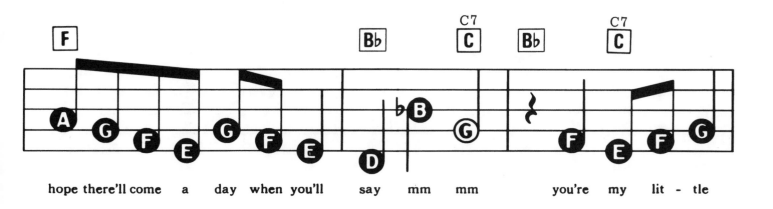

hope there'll come a day when you'll say mm mm you're my lit – tle

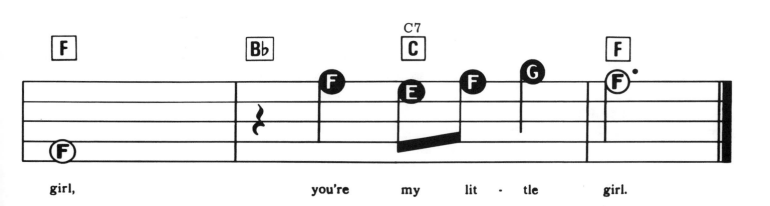

girl, you're my lit – tle girl.

Helter Skelter

Registration 4
Rhythm: Rock

Words and Music by John Lennon
and Paul McCartney

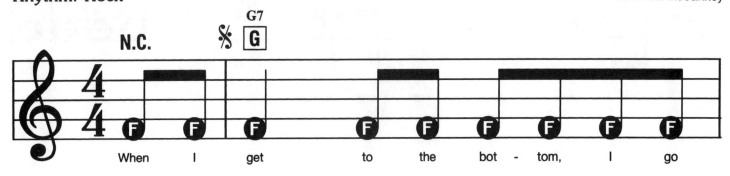

When I get to the bot - tom, I go

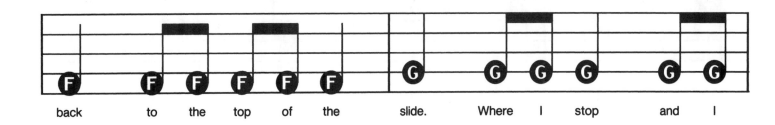

back to the top of the slide. Where I stop and I

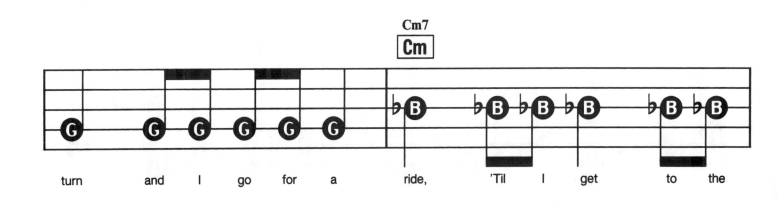

turn and I go for a ride, 'Til I get to the

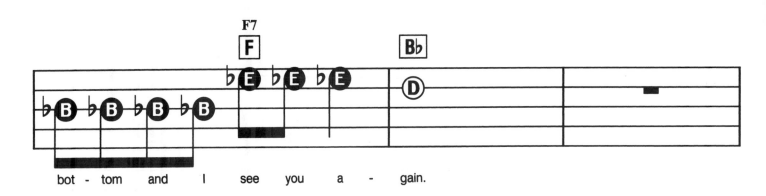

bot - tom and I see you a - gain.

G

shout

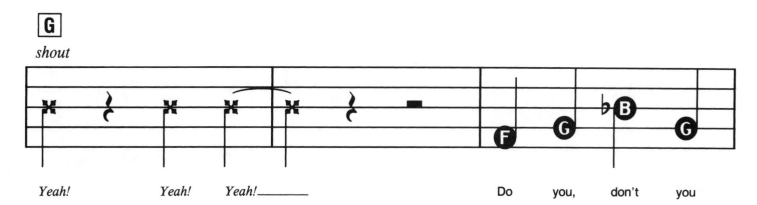

Yeah!   Yeah!   Yeah!_____   Do   you,   don't   you

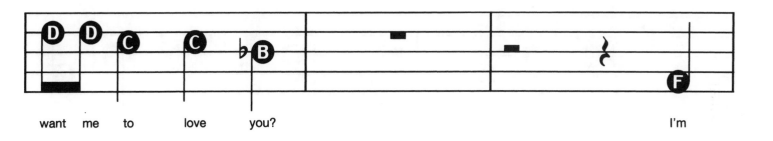

want   me   to   love   you?   I'm

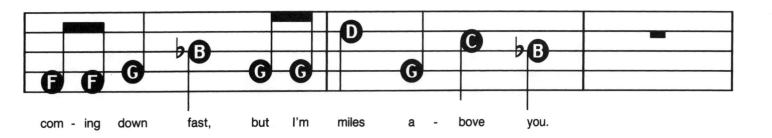

com - ing   down   fast,   but   I'm   miles   a - bove   you.

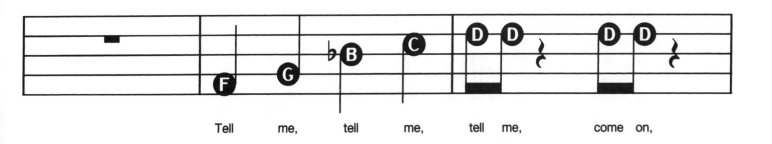

Tell   me,   tell   me,   tell   me,   come   on,

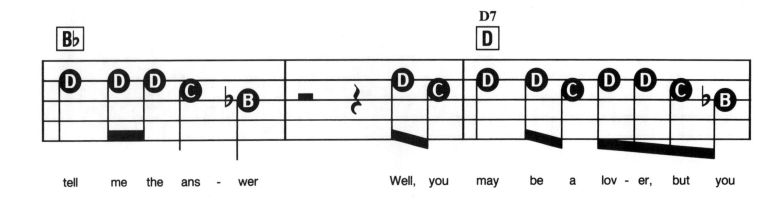

tell me the ans - wer   Well, you may be a lov - er, but you

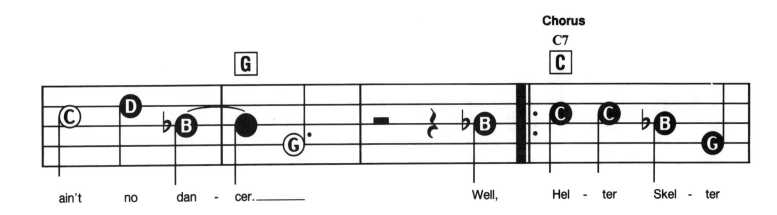

ain't no dan - cer._____   Well, Hel - ter Skel - ter

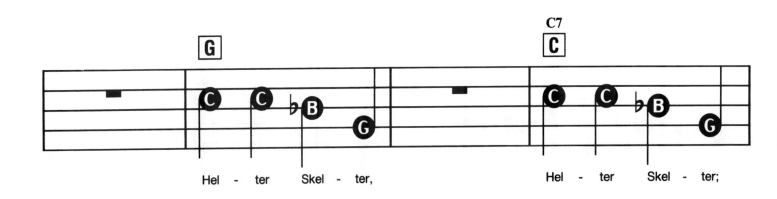

Hel - ter Skel - ter,   Hel - ter Skel - ter;

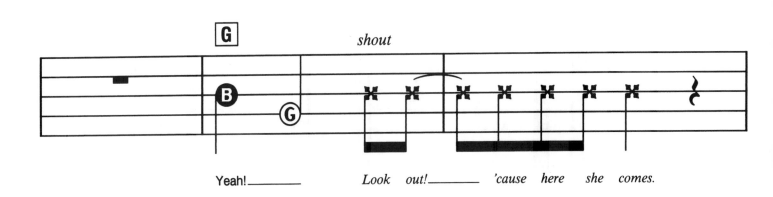

Yeah!_____   *Look out!*_____ *'cause here she comes.*

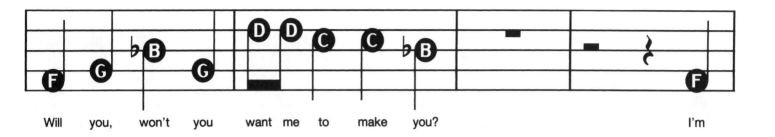

Will you, won't you want me to make you? I'm

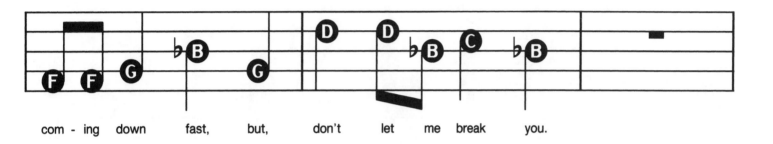

com - ing down fast, but, don't let me break you.

B♭

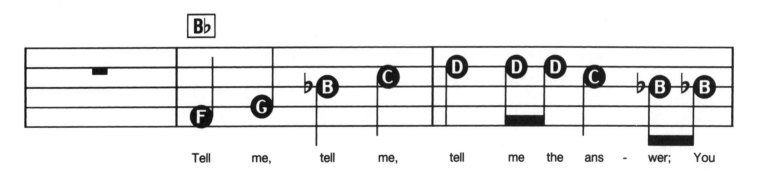

Tell me, tell me, tell me the ans - wer; You

D7

D

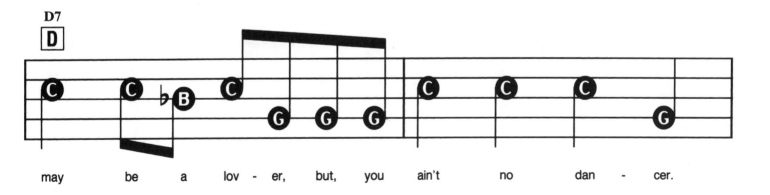

may be a lov - er, but, you ain't no dan - cer.

G

shout

D.S.
(Return to % and
Fade on Chorus)

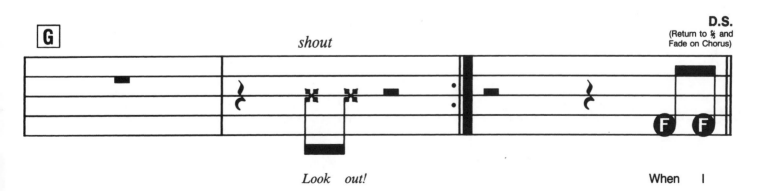

Look out! When I

Here Comes the Sun

Registration 7
Rhythm: Rock

Words and Music by
George Harrison

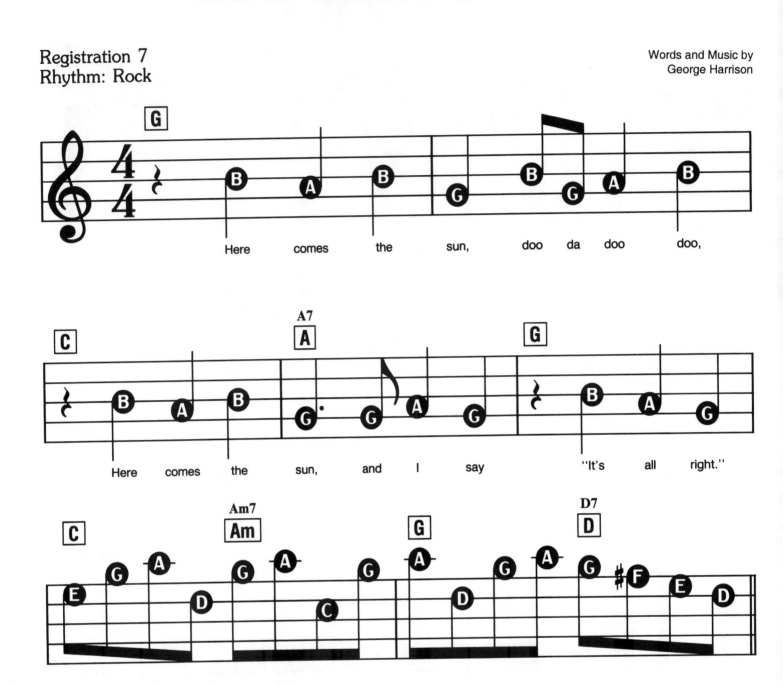

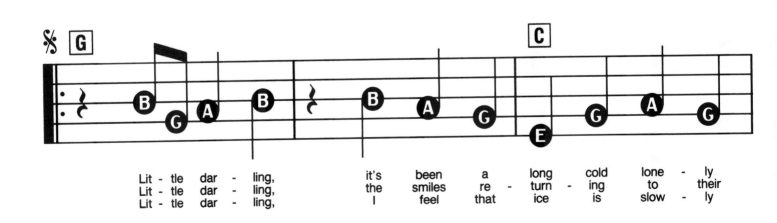

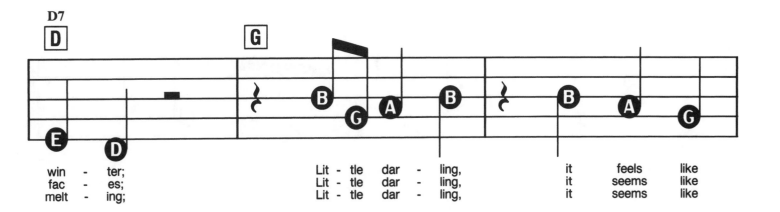

winter;
faces;
melting;

Lit - tle dar - ling,
Lit - tle dar - ling,
Lit - tle dar - ling,

it feels like
it seems like
it seems like

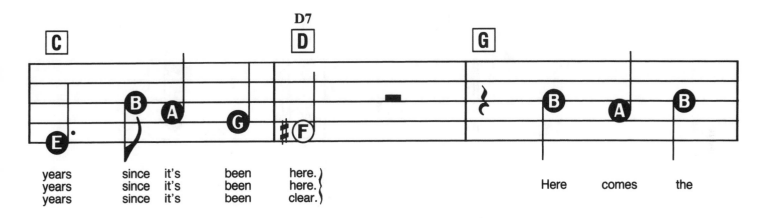

years since it's been here.⎫
years since it's been here.⎬
years since it's been clear.⎭

Here comes the

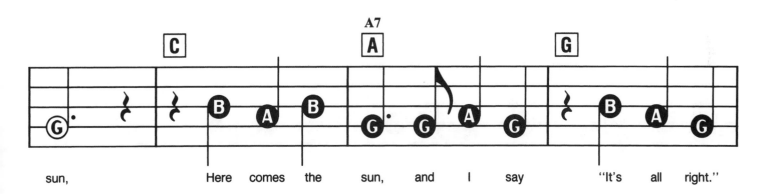

sun,   Here comes the sun, and I say "It's all right."

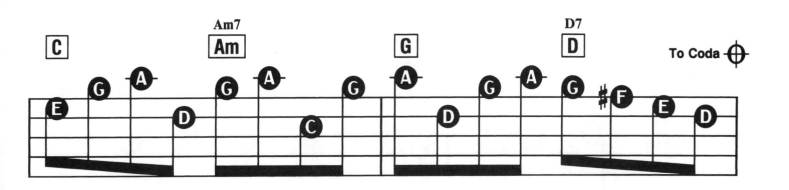

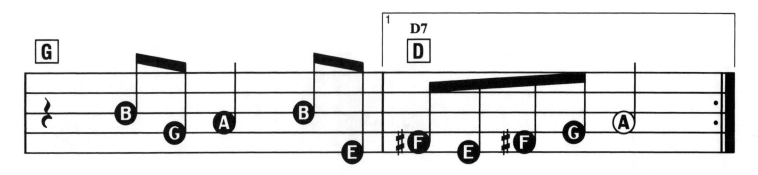

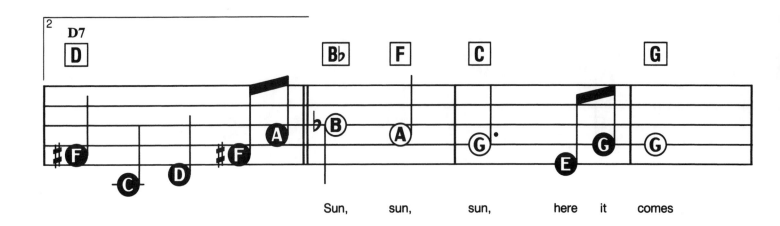

Sun,   sun,   sun,   here   it   comes

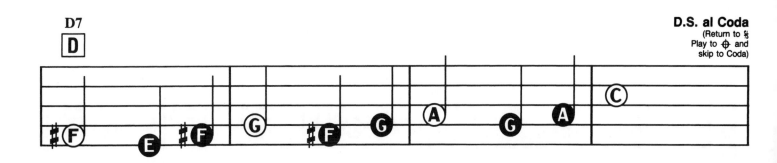

D.S. al Coda
(Return to ℅
Play to ⊕ and
skip to Coda)

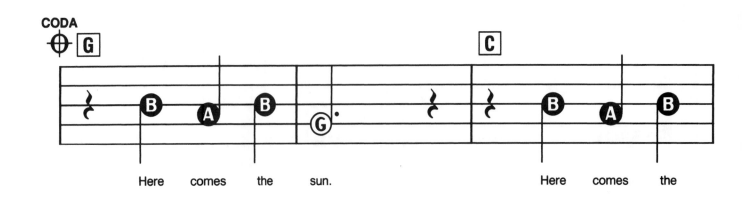

Here   comes   the   sun.   Here   comes   the

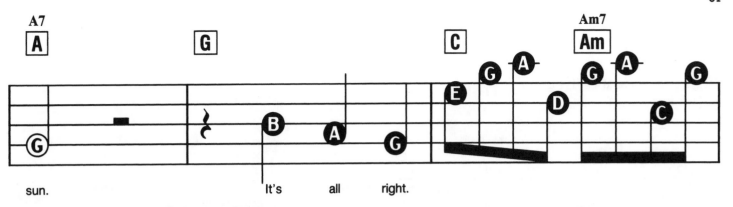

sun.   It's   all   right.

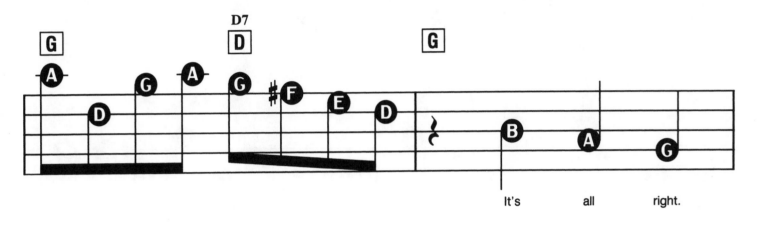

It's   all   right.

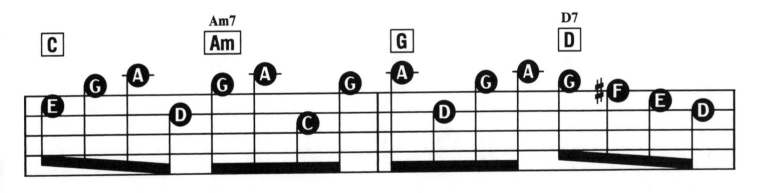

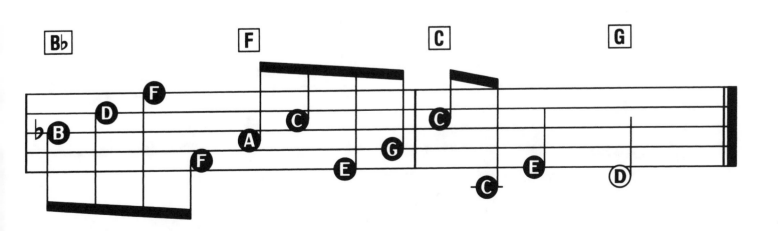

Hey Bulldog

Registration 8
Rhythm: 8 Beat or Rock

Words and Music by John Lennon
and Paul McCartney

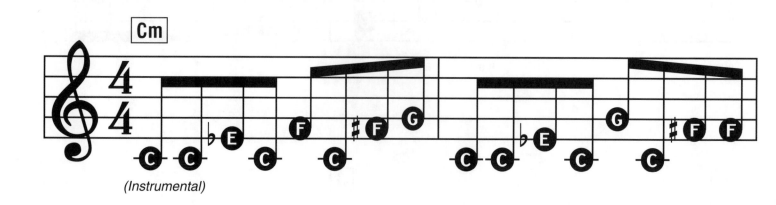

(Instrumental)

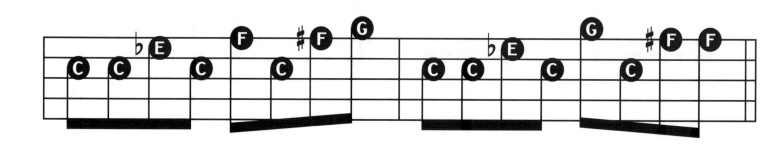

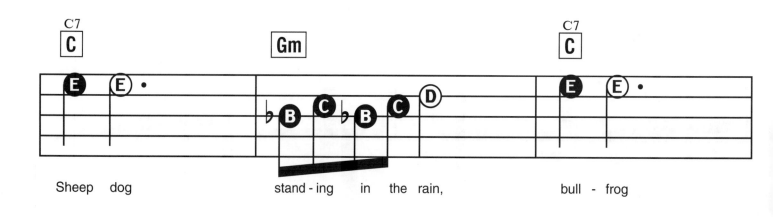

Sheep dog   stand - ing in the rain,   bull - frog

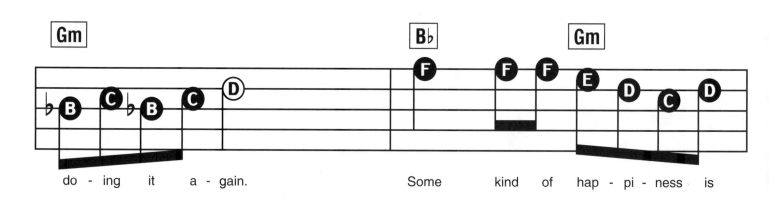

do - ing it a - gain.   Some kind of hap - pi - ness is

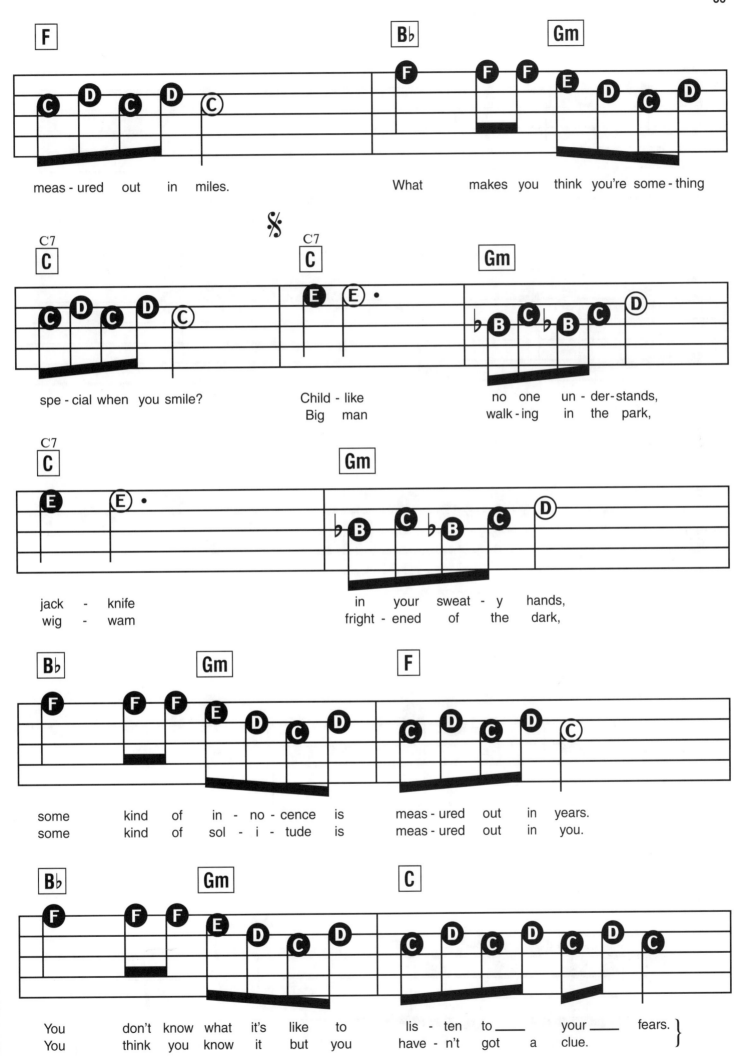

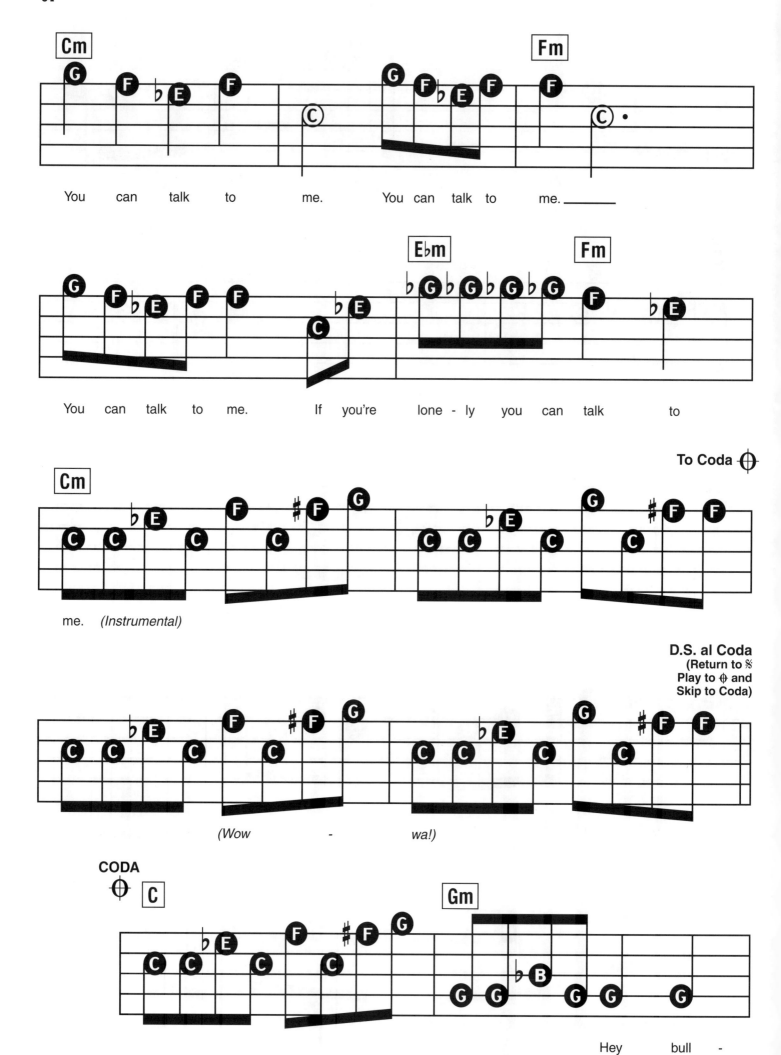

You can talk to me. You can talk to me. _____

You can talk to me. If you're lone - ly you can talk to

To Coda ⊕

me. *(Instrumental)*

D.S. al Coda
(Return to %
Play to ⊕ and
Skip to Coda)

(Wow - wa!)

CODA ⊕

Hey bull -

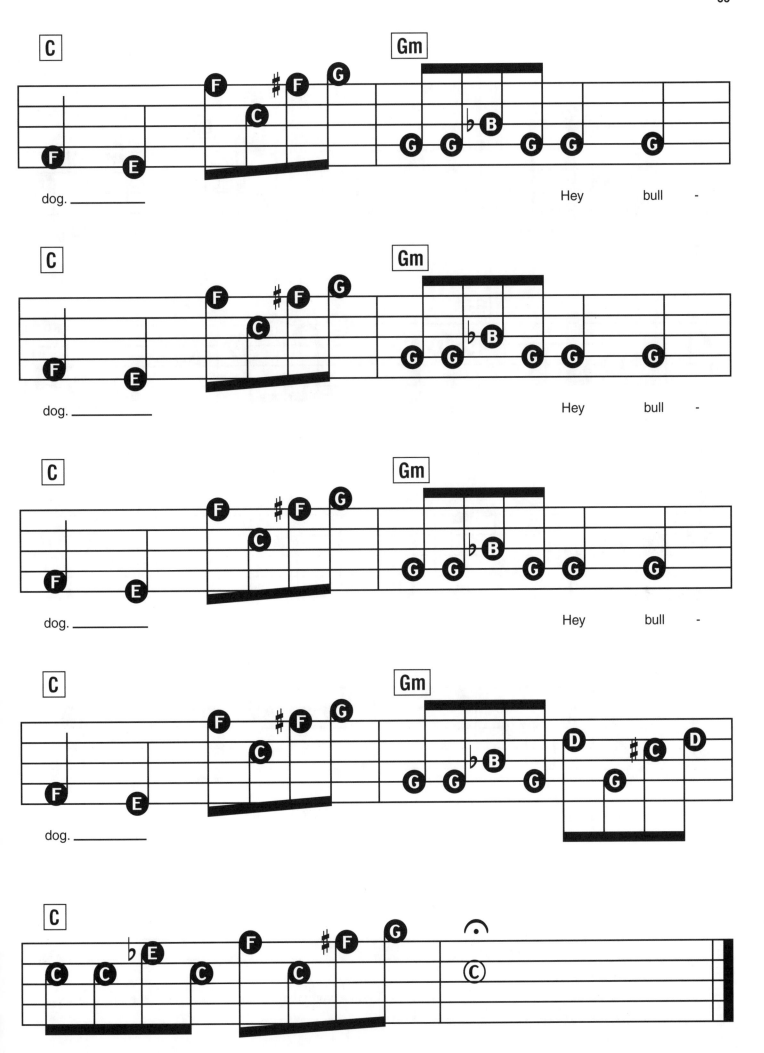

Hey Jude

Registration 2
Rhythm: Pops or 8 Beat

Words and Music by John Lennon
and Paul McCartney

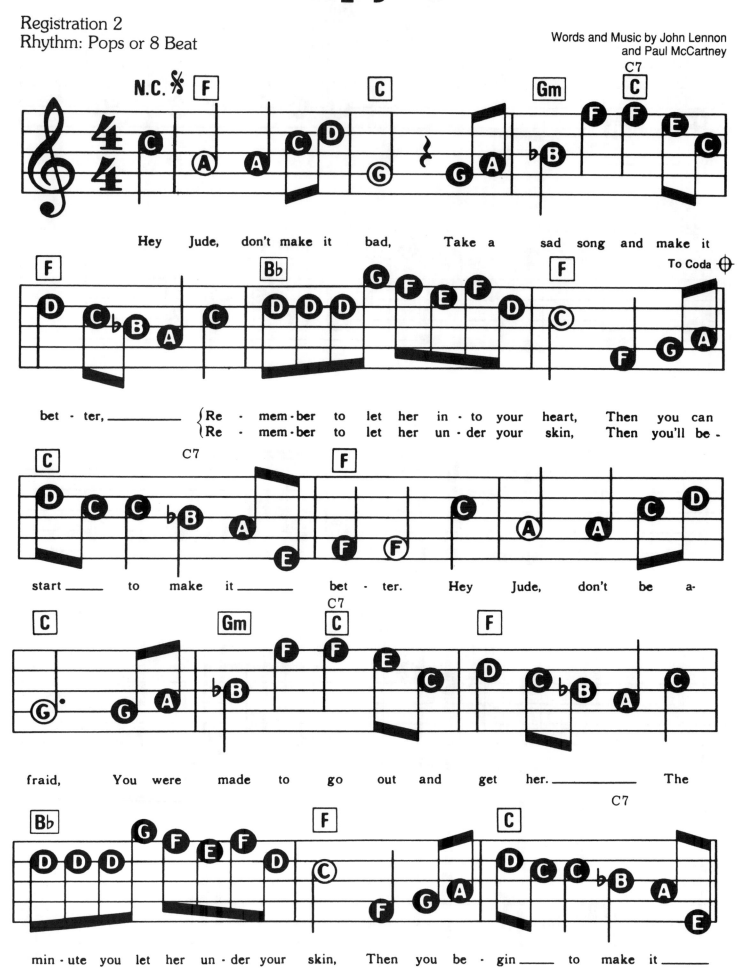

87

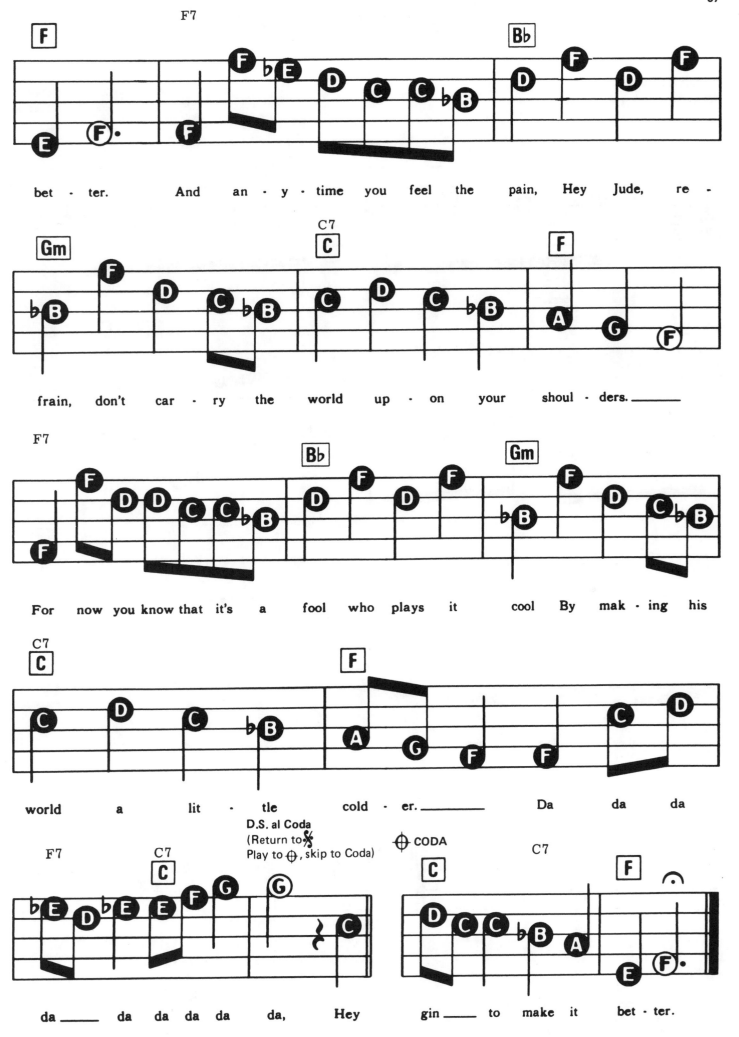

I Am the Walrus

Registration 5
Rhythm: Rock

Words and Music by John Lennon
and Paul McCartney

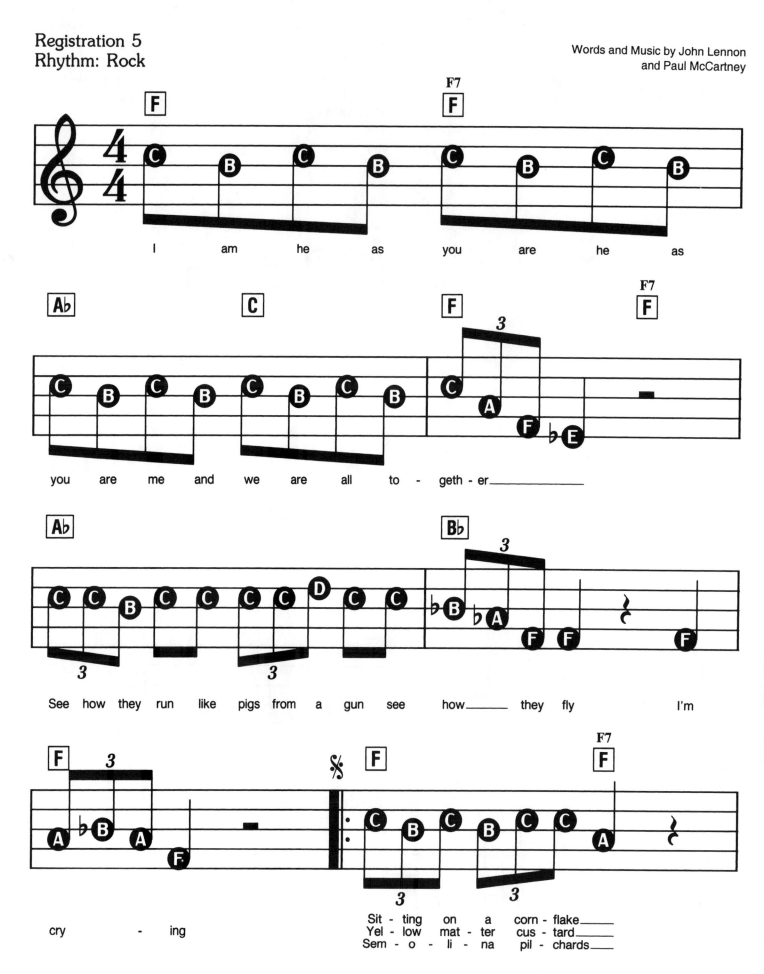

89

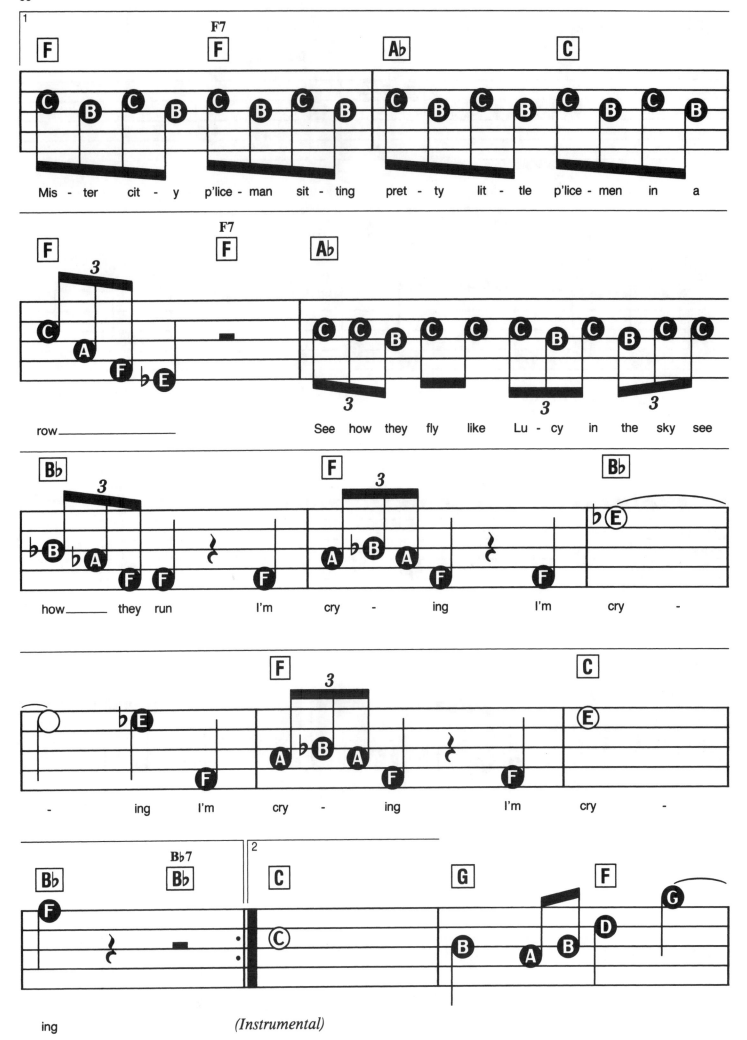

Mis - ter cit - y p'lice - man sit - ting pret - ty lit - tle p'lice - men in a

row_____ See how they fly like Lu - cy in the sky see

how_____ they run I'm cry - ing I'm cry -

- ing I'm cry - ing I'm cry -

ing   (Instrumental)

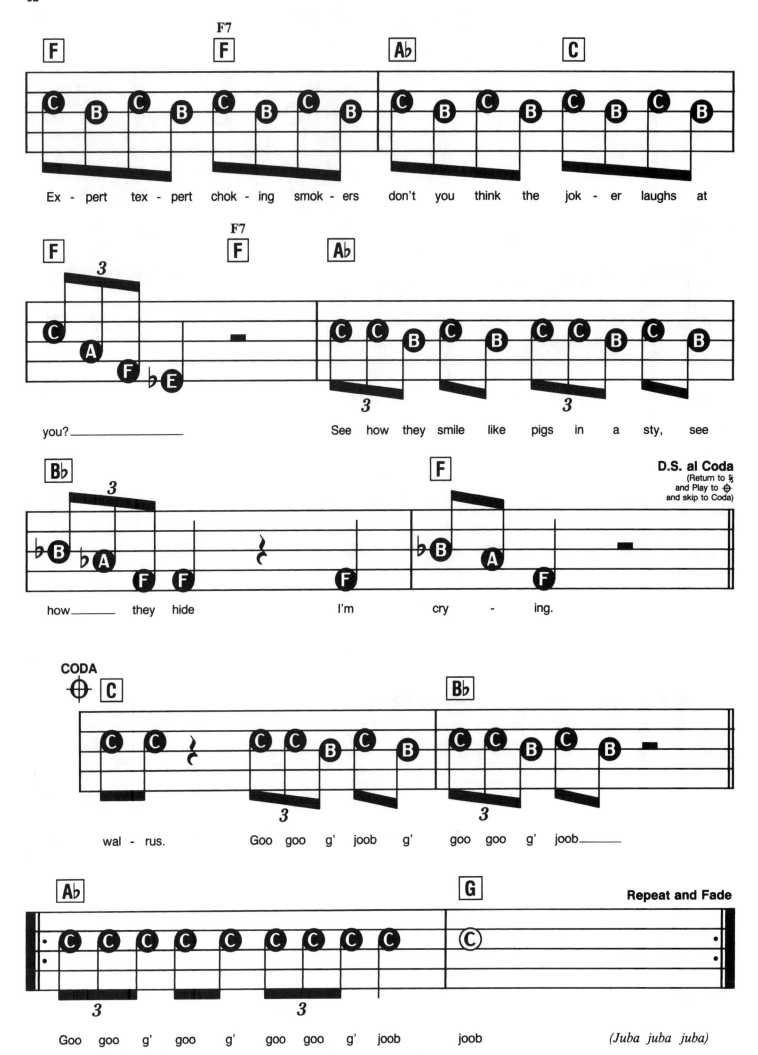

I Want You
(She's So Heavy)

Words and Music by John Lennon
and Paul McCartney

Registration 1
Rhythm: Slow Rock or Rock

94

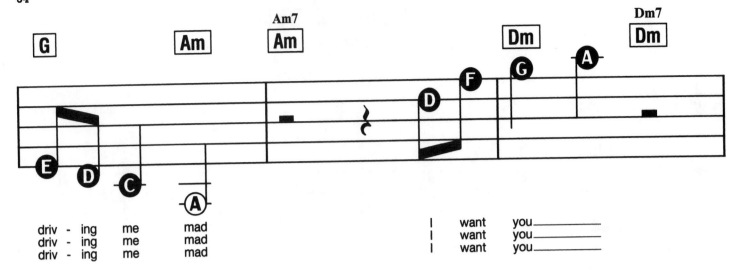

driving me mad
driving me mad
driving me mad

I want you
I want you
I want you

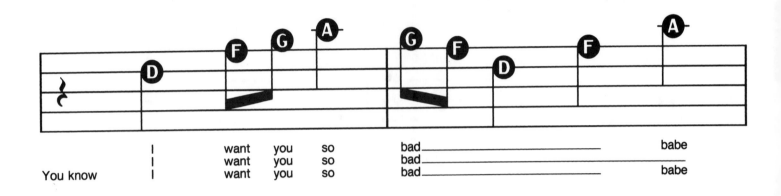

You know

I want you so
I want you so
I want you so

bad   babe
bad
bad   babe

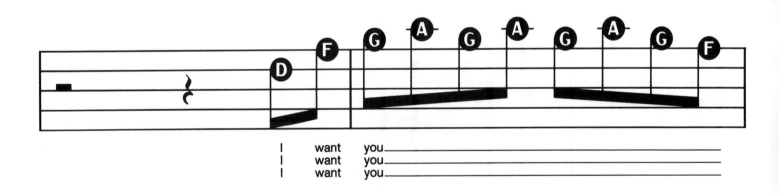

I want you
I want you
I want you

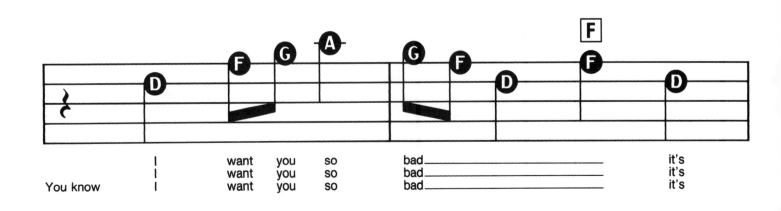

You know

I want you so
I want you so
I want you so

bad   it's
bad   it's
bad   it's

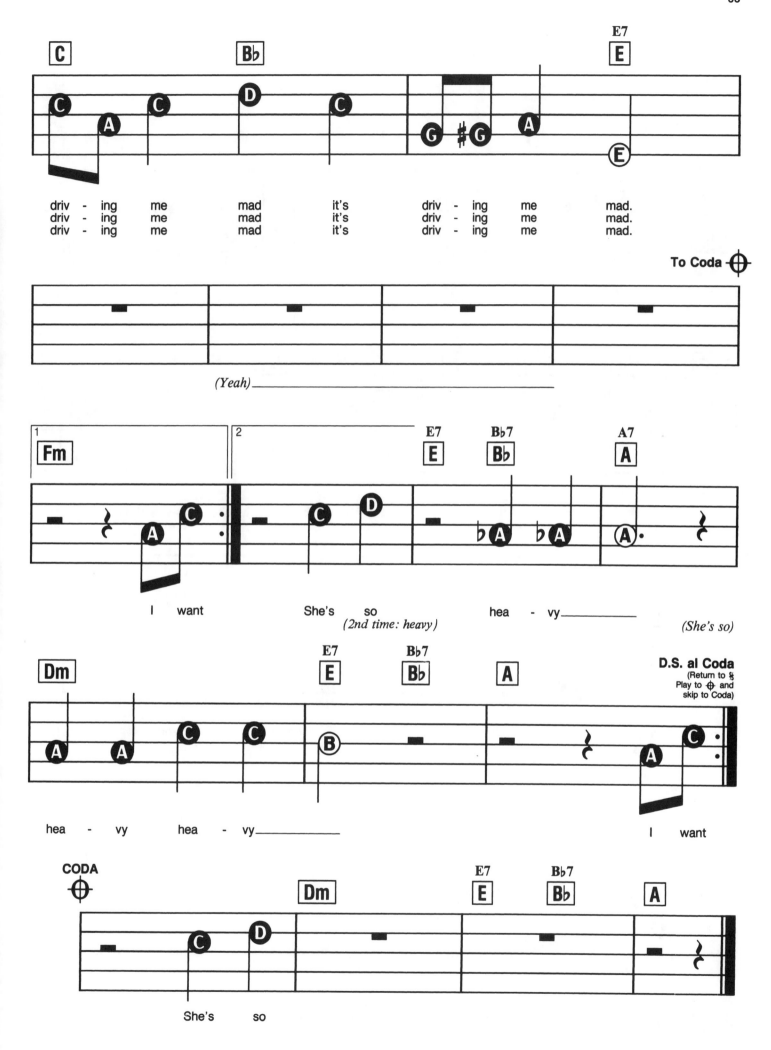

95

I Will

Registration 4
Rhythm: Rock or Slow Rock

Words and Music by John Lennon
and Paul McCartney

97

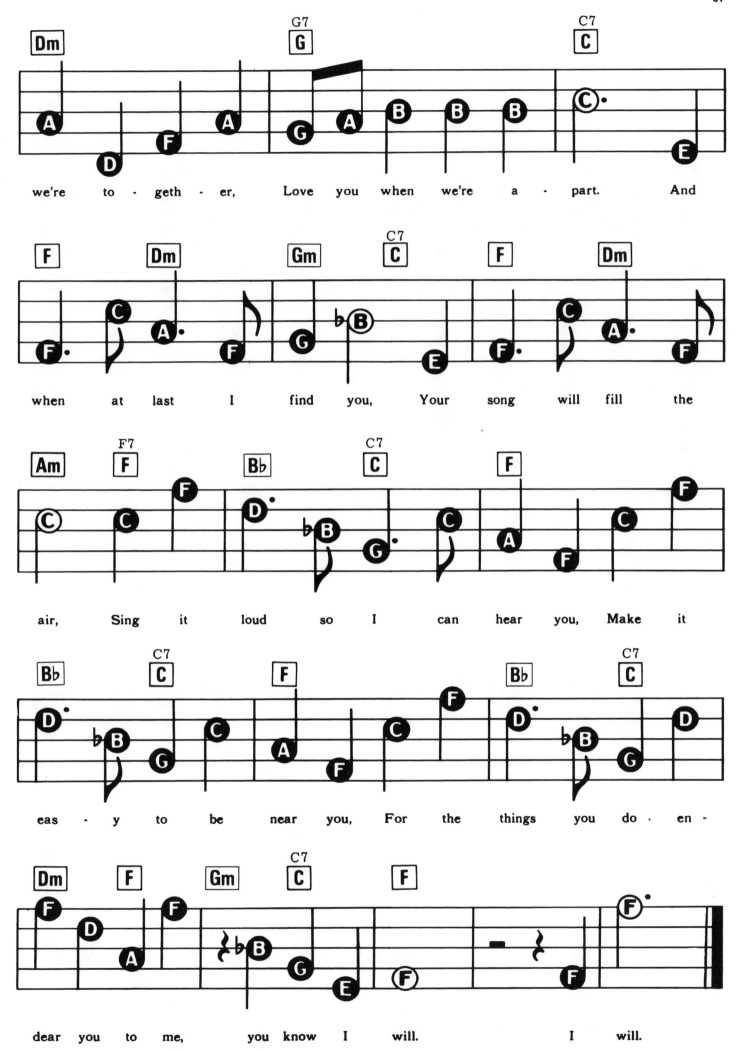

I'm Down

Registration 4
Rhythm: 8 Beat or Rock

Words and Music by John Lennon
and Paul McCartney

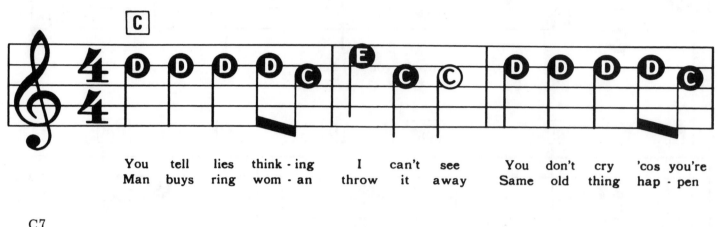

You tell lies think-ing I can't see You don't cry 'cos you're
Man buys ring wom-an throw it away Same old thing hap-pen

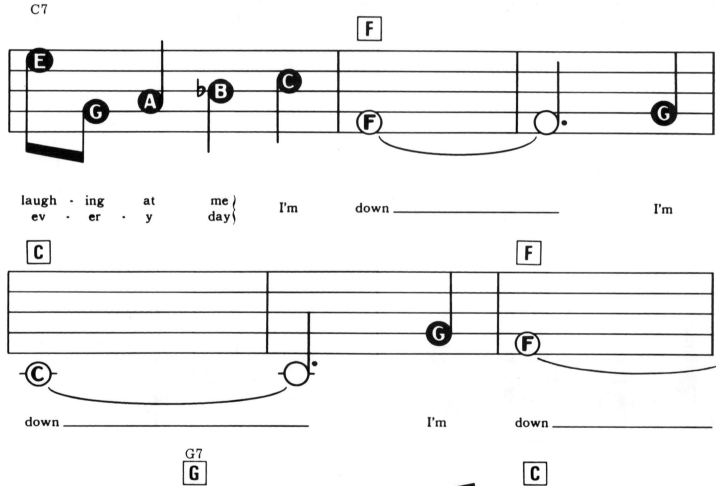

laugh-ing at me }
ev-er-y day } I'm down _____ I'm

down _____ I'm down _____

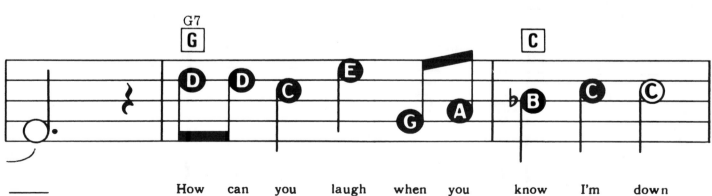

_____ How can you laugh when you know I'm down

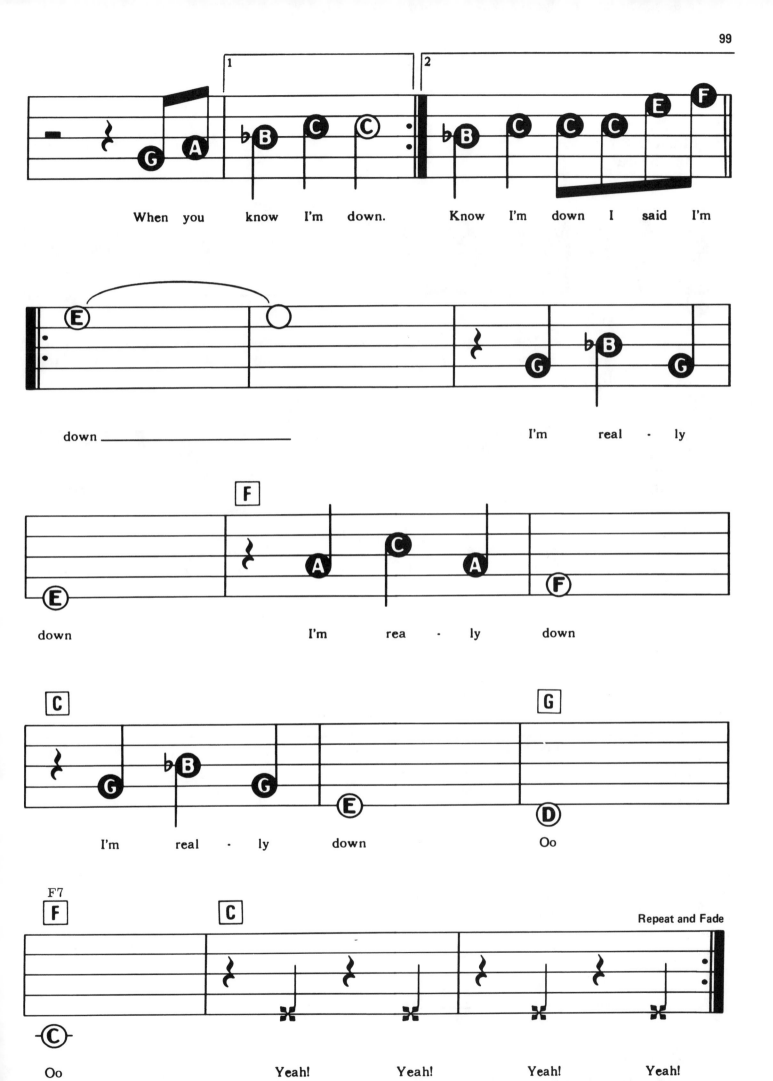

The Inner Light

Registration 3
Rhythm: 8 Beat

Words and Music by
George Harrison

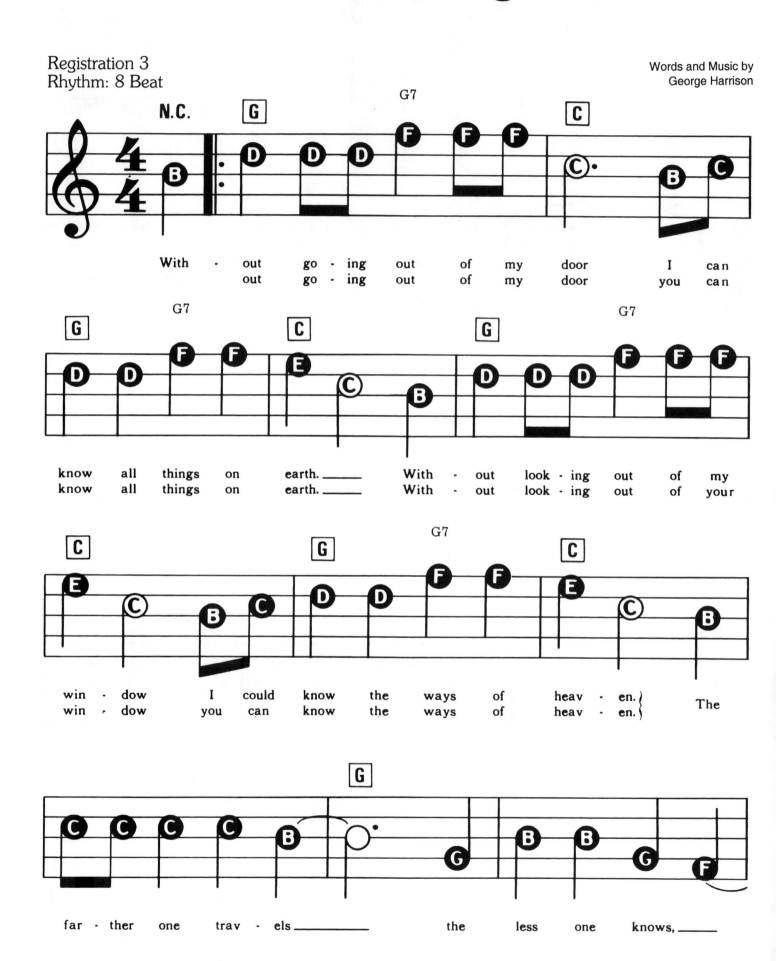

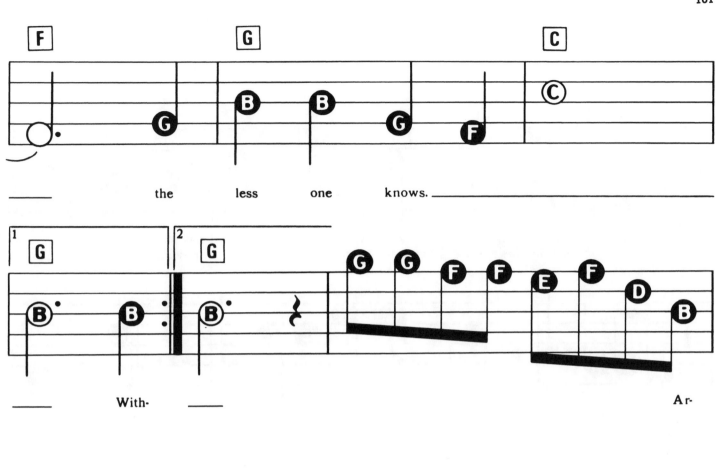

the less one knows.

With-

Ar-

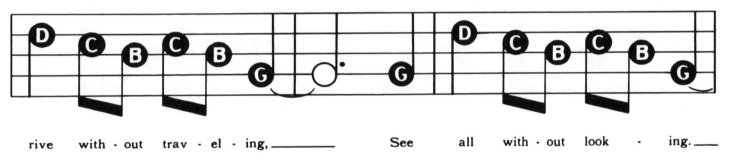

rive with-out trav-el-ing,_____ See all with-out look-ing._____

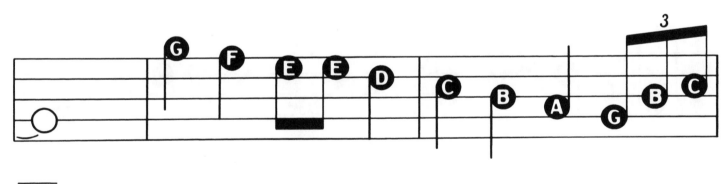

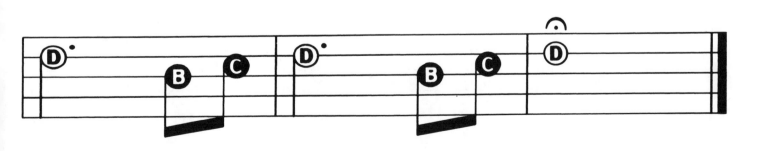

It's All Too Much

Registration 5
Rhythm: 8 Beat

Words and Music by
George Harrison

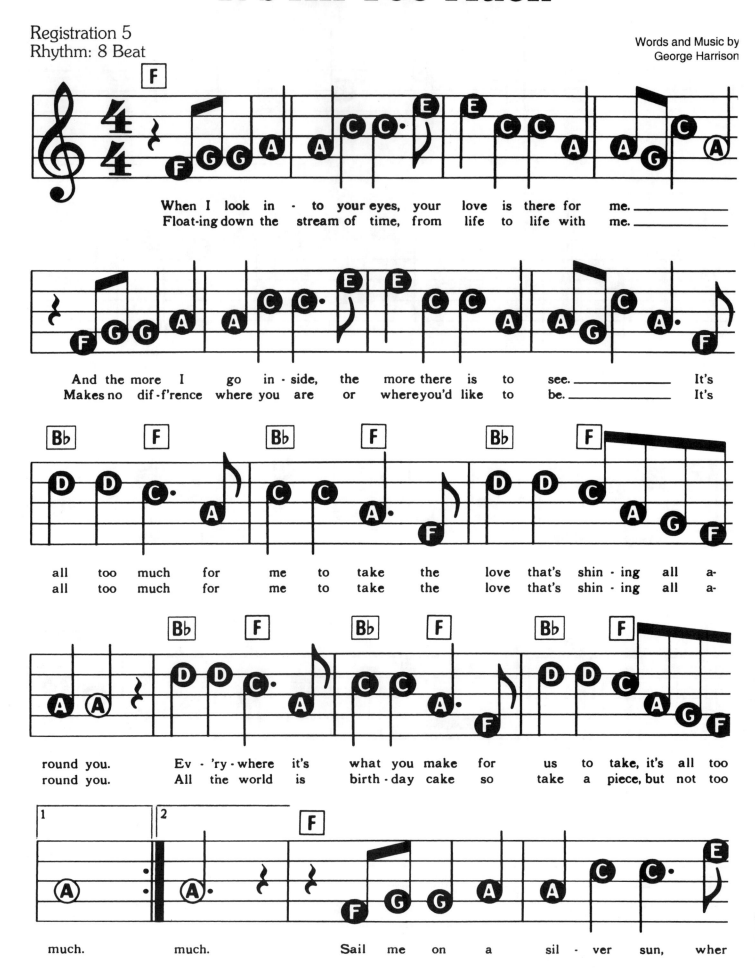

103

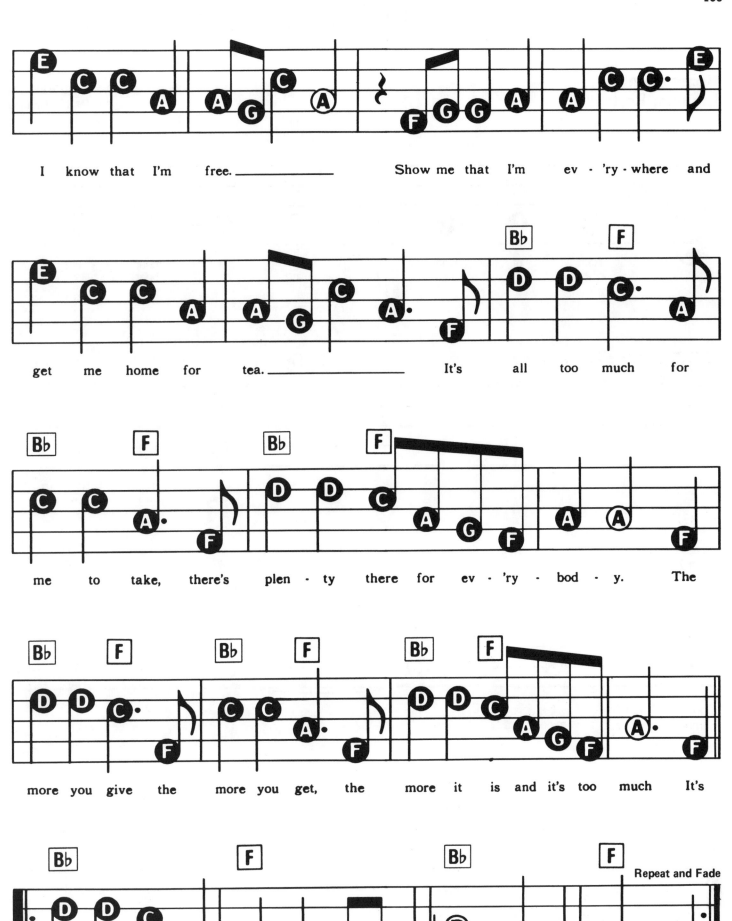

Julia

Registration 7
Rhythm: Rock

Words and Music by John Lennon
and Paul McCartney

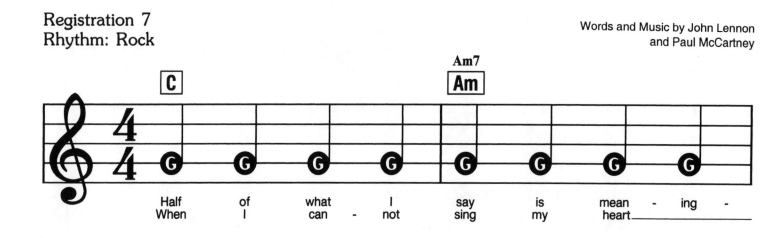

Half of what I say is mean - ing -
When I can - not sing my heart_____

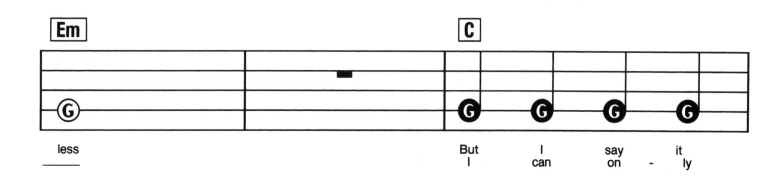

less
_____

But I say it
I can on - ly

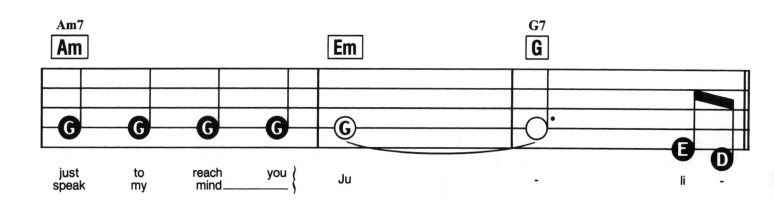

just to reach you { Ju
speak to my mind_____   -   li -

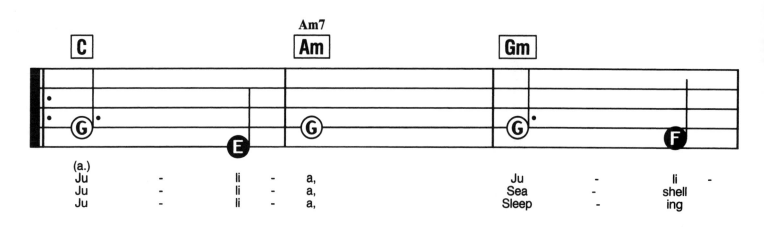

(a.)
Ju - li - a,   Ju - li -
Ju - li - a,   Sea - shell
Ju - li - a,   Sleep - ing

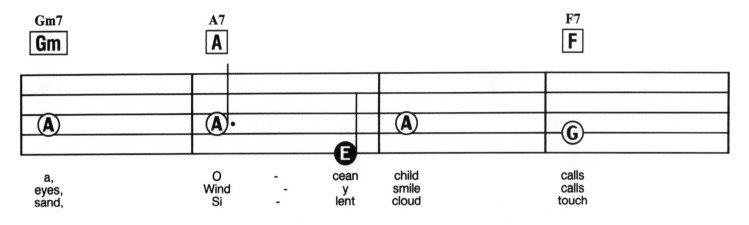

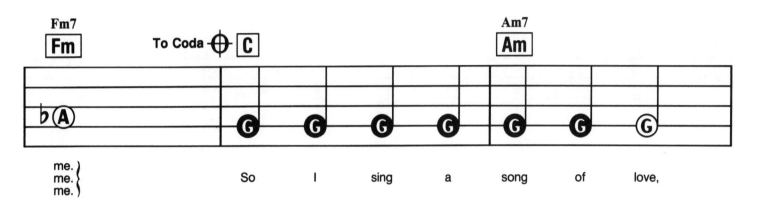

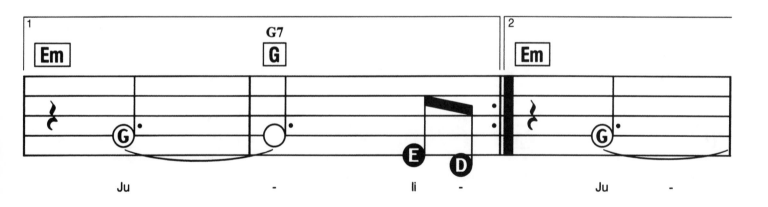

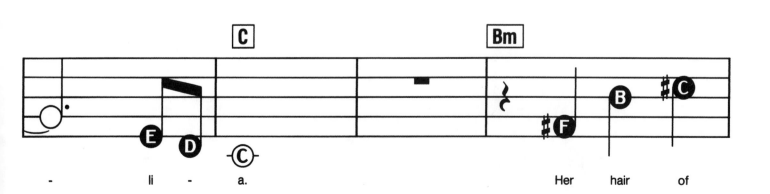

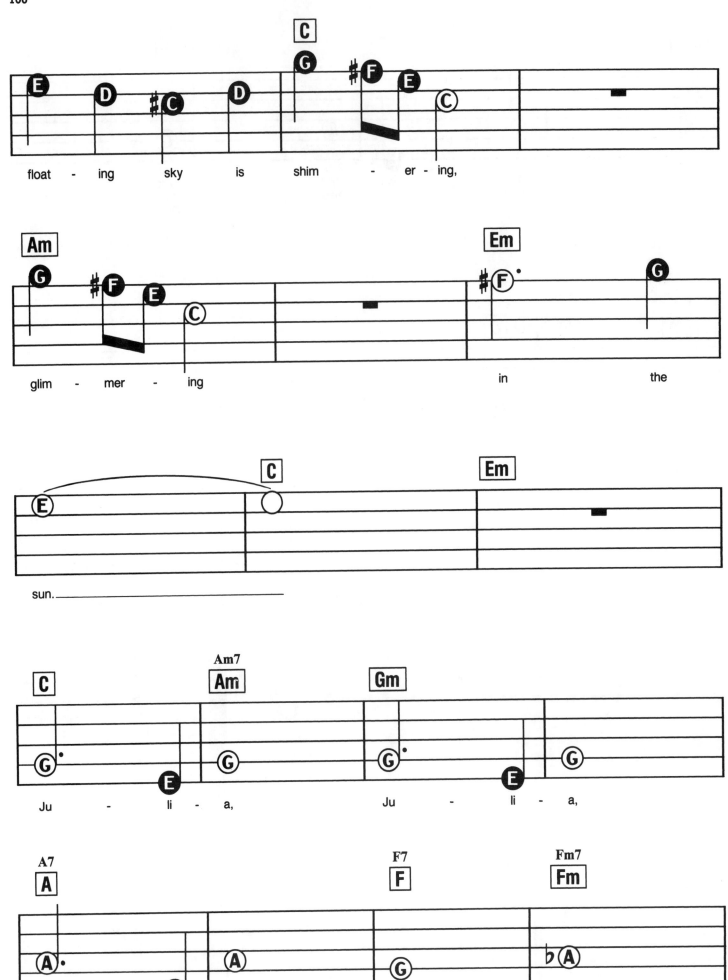

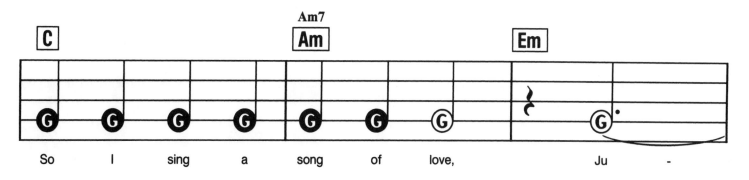

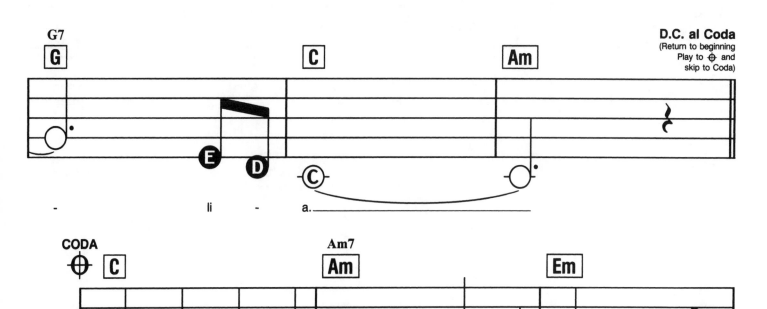

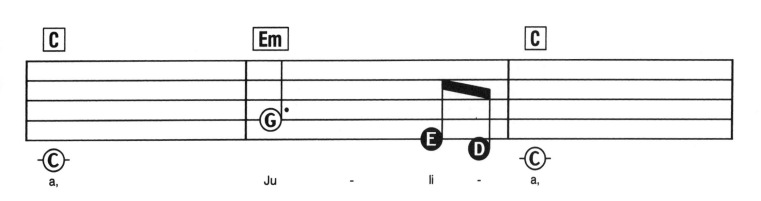

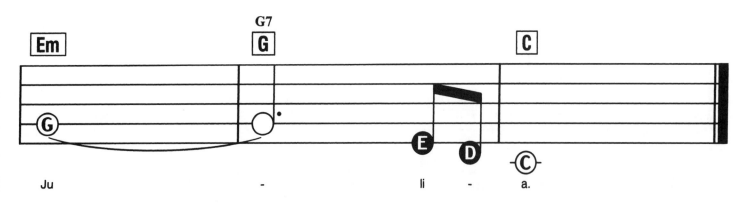

Lady Madonna

Registration 4
Rhythm: Rock

Words and Music by John Lennon
and Paul McCartney

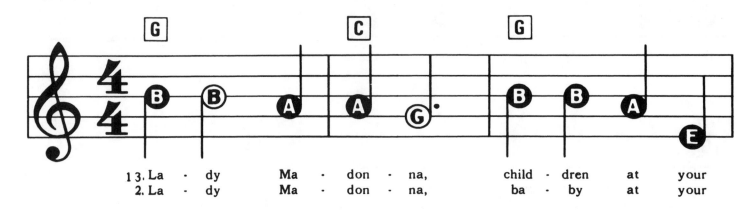

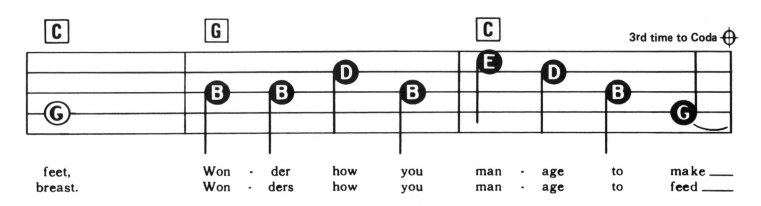

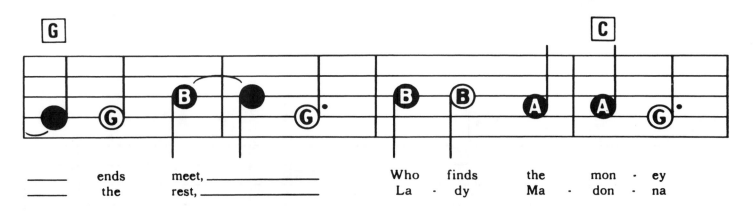

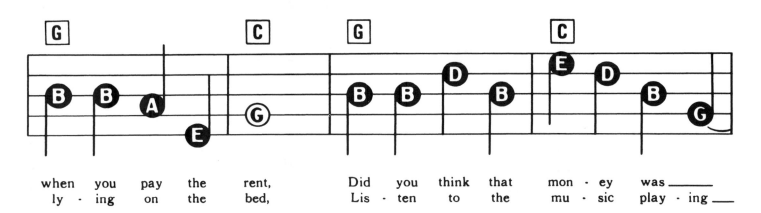

Let It Be

Registration 3
Rhythm: Rock

Words and Music by John Lennon
and Paul McCartney

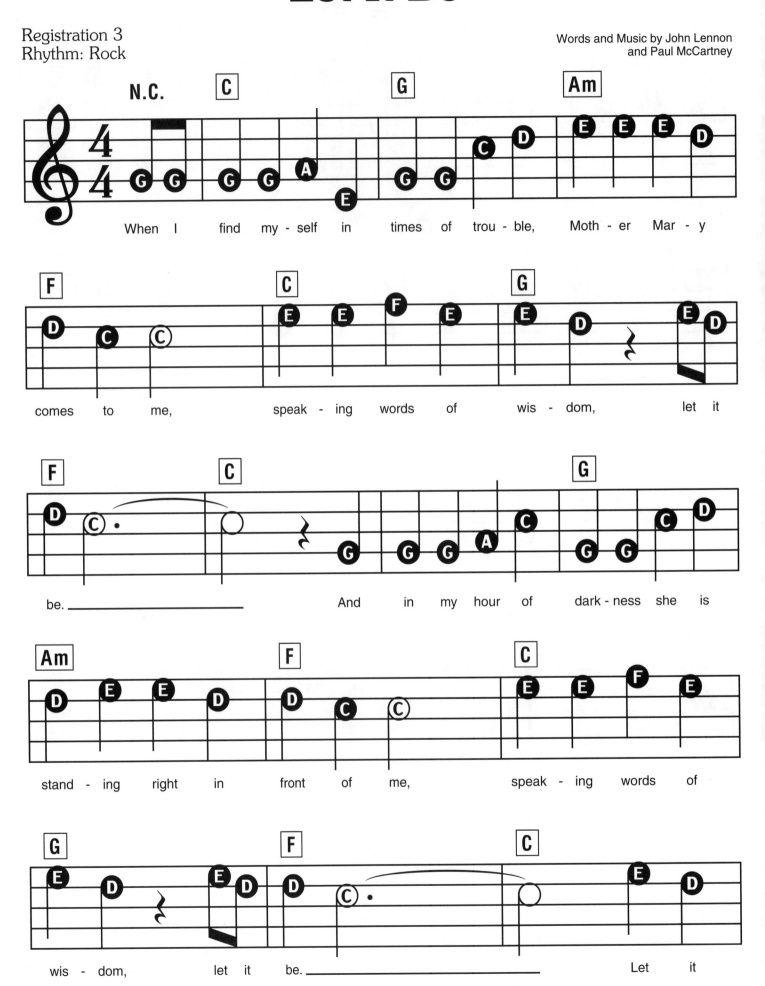

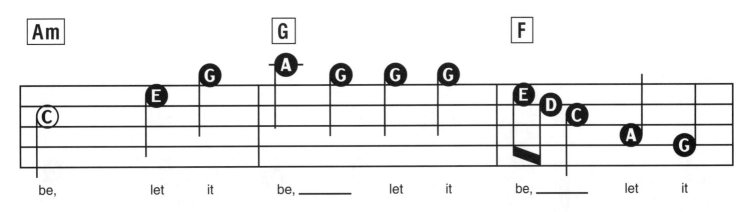

be,   let it   be, _____ let it   be, _____ let it

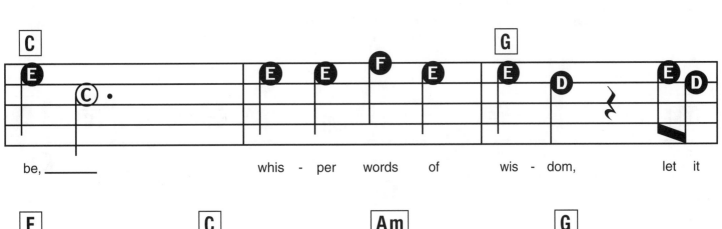

be, _____   whis - per words of   wis - dom,   let it

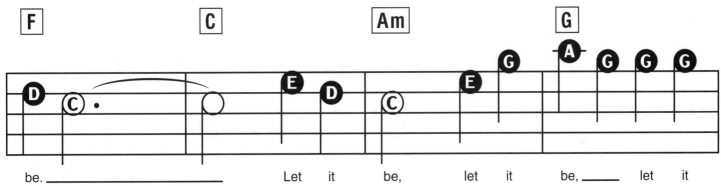

be. _____   Let it be,   let it be, _____ let it

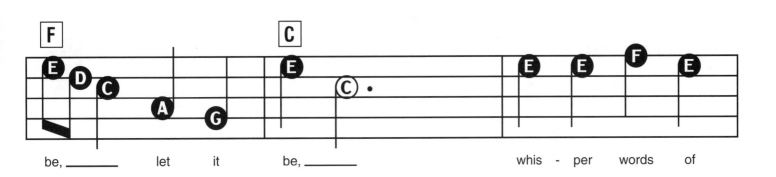

be, _____ let it   be, _____   whis - per words of

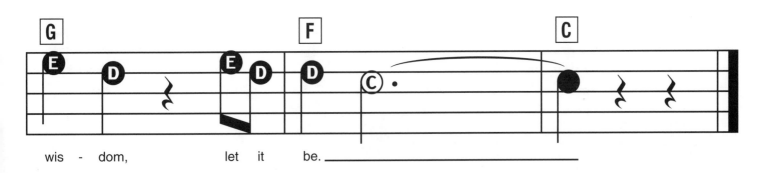

wis - dom,   let it be. _____

The Long and Winding Road

Registration 1
Rhythm: Ballad

Words and Music by John Lennon
and Paul McCartney

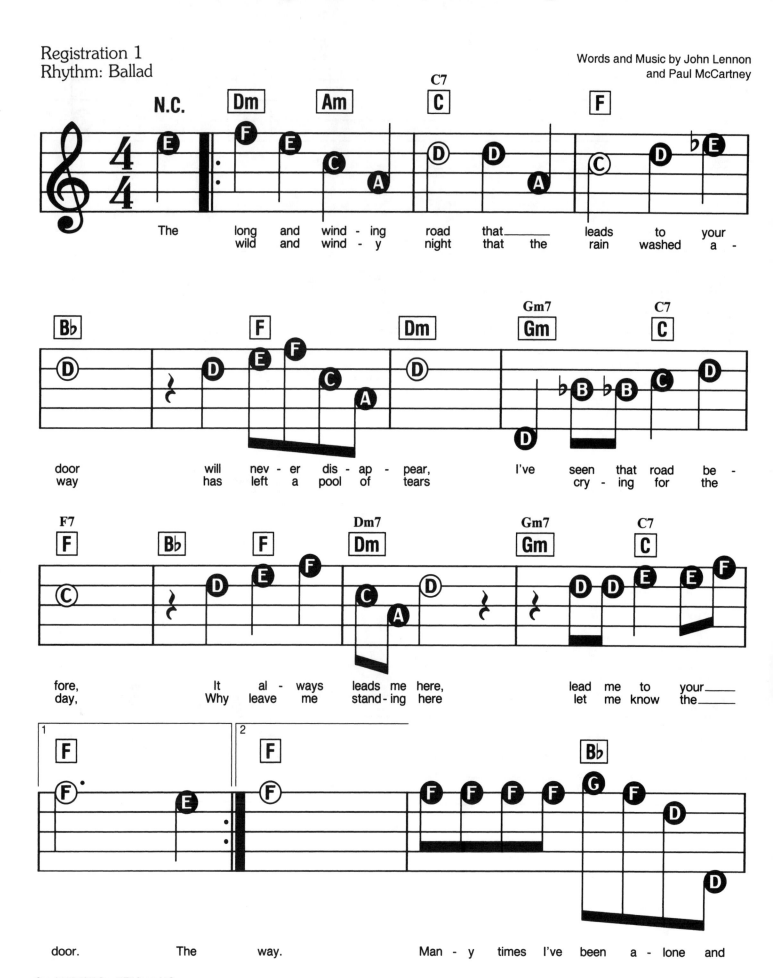

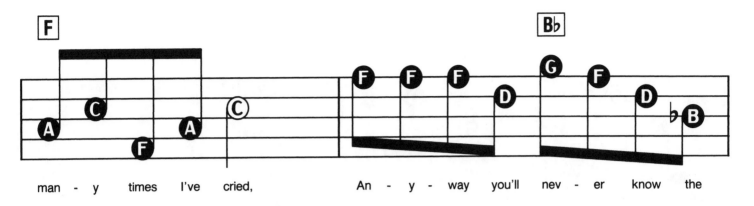

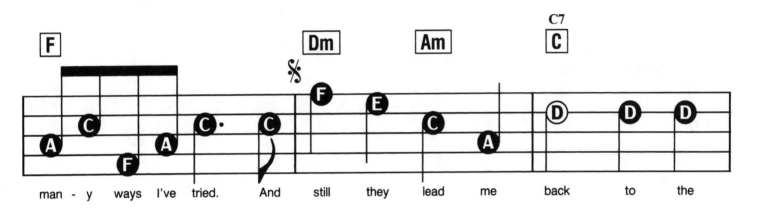

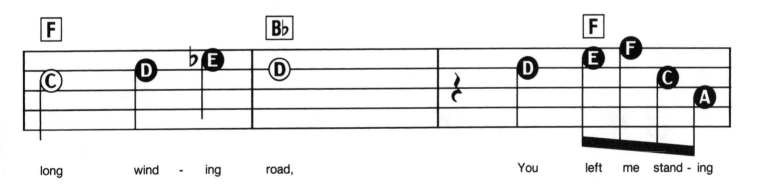

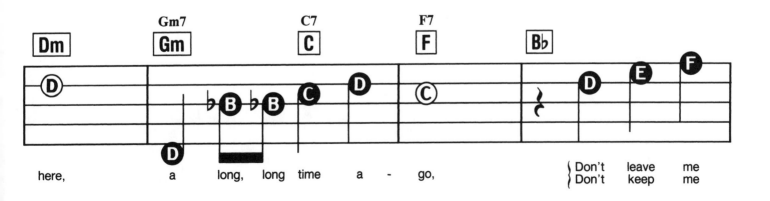

114

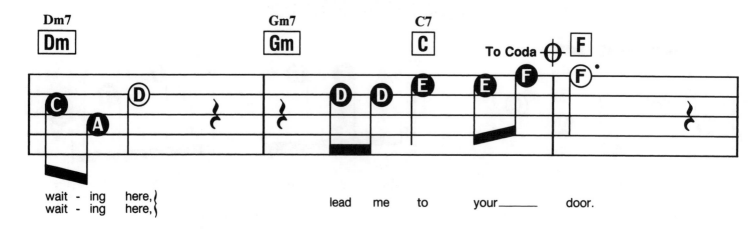

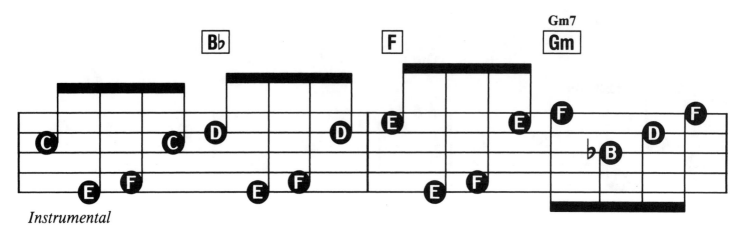

Instrumental

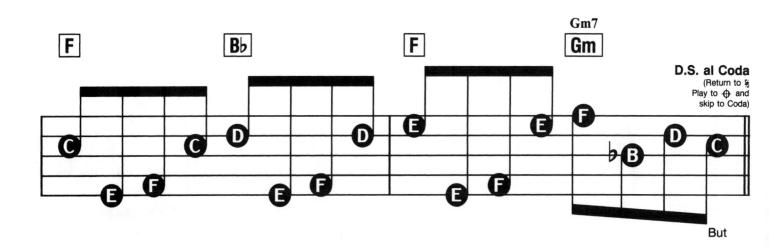

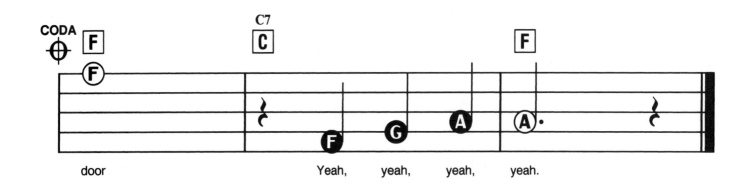

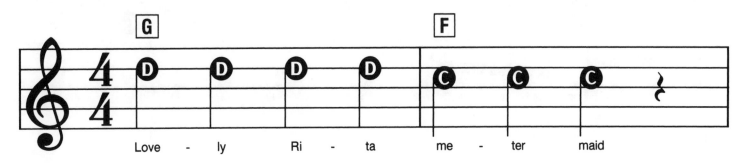

Lovely Rita

Registration 4
Rhythm: Rock or 16 Beat

Words and Music by John Lennon
and Paul McCartney

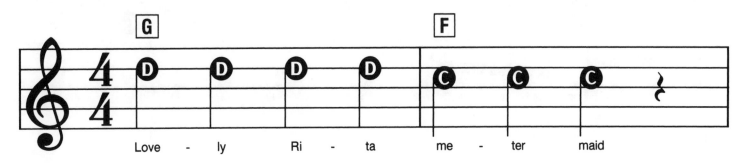

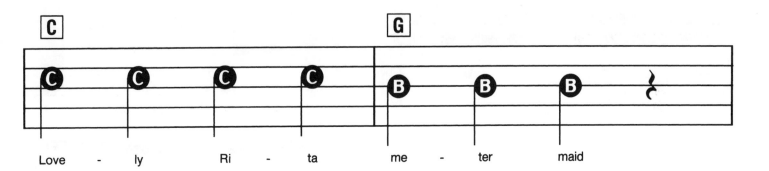

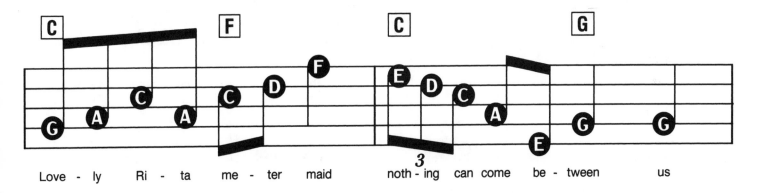

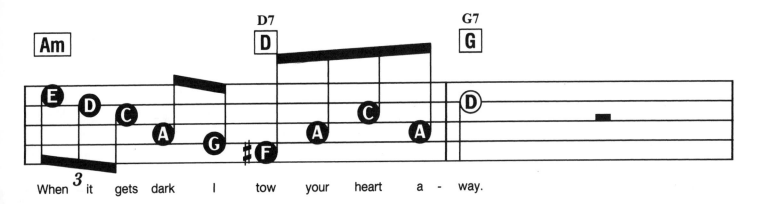

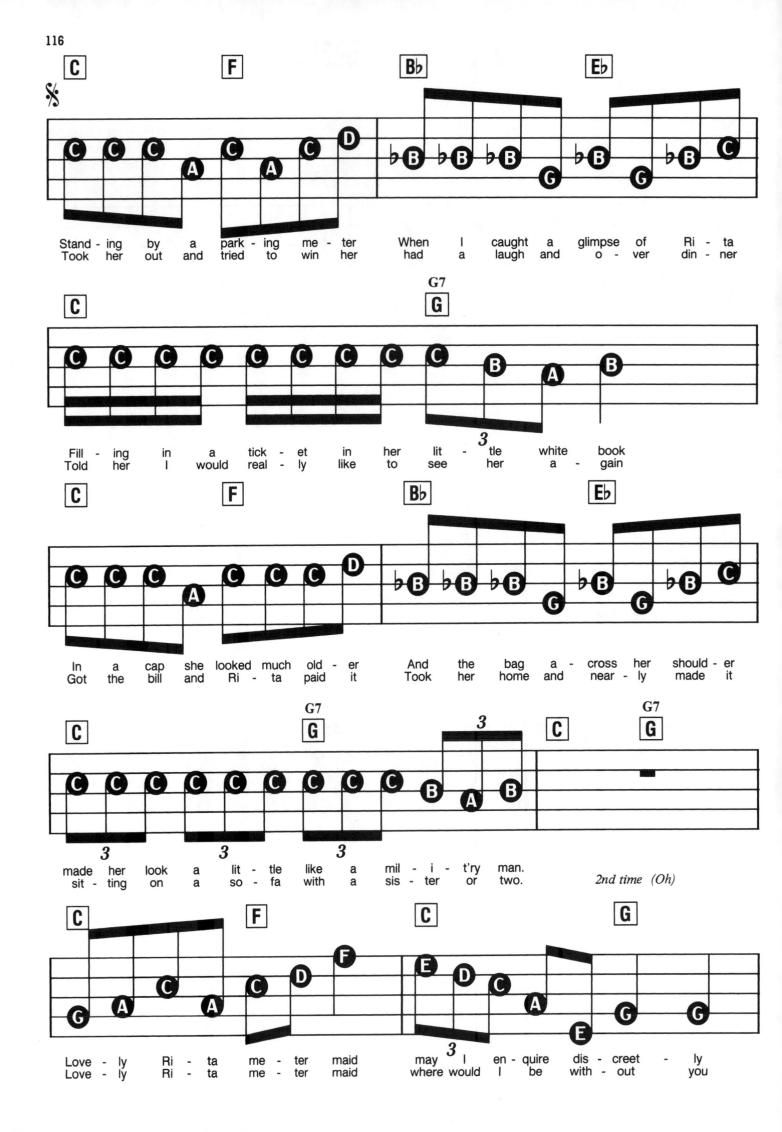

117

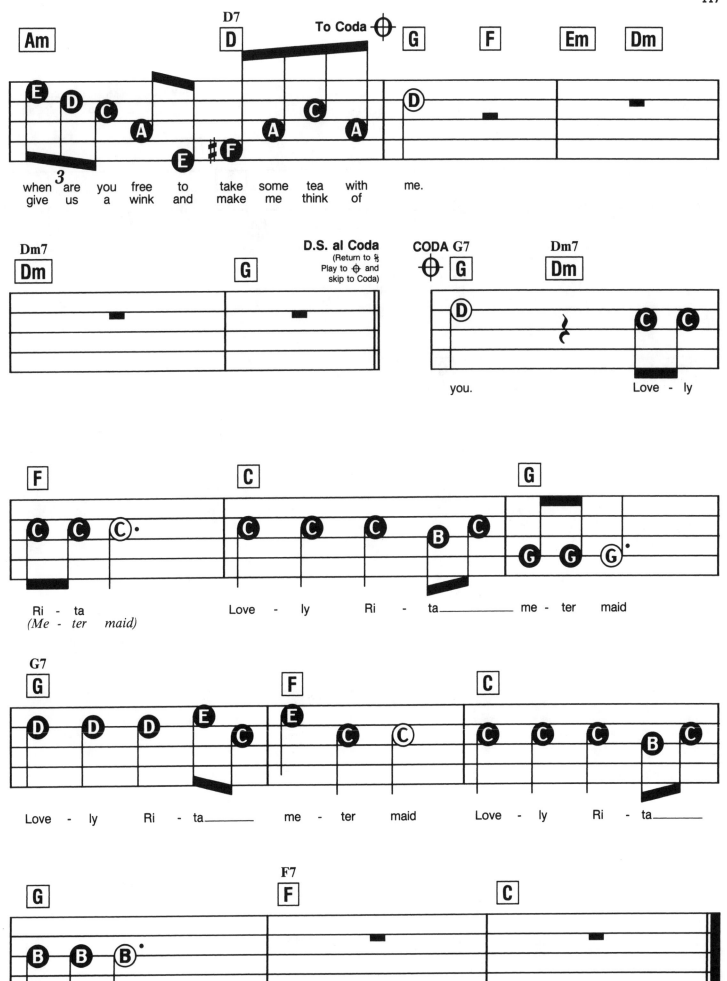

Lucy in the Sky with Diamonds

Registration 8
Rhythm: Waltz

Words and Music by John Lennon
and Paul McCartney

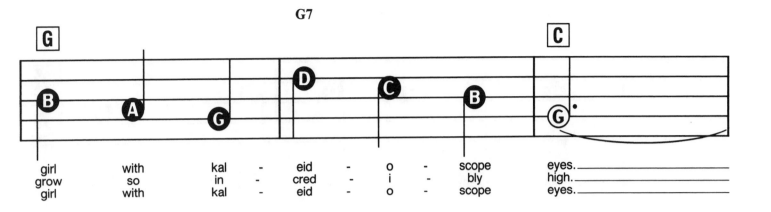

girl | with | kal | - | eid | - | o | - | scope | eyes. _____
grow | so | in | - | cred | - | i | - | bly | high. _____
girl | with | kal | - | eid | - | o | - | scope | eyes. _____

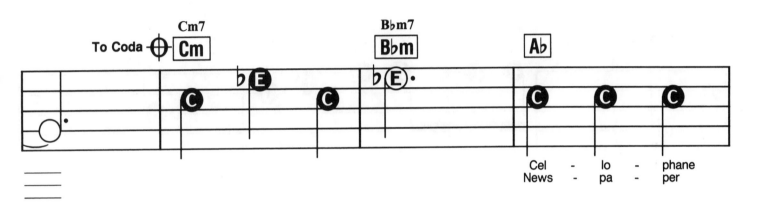

_____
_____

Cel | - | lo | - | phane
News | - | pa | - | per

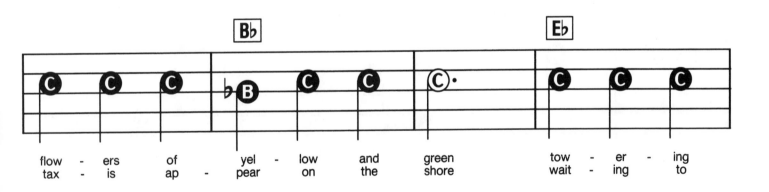

flow | - | ers | of | yel | - | low | and | green | tow | - | er | - | ing
tax | - | is | ap | - | pear | on | the | shore | wait | - | ing | to

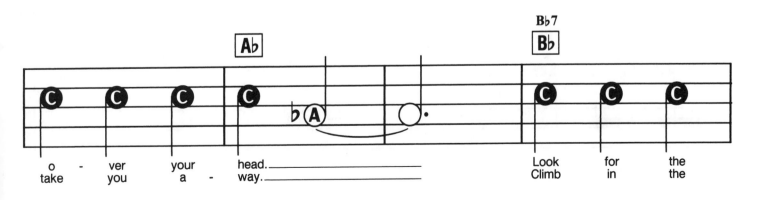

o | - | ver | your | head. _____
take | you | a | - | way. _____

Look | for | the
Climb | in | the

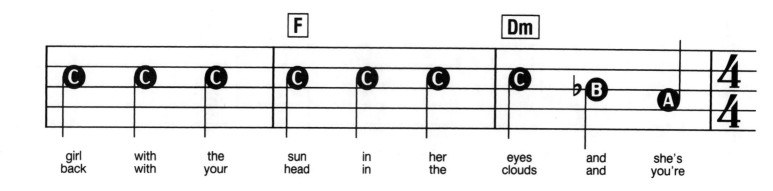

girl with the sun in her eyes and she's
back with your head in the clouds and you're

Rhythm: Rock

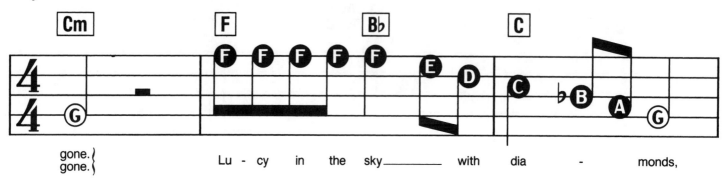

gone.
gone. Lu - cy in the sky_____ with dia - monds,

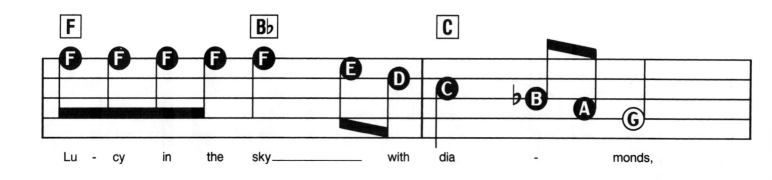

Lu - cy in the sky_____ with dia - monds,

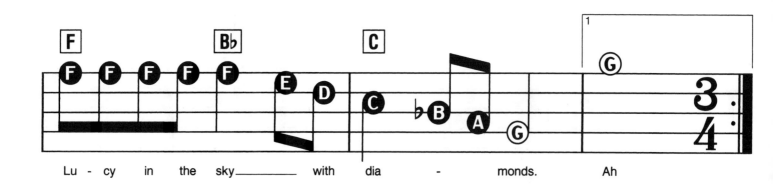

Lu - cy in the sky_____ with dia - monds. Ah

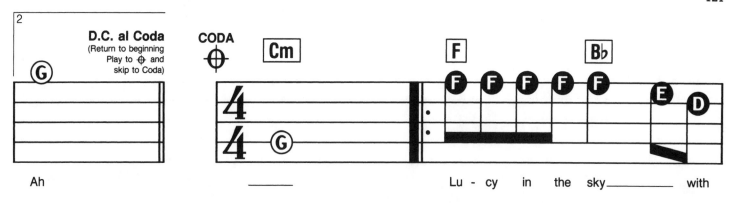

Ah _____ Lu - cy in the sky_____ with

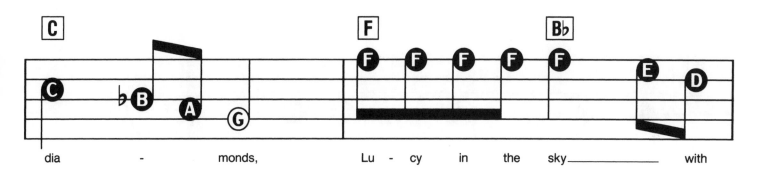

dia - monds, Lu - cy in the sky_____ with

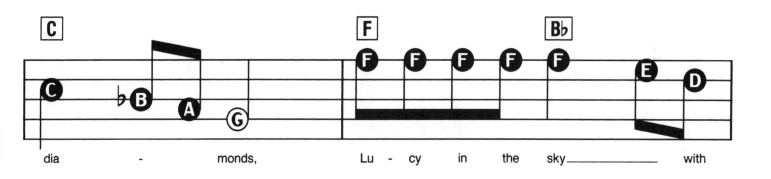

dia - monds, Lu - cy in the sky_____ with

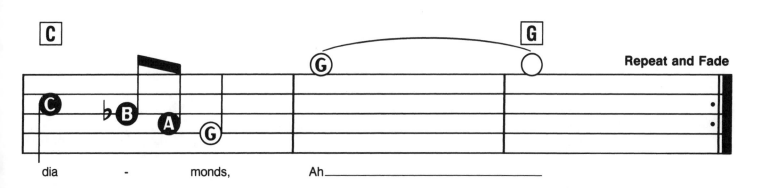

dia - monds, Ah_____

Maggie Mae

Registration 4
Rhythm: 8 Beat or Rock

By George Harrison, John Lennon,
Paul McCartney and Richard Starkey

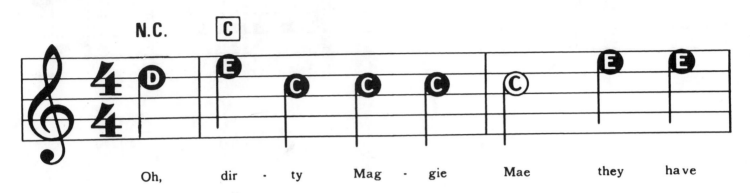

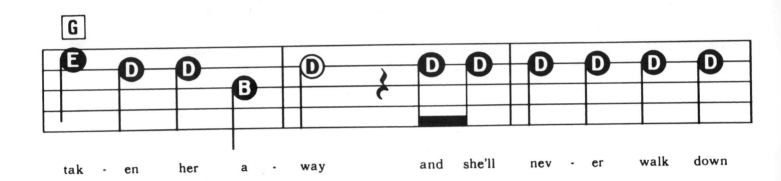

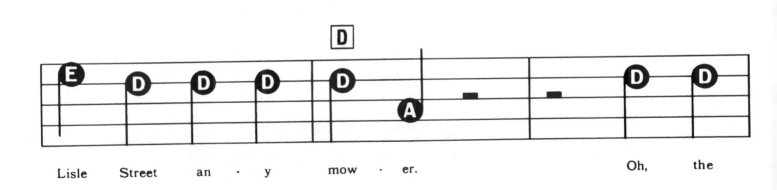

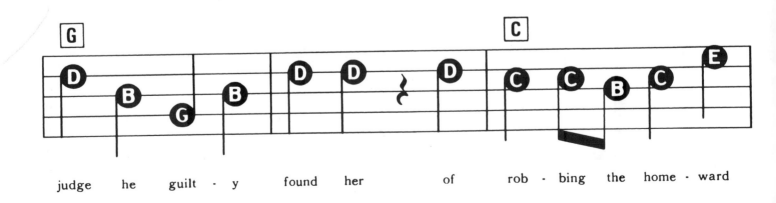

123

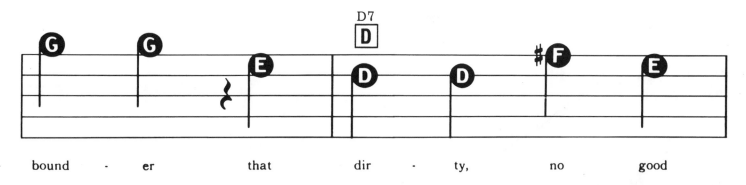

bound - er that dir - ty, no good

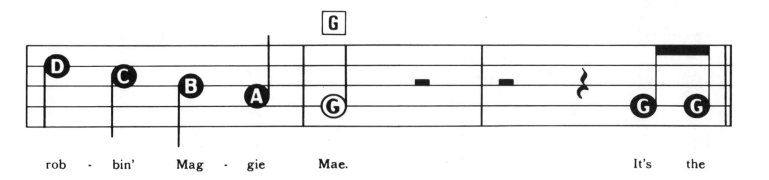

rob - bin' Mag - gie Mae. It's the

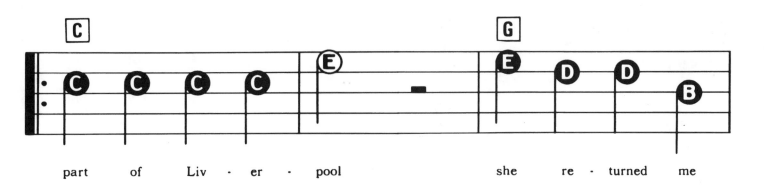

part of Liv - er - pool she re - turned me

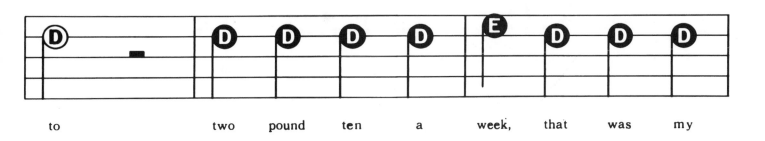

to two pound ten a week, that was my

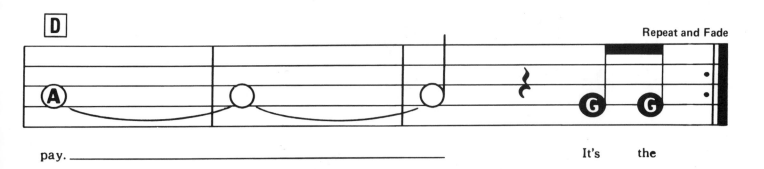

Repeat and Fade

pay. _____ It's the

Magical Mystery Tour

Registration 2
Rhythm: Rock

Words and Music by John Lennon
and Paul McCartney

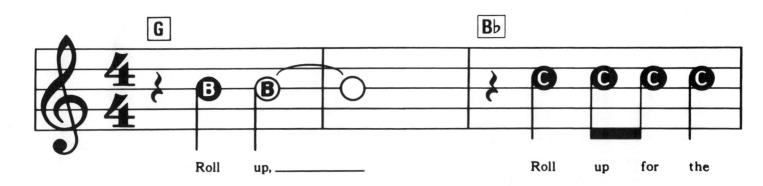

Roll up, _____ Roll up for the

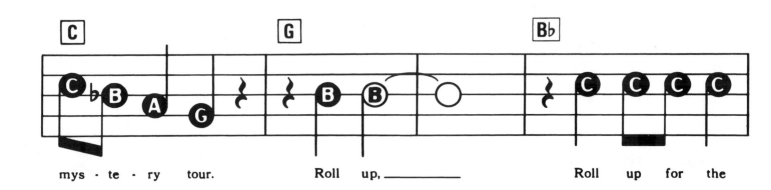

mys - te - ry tour. Roll up, _____ Roll up for the

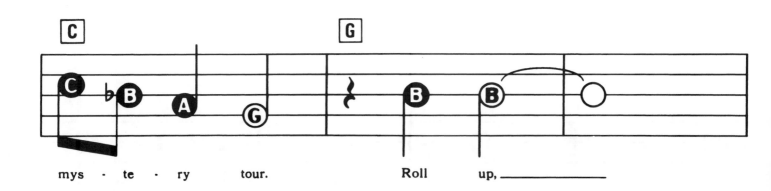

mys - te - ry tour. Roll up, _____

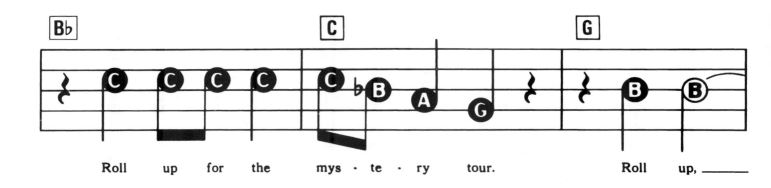

Roll up for the mys - te - ry tour. Roll up, _____

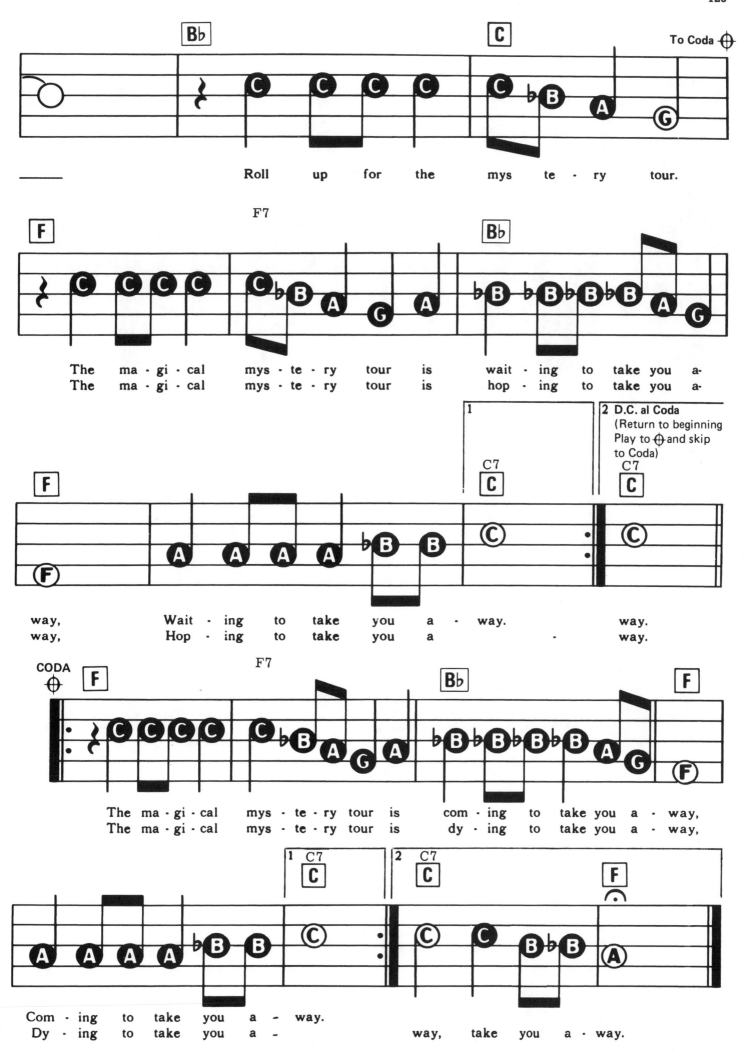

Martha My Dear

Registration 8
Rhythm: Swing or Shuffle

Words and Music by John Lennon
and Paul McCartney

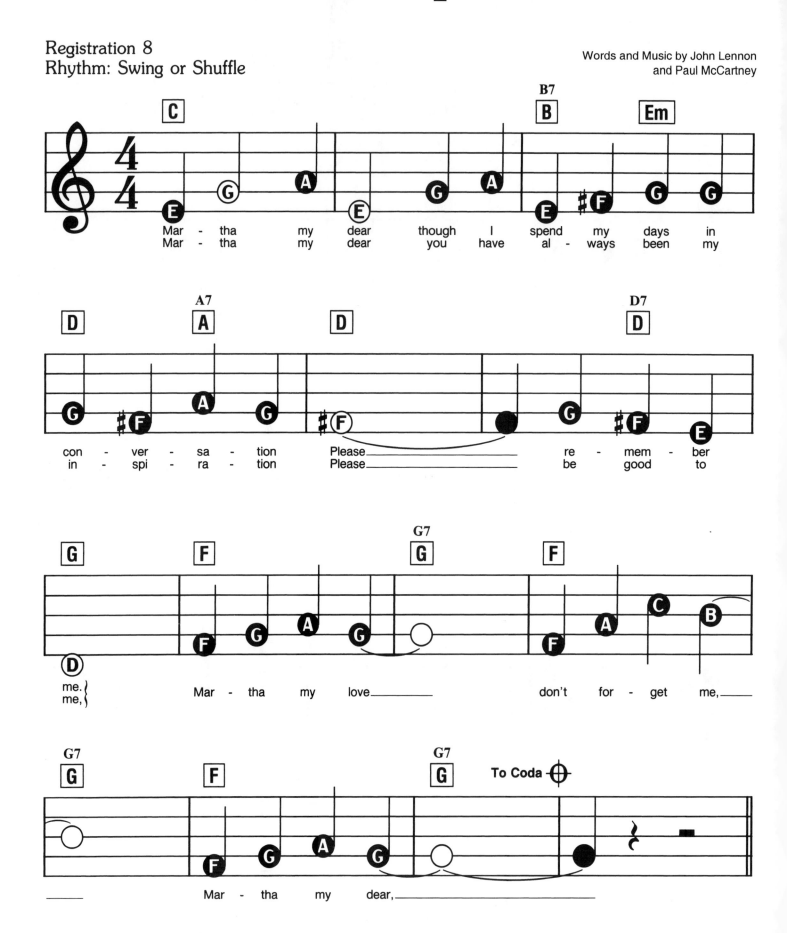

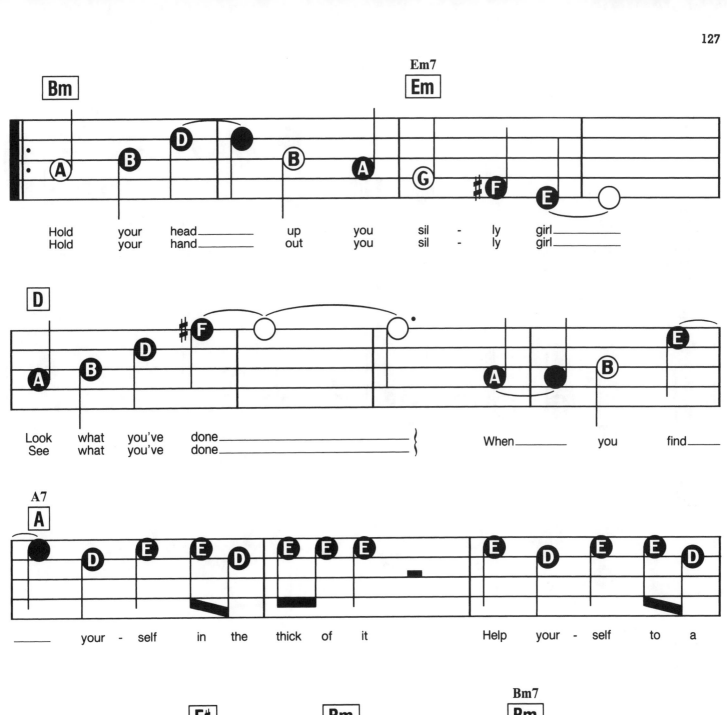

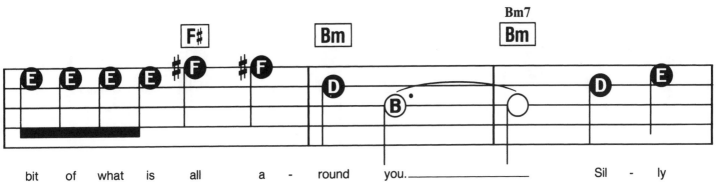

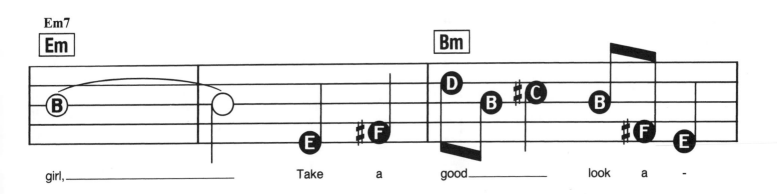

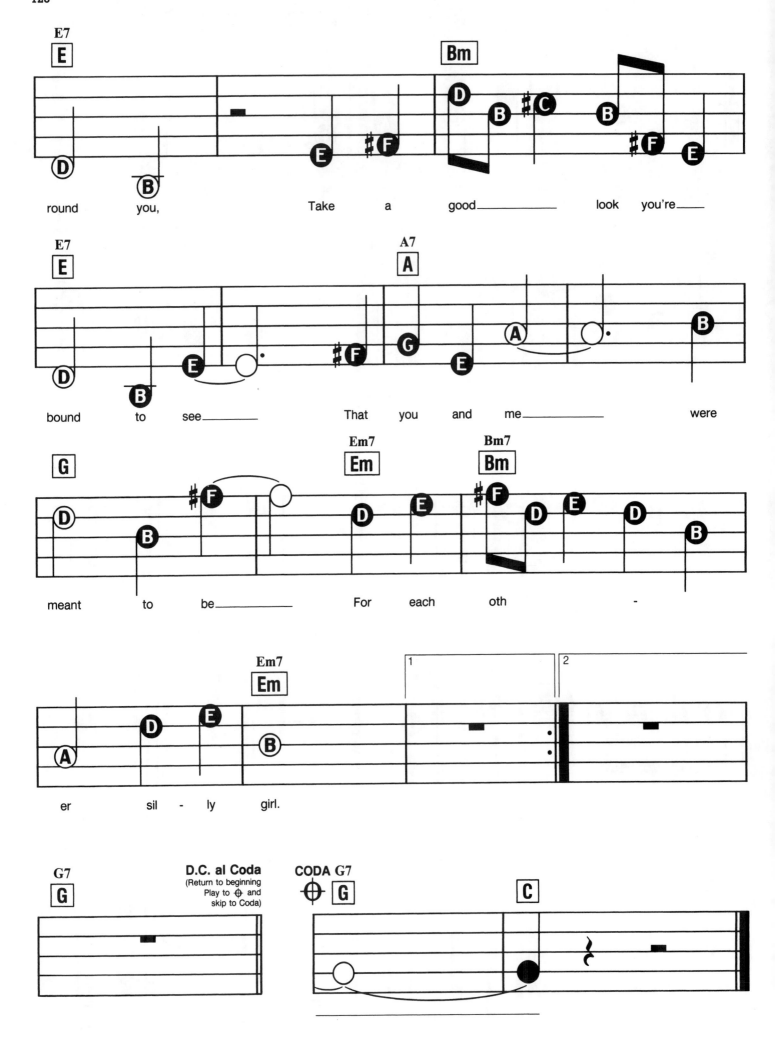

Maxwell's Silver Hammer

Registration 1
Rhythm: Rock or Shuffle

Words and Music by John Lennon
and Paul McCartney

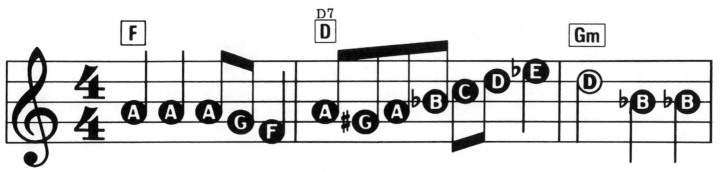

Joan was quiz-zi-cal Stud-ied pat-a-phy-i-cal science in the
Back in school a-gain, Max-well plays the fool a-gain Teacher gets an-
P. C. thirty-one said, We've caught a' dir-ty one,' Max-well stands a-

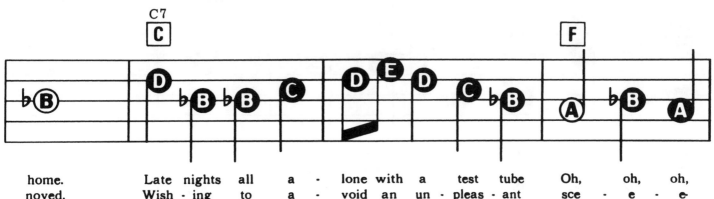

home. Late nights all a - lone with a test tube Oh, oh, oh,
noyed. Wish-ing to a-void an un-pleas-ant sce - e - e
lone. Paint-ing test-i-mon-i-al pic-tures, Oh, oh, oh,

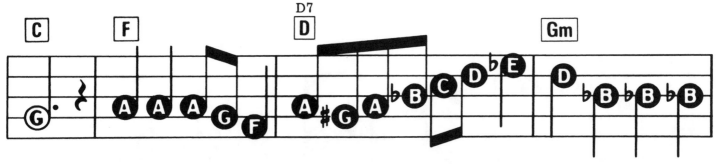

oh. Max-well Ed-i-son Ma-jor-ing in med-i-cine, calls her on the
ene. She tells Max to stay when the class has gone a-way, So he waits be-
oh. Rose and Val-er-ie Scream-ing from the gal-ler-y Say he must go

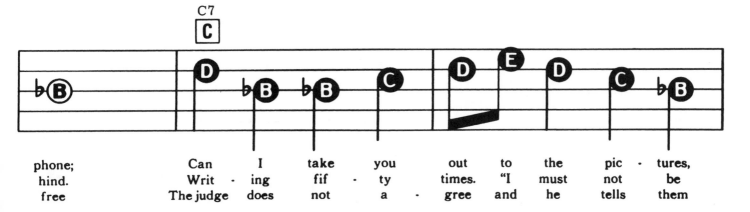

phone; Can I take you out to the pic-tures,
hind. Writ-ing fif-ty times. "I must not be
free The judge does not a-gree and he tells them

130

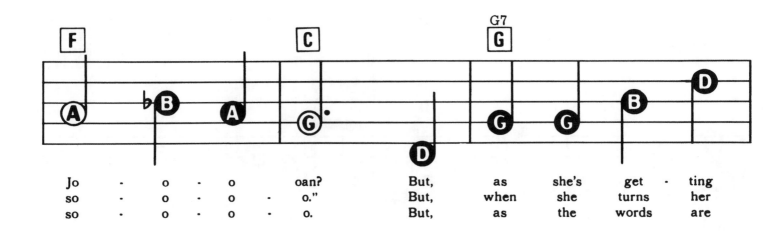

Jo - o - o oan? But, as she's get - ting
so - o - o - o." But, when she turns her
so - o - o - o. But, as the words are

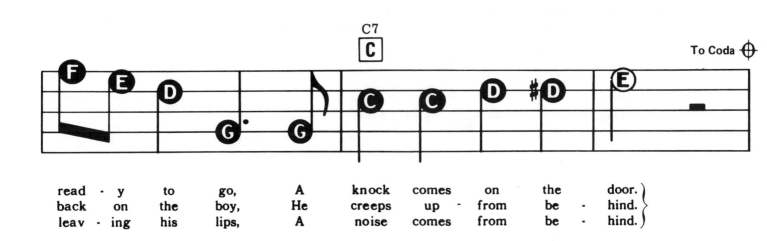

read - y to go, A knock comes on the door.
back on the boy, He creeps up - from be - hind.
leav - ing his lips, A noise comes from be - hind.

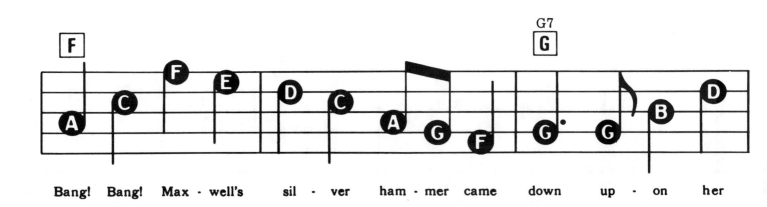

Bang! Bang! Max - well's sil - ver ham - mer came down up - on her

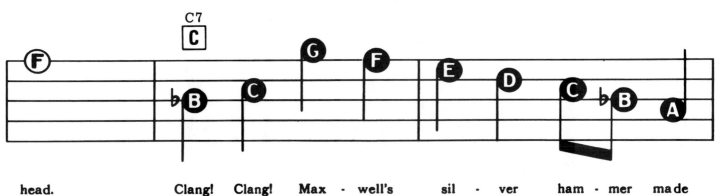

head. Clang! Clang! Max - well's sil - ver ham - mer made

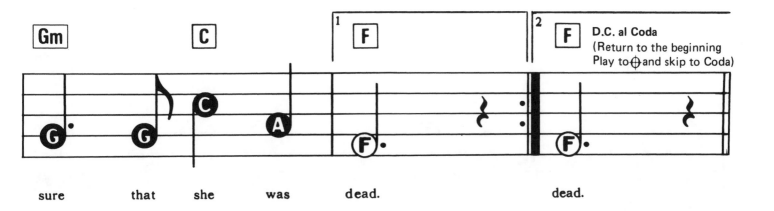

sure   that   she   was   dead.   dead.

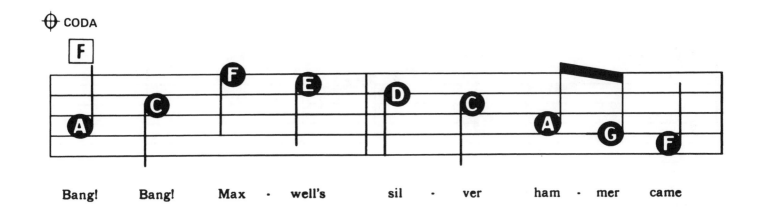

Bang!   Bang!   Max - well's   sil - ver   ham - mer   came

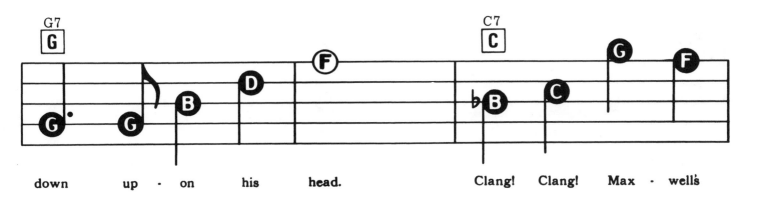

down   up - on   his   head.   Clang!   Clang!   Max - well's

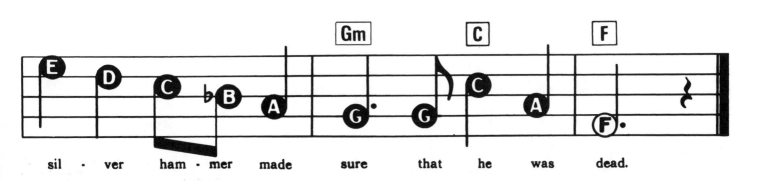

sil - ver   ham - mer   made   sure   that   he   was   dead.

Mean Mr. Mustard

Registration 4
Rhythm: Rock

Words and Music by John Lennon
and Paul McCartney

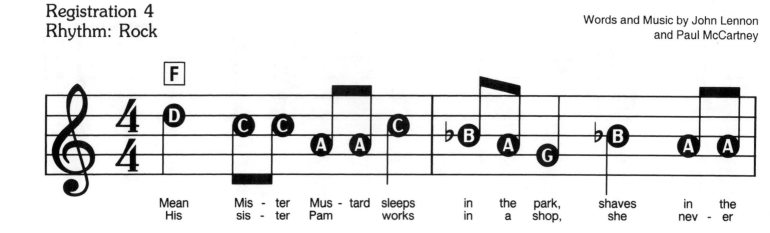

Mean Mis-ter Mus-tard sleeps in the park, shaves in the
His sis-ter Pam works in a shop, she nev-er

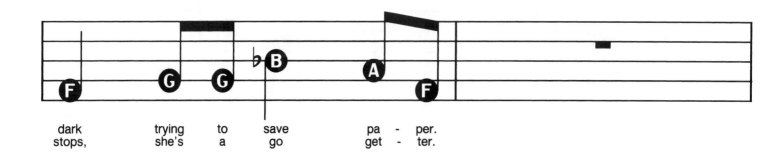

dark, try-ing to save pa - per.
stops, she's a go get - ter.

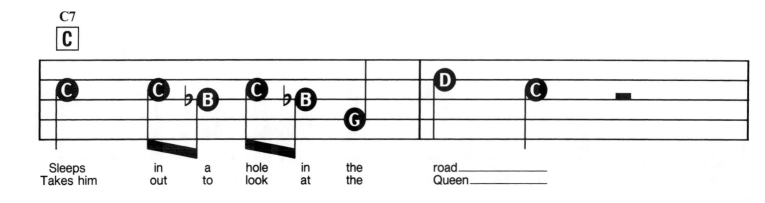

Sleeps in a hole in the road_____
Takes him out to look at the Queen_____

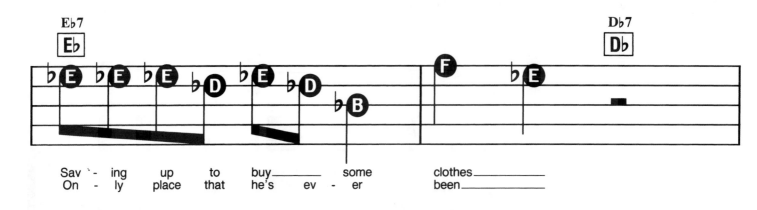

Sav`- ing up to buy_____ some clothes_____
On - ly place that he's ev - er been_____

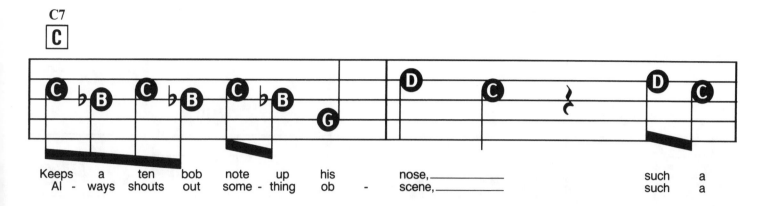

Keeps a ten bob note up his nose,_____ such a
Al - ways shouts out some - thing ob - scene,_____ such a

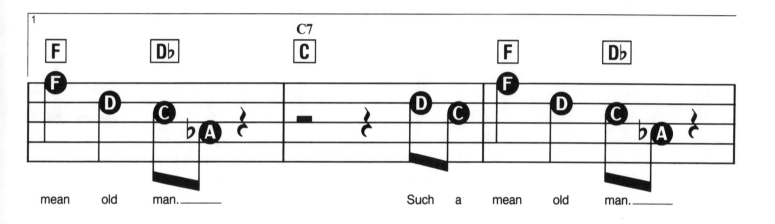

mean old man._____ Such a mean old man._____

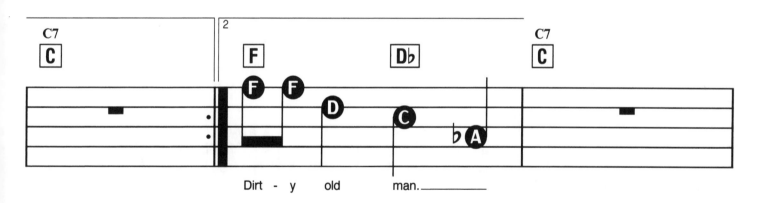

Dirt - y old man._____

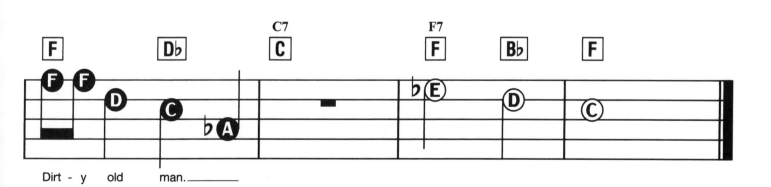

Dirt - y old man._____

Mother Nature's Son

Registration 4
Rhythm: 8 Beat or Rock

Words and Music by John Lennon
and Paul McCartney

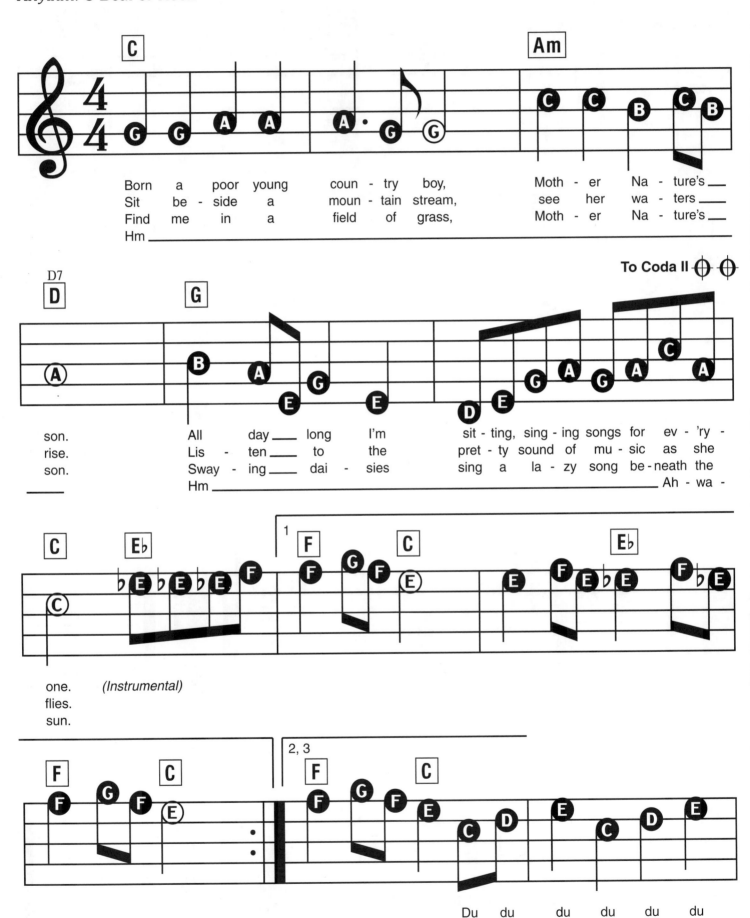

Born   a   poor   young   coun - try   boy,
Sit   be - side   a   moun - tain   stream,
Find   me   in   a   field   of   grass,
Hm _____

Moth - er   Na - ture's ___
see   her   wa - ters ___
Moth - er   Na - ture's ___

To Coda II

son.
rise.
son.
___

All   day ___   long   I'm
Lis - ten ___   to   the
Sway - ing ___   dai - sies
Hm _____

sit - ting, sing - ing songs for   ev - 'ry-
pret - ty   sound of   mu - sic   as   she
sing   a   la - zy song be - neath the
Ah - wa -

one.   *(Instrumental)*
flies.
sun.

Du   du   du   du   du   du

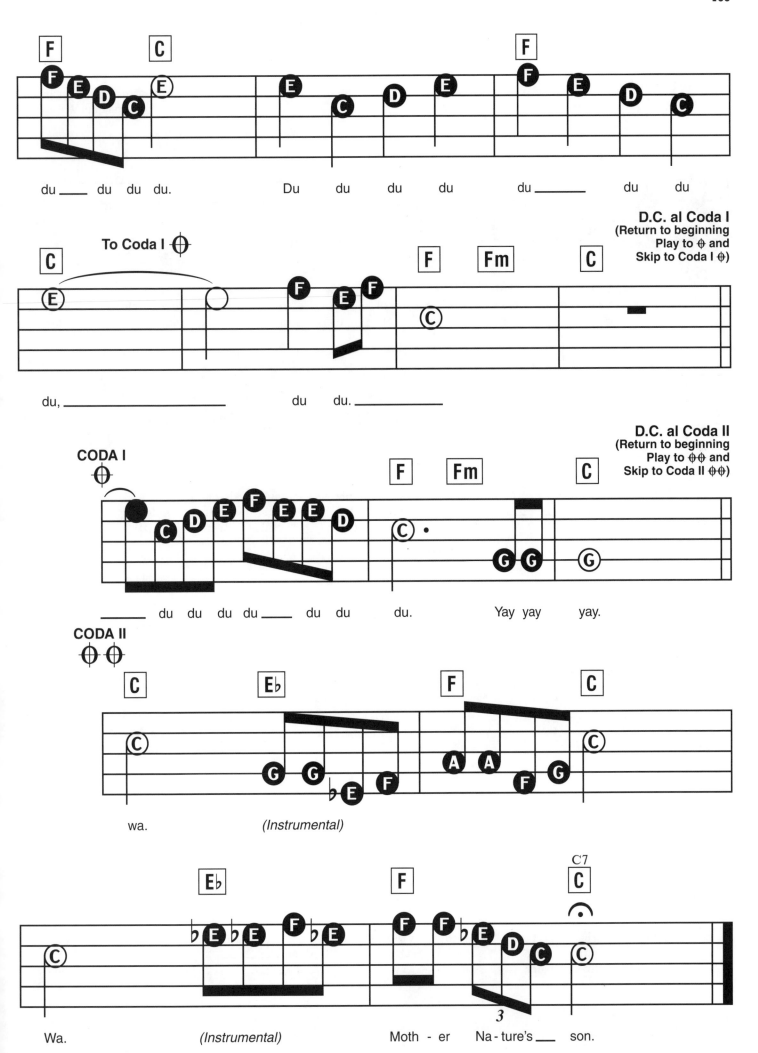

Ob-La-Di, Ob-La-Da

Registration 5
Rhythm: Rock

Words and Music by John Lennon
and Paul McCartney

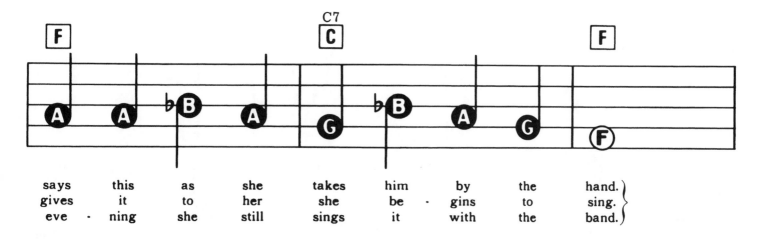

says this as she takes him by the hand.
gives it to her she be - gins to sing.
eve - ning to she still sings it with the band.

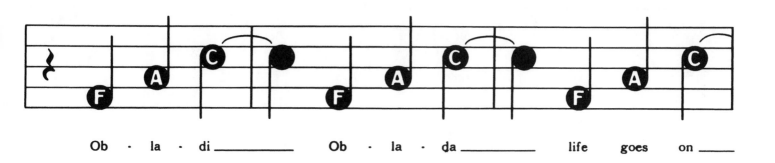

Ob - la - di _____ Ob - la - da _____ life goes on _____

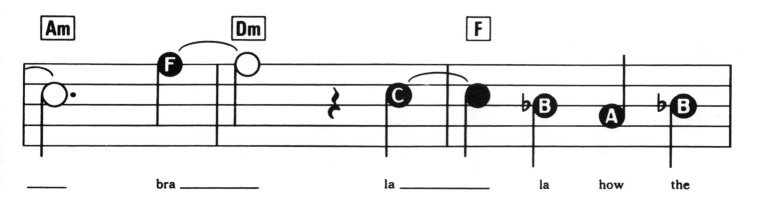

_____ bra _____ la _____ la how the

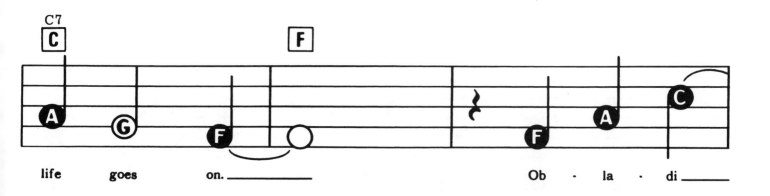

life goes on. _____ Ob - la - di _____

138

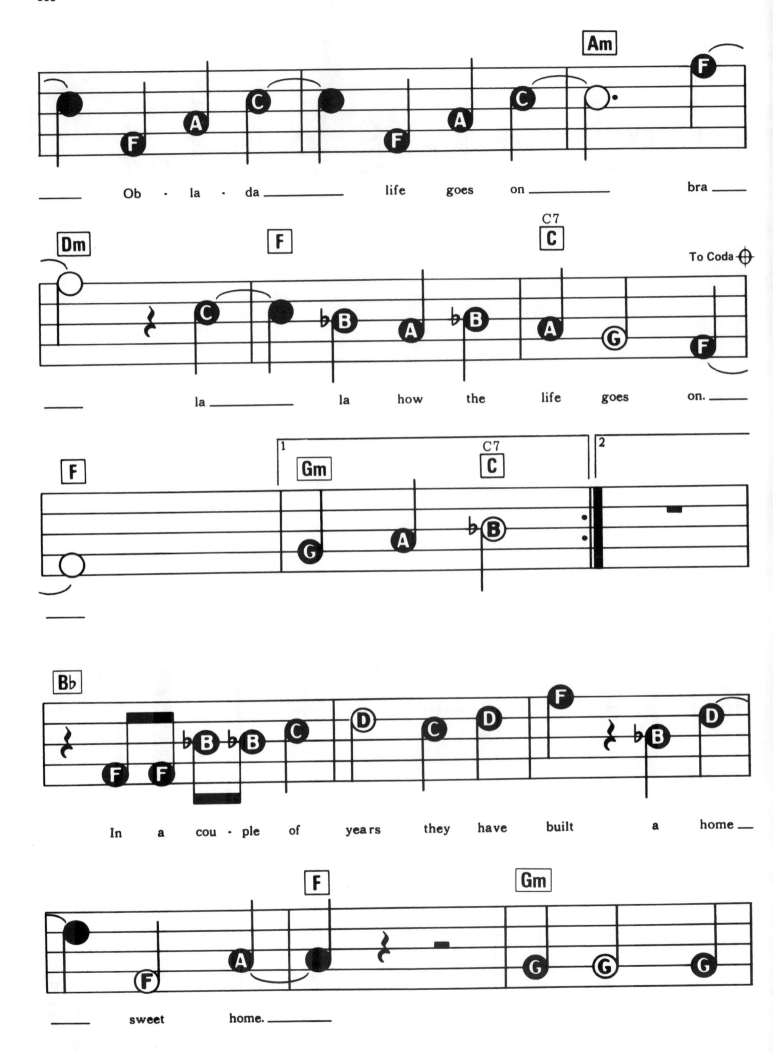

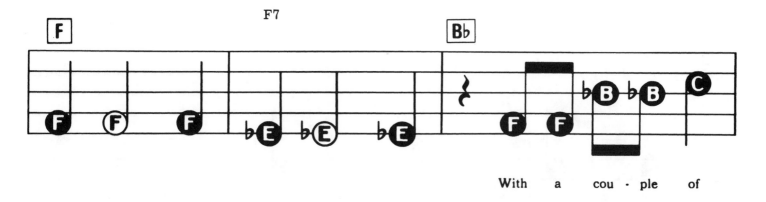

With a cou-ple of

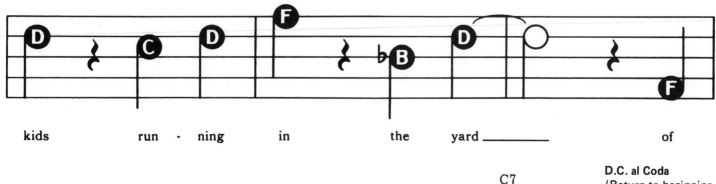

kids run-ning in the yard _____ of

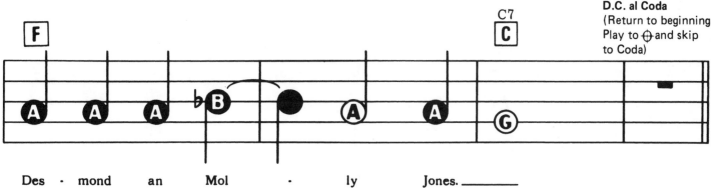

Des-mond an Mol-ly Jones. _____

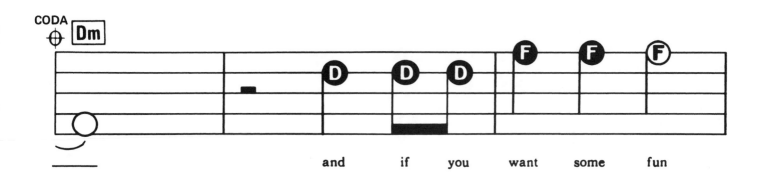

and if you want some fun

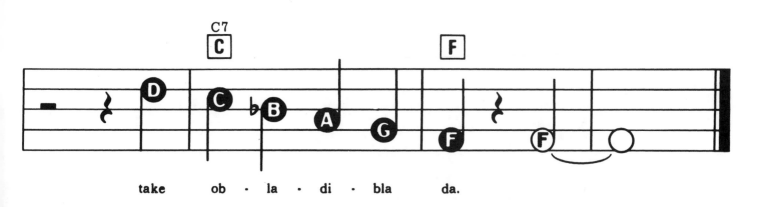

take ob-la-di-bla da.

Oh! Darling

Registration 2
Rhythm: Slow Rock

Words and Music by John Lennon
and Paul McCartney

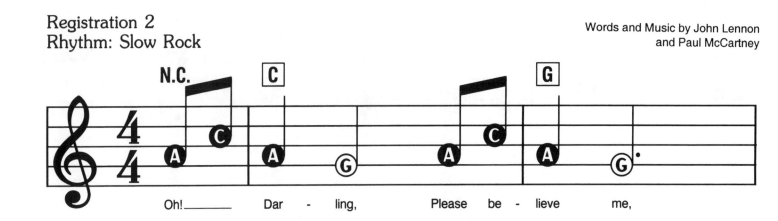

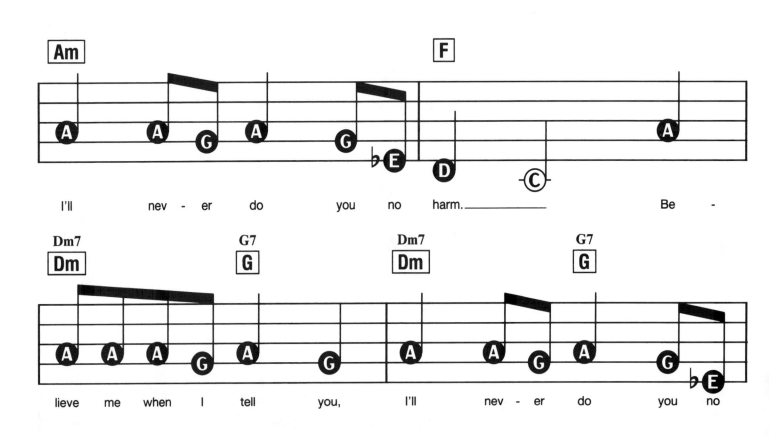

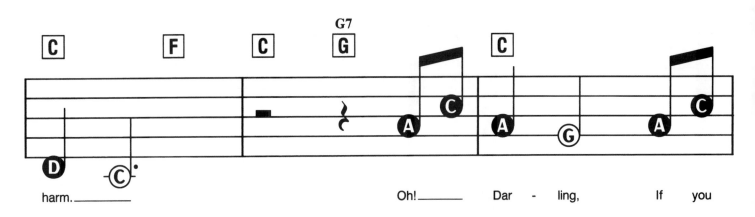

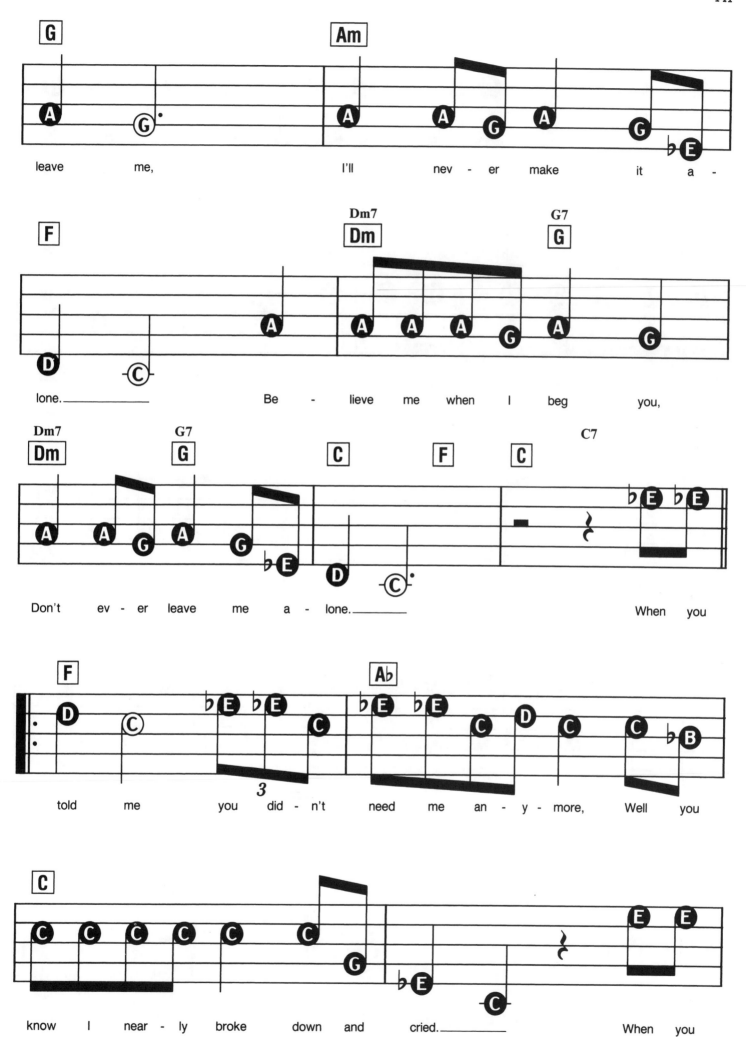

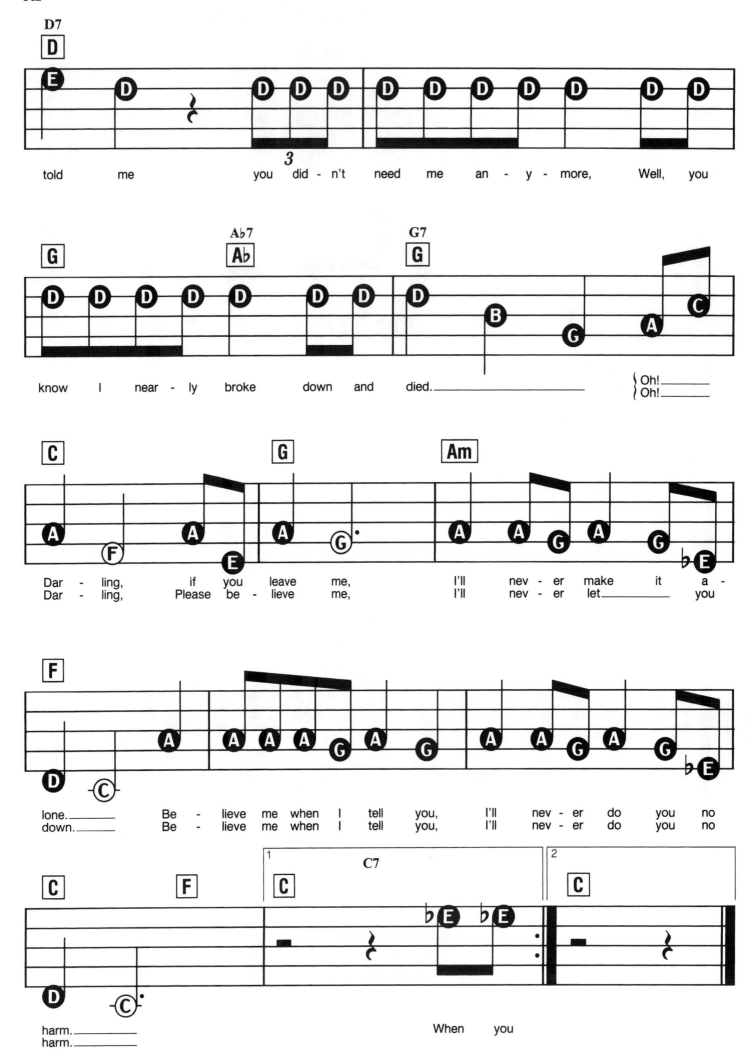

G
Am
leave me, I'll nev - er make it a -
F
Dm7
Dm
G7
G
lone. Be - lieve me when I beg you,
Dm7
Dm
G7
G
C
F
C
C7
Don't ev - er leave me a - lone. When you
F
A♭
3
told me you did - n't need me an - y - more, Well you
C
know I near - ly broke down and cried. When you

Old Brown Shoe

Registration 1
Rhythm: 8 Beat or Rock

Words and Music by
George Harrison

144

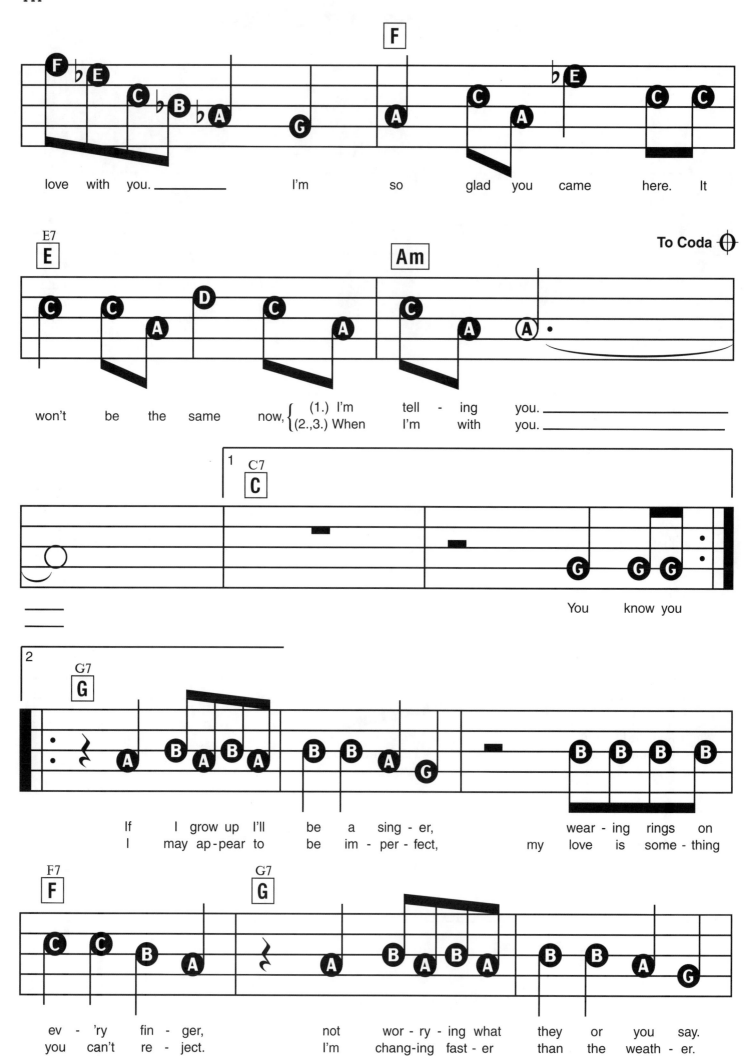

145

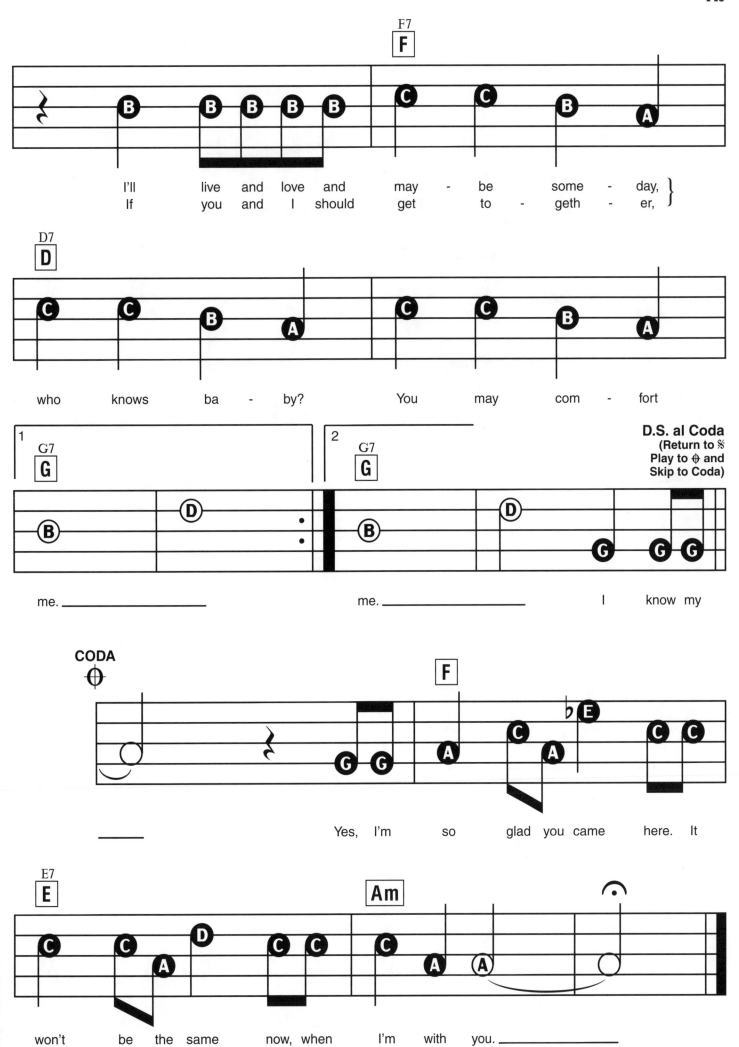

Penny Lane

Registration 2
Rhythm: Rock

Words and Music by John Lennon
and Paul McCartney

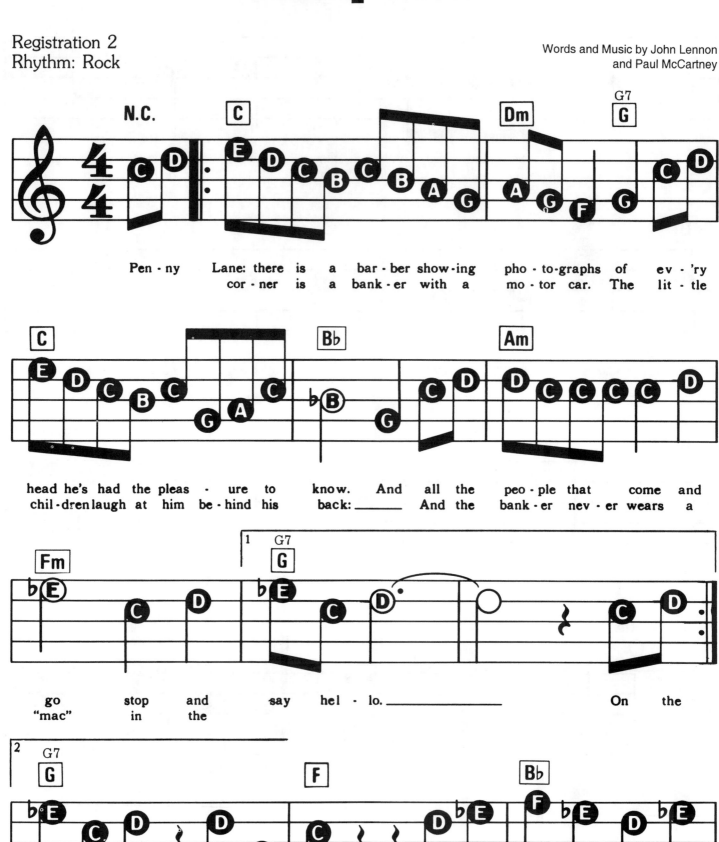

147

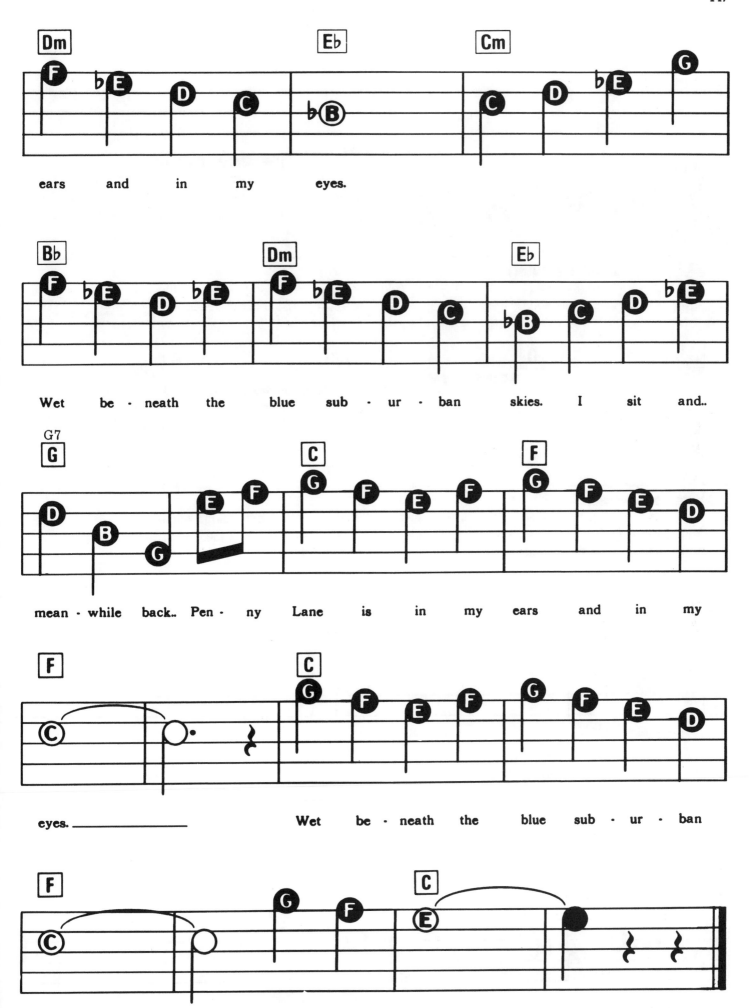

Piggies

Registration 8
Rhythm: Rock

Words and Music by
George Harrison

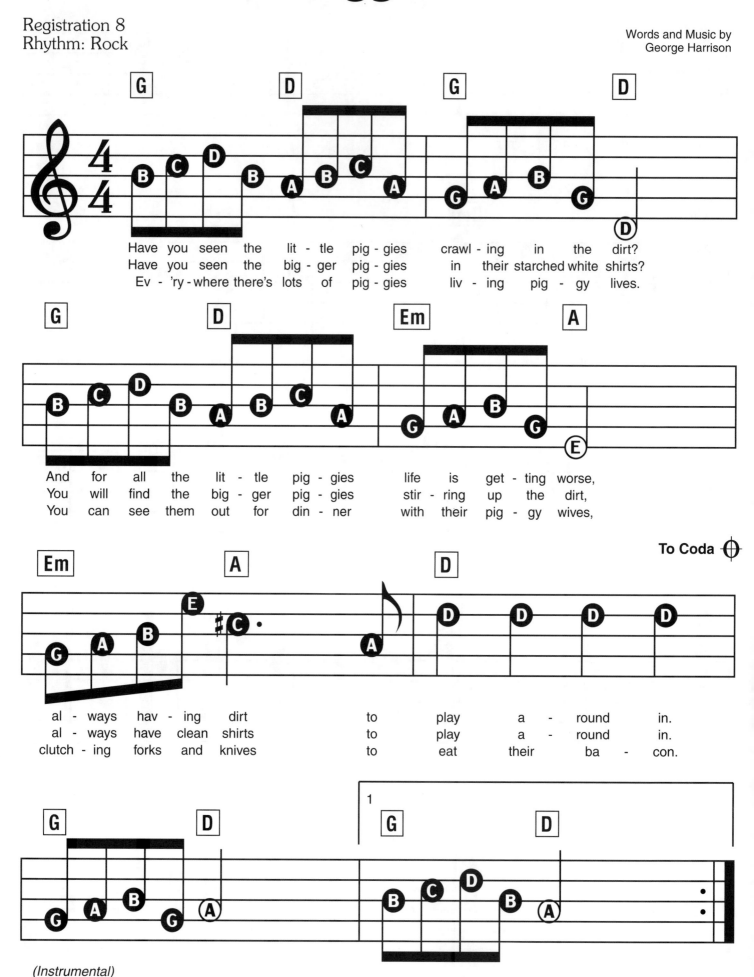

(Instrumental)

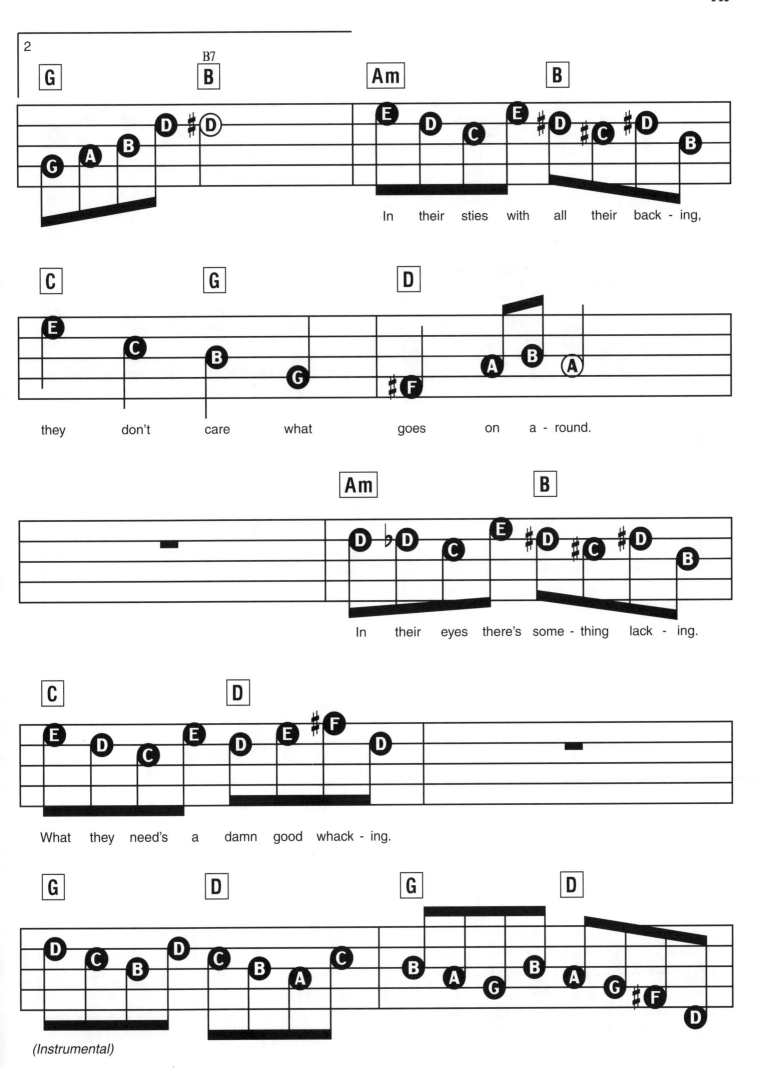

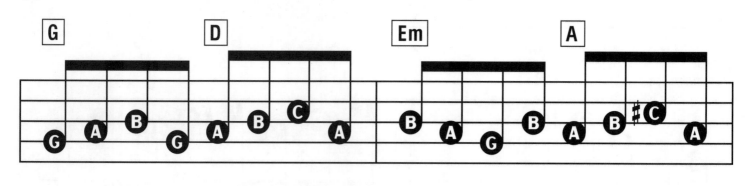

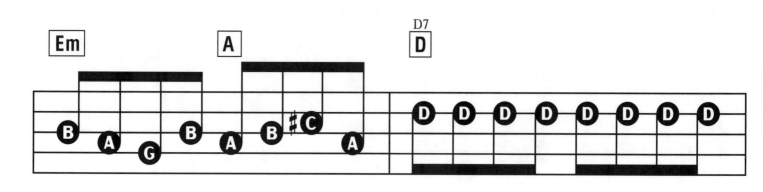

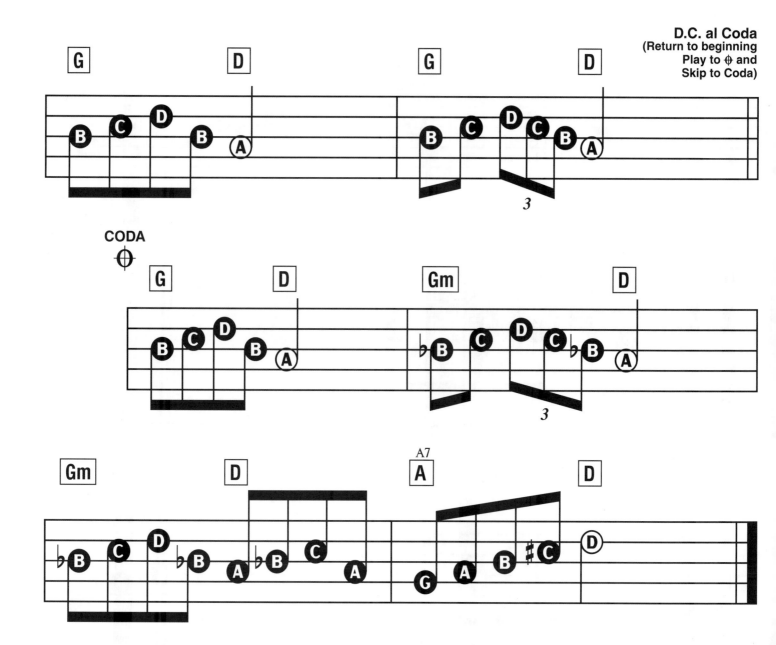

Revolution

Registration 7
Rhythm: Shuffle or Swing

Words and Music by John Lennon
and Paul McCartney

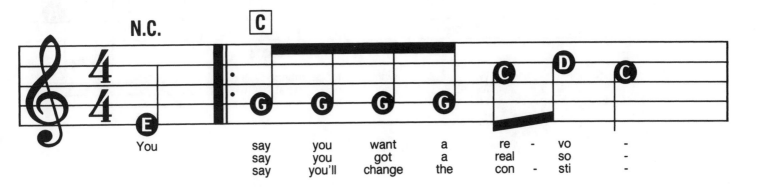

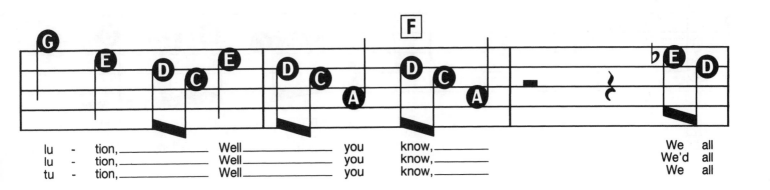

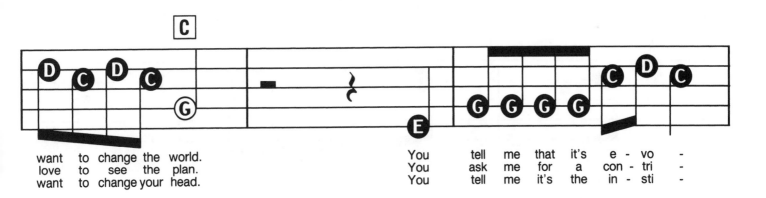

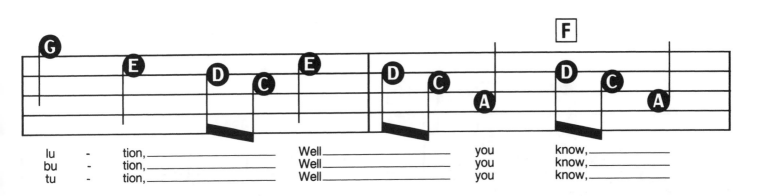

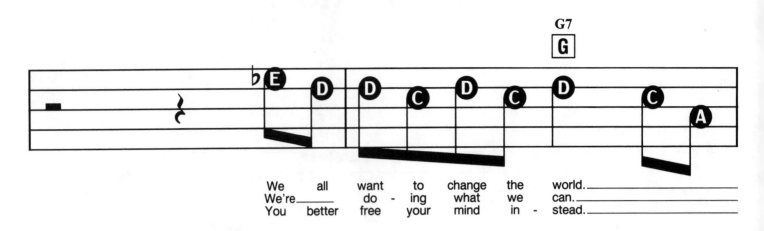

We all want to change the world._____
We're_____ do - ing what we can._____
You better free your mind in - stead._____

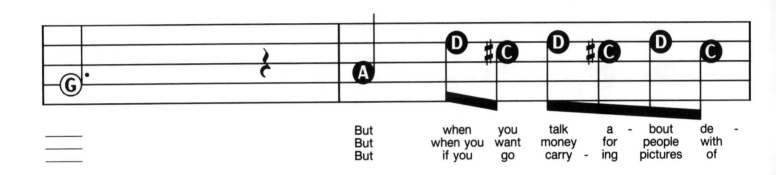

_____   But   when   you   talk   a - bout   de-
_____   But   when you want   money   for   people   with
_____   But   if you   go   carry - ing   pictures   of

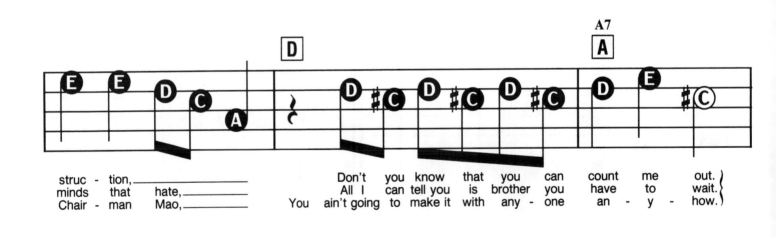

struc - tion,_____
minds   that   hate,_____
Chair - man   Mao,_____

Don't   you   know   that   you   can   count   me   out.
All I   can tell you   is   brother you   have   to   wait.}
You   ain't going to make it with   any - one   an - y - how.)

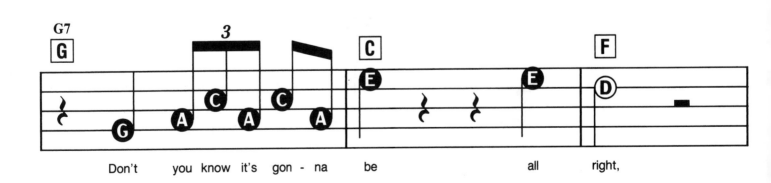

Don't   you know it's gon - na   be   all   right,

153

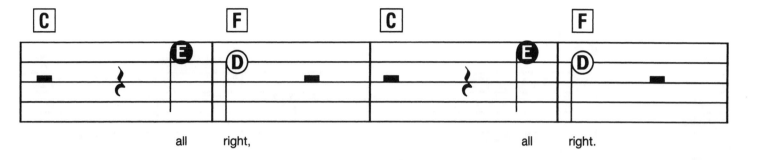

all   right,   all   right.

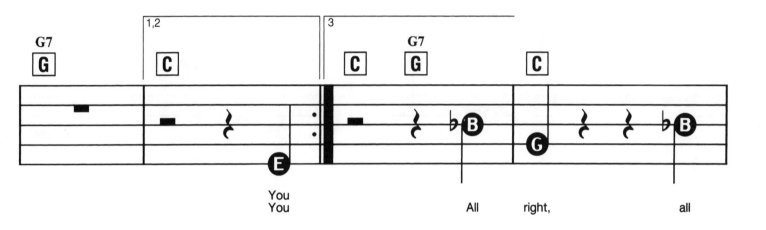

You
You   All   right,   all

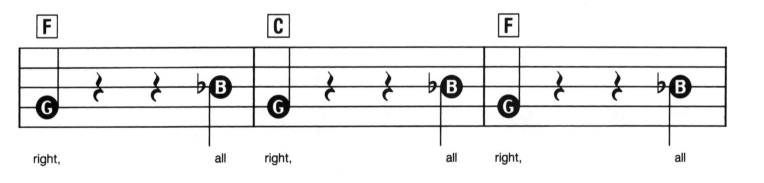

right,   all   right,   all   right,   all

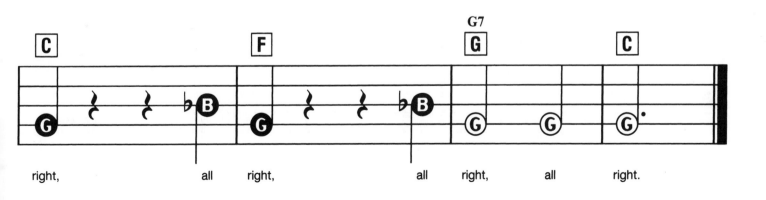

right,   all   right,   all   right,   all   right.

Polythene Pam

Registration 5
Rhythm: Rock

Words and Music by John Lennon
and Paul McCartney

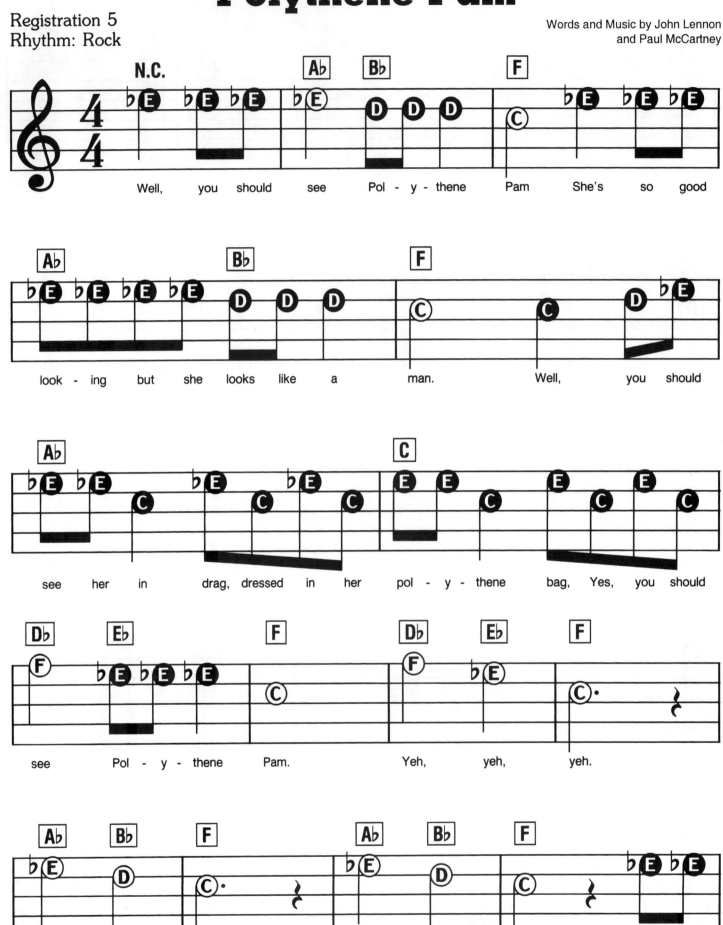

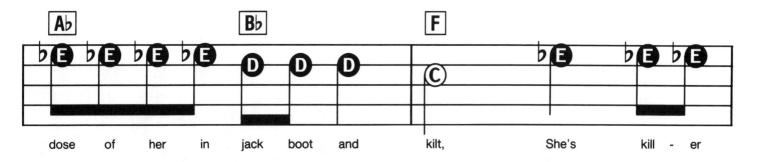

dose of her in jack boot and kilt, She's kill - er

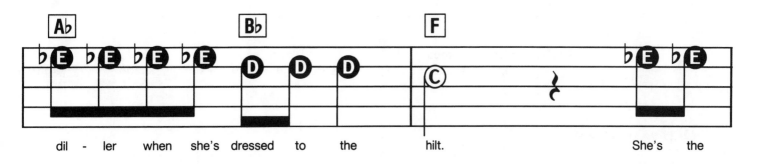

dil - ler when she's dressed to the hilt. She's the

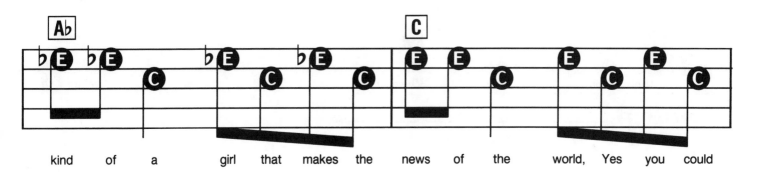

kind of a girl that makes the news of the world, Yes you could

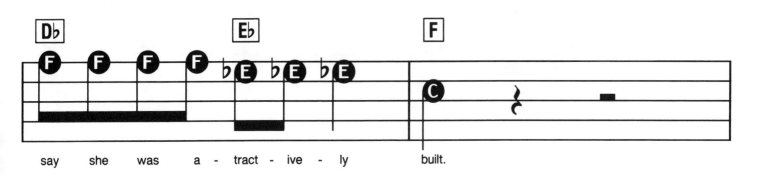

say she was a - tract - ive - ly built.

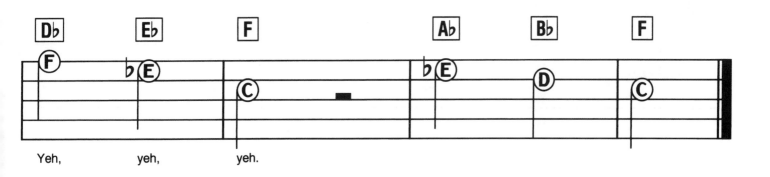

Yeh, yeh, yeh.

Rain

Registration 2
Rhythm: Rock or Latin

Words and Music by John Lennon
and Paul McCartney

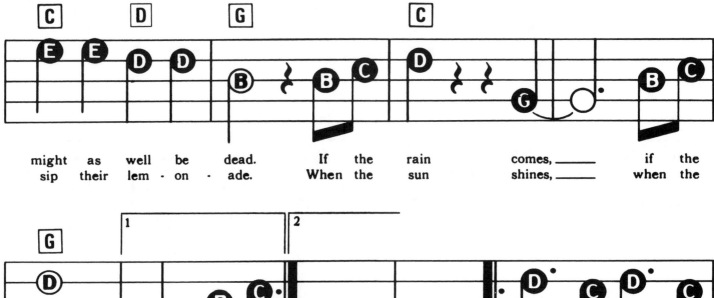

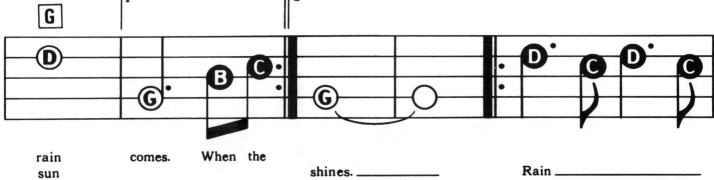

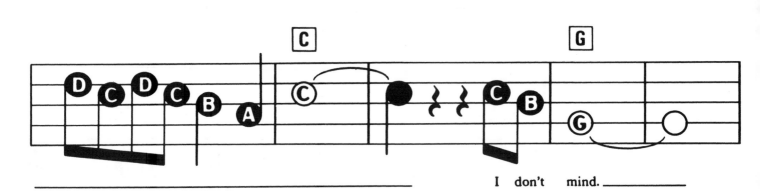

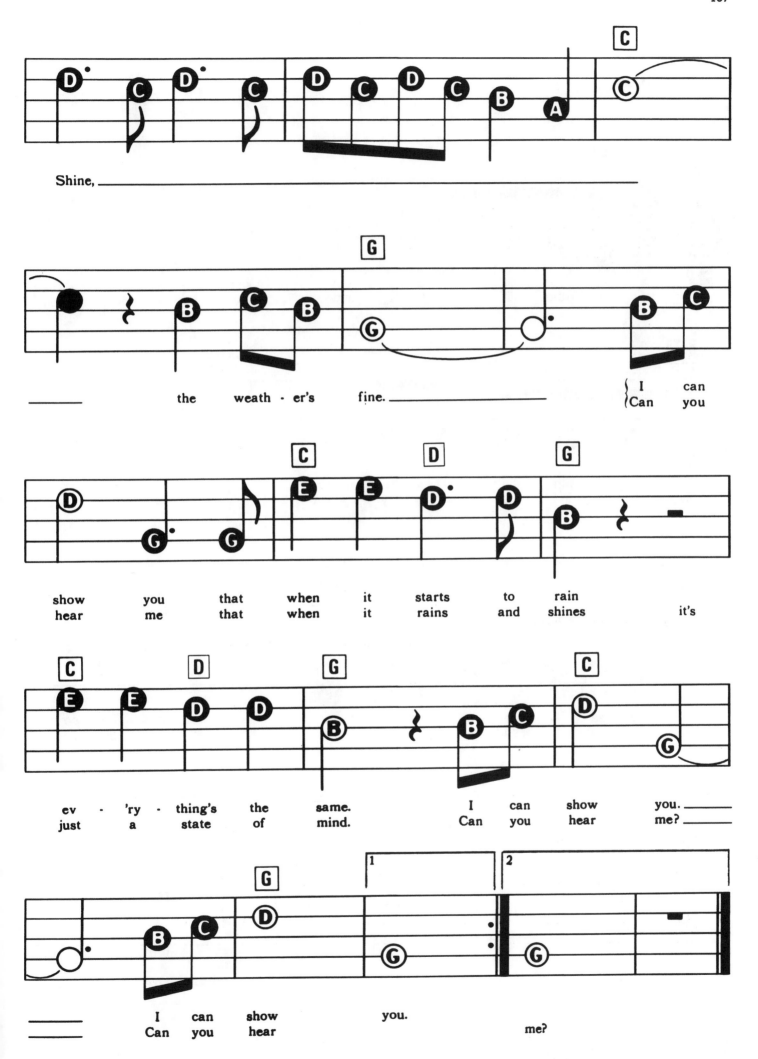

Real Love

Registration 2
Rhythm: 8 Beat

Words and Music by
John Lennon

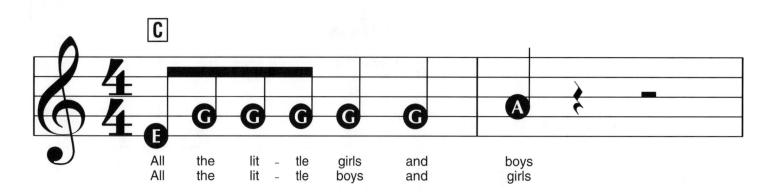

All the lit – tle girls and boys
All the lit – tle boys and girls

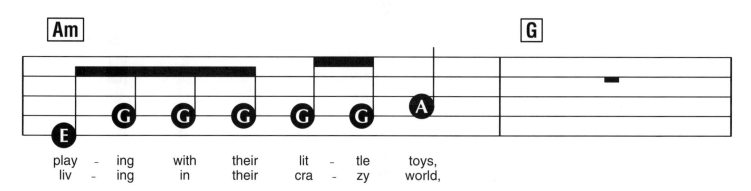

play – ing with their lit – tle toys,
liv – ing in their cra – zy world,

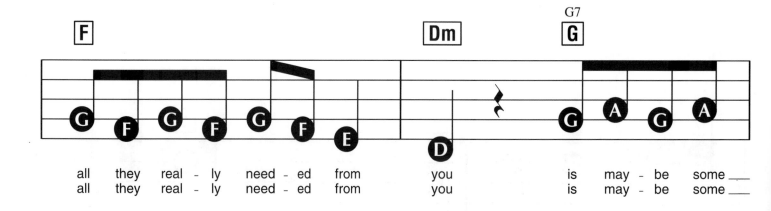

all they real – ly need – ed from you is may – be some ___
all they real – ly need – ed from you is may – be some ___

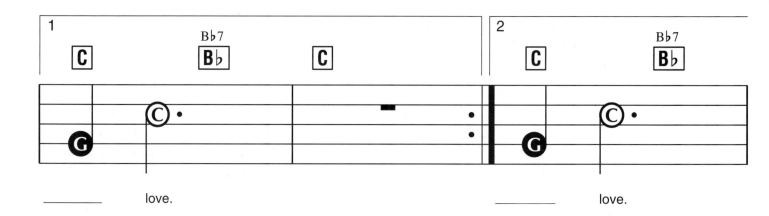

___ love.   ___ love.

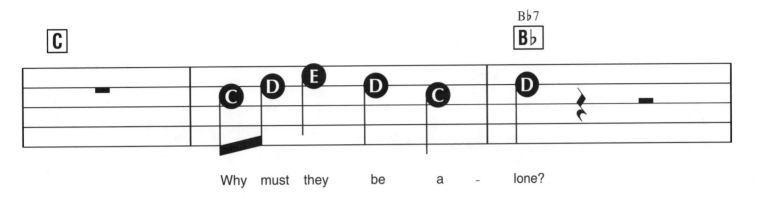

Why must they be a - lone?

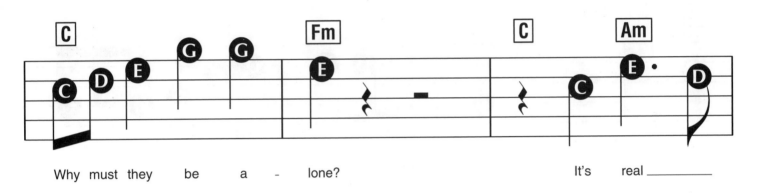

Why must they be a - lone?   It's real _____

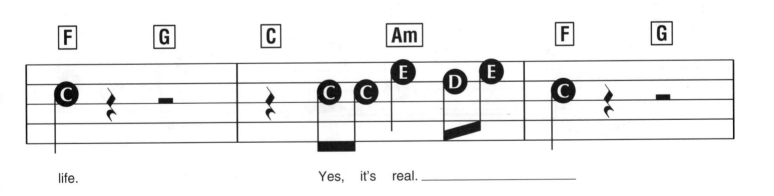

life.   Yes, it's real. _____

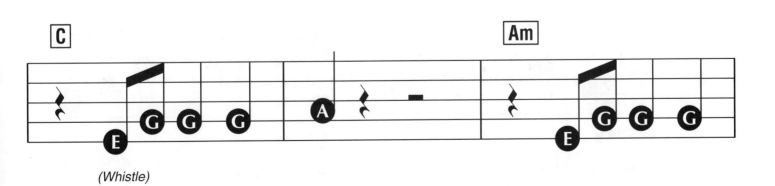

(Whistle)

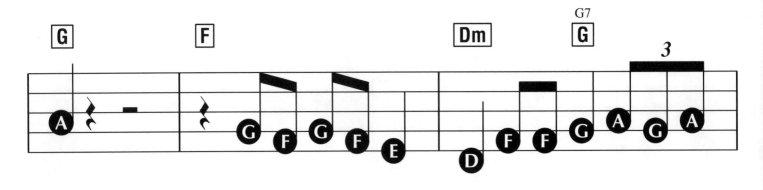

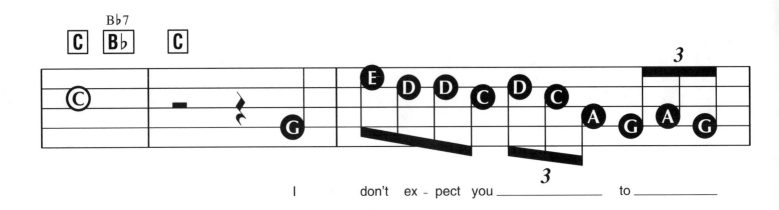

I don't ex - pect you _____ to _____

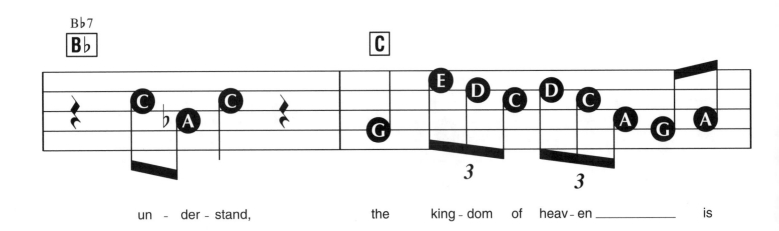

un - der - stand, the king - dom of heav - en _____ is

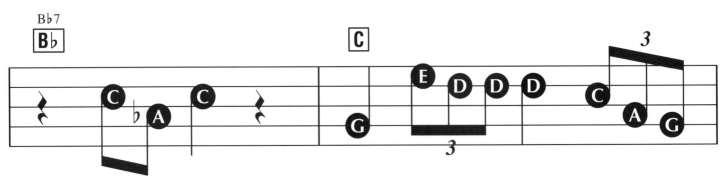

in your hands. I don't ex - pect you _____

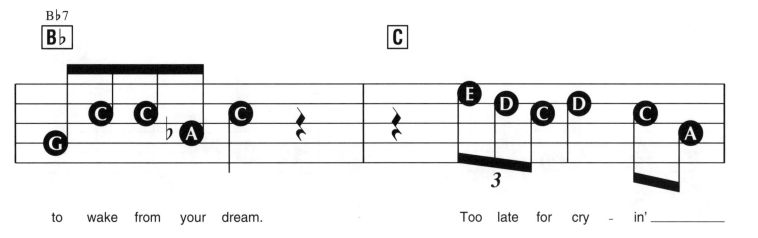

to wake from your dream. Too late for cry - in' _____

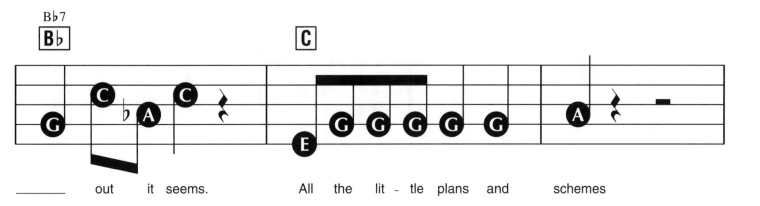

_____ out it seems. All the lit - tle plans and schemes

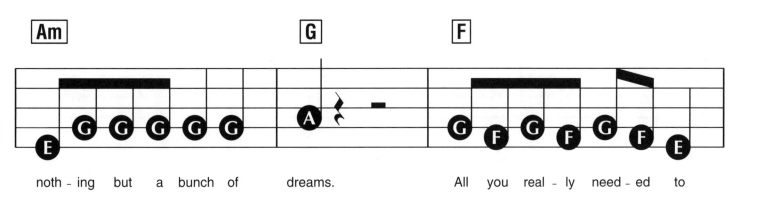

noth - ing but a bunch of dreams. All you real - ly need - ed to

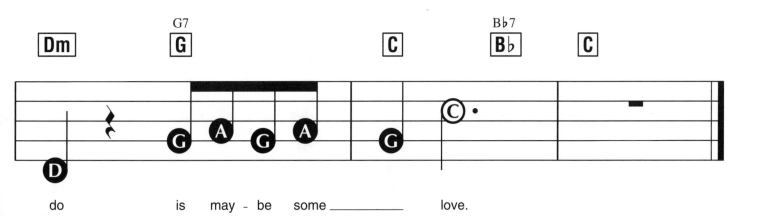

do   is may - be some _____ love.

Rocky Raccoon

Registration 5
Rhythm: Fox Trot or Swing

Words and Music by John Lennon
and Paul McCartney

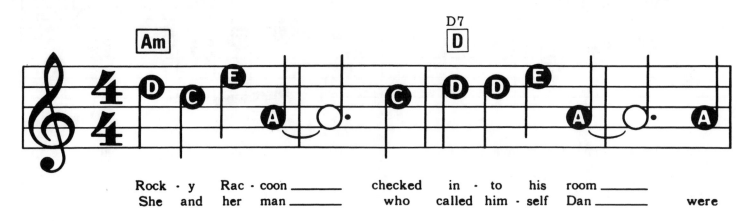

Rock - y Rac - coon _____ checked in - to his room _____
She and her man _____ who called him - self Dan _____ were

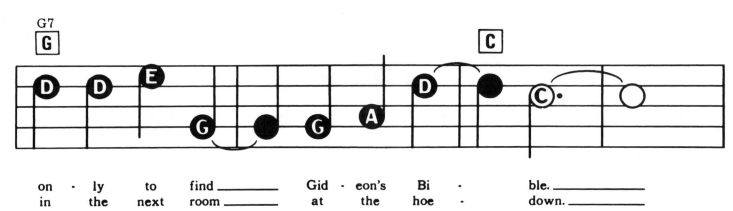

on - ly to find _____ Gid - eon's Bi - ble. _____
in the next room _____ at the hoe - down. _____

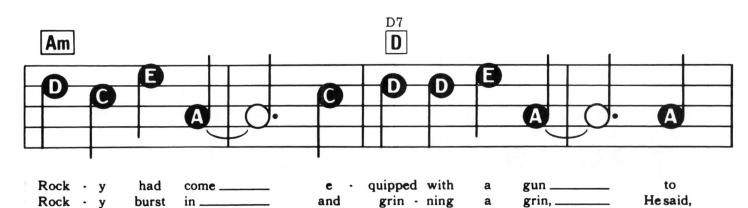

Rock - y had come _____ e - quipped with a gun _____ to
Rock - y burst in _____ and grin - ning a grin, _____ He said,

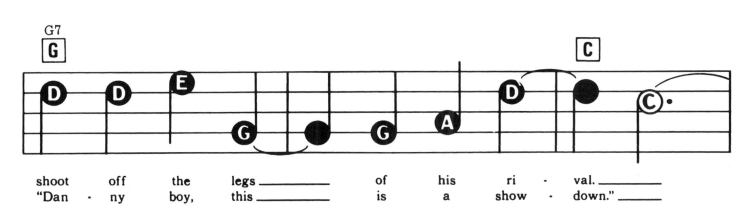

shoot off the legs _____ of his ri - val. _____
"Dan - ny boy, this _____ is a show - down." _____

Savoy Truffle

Registration 4
Rhythm: 8 Beat or Rock

Words and Music by
George Harrison

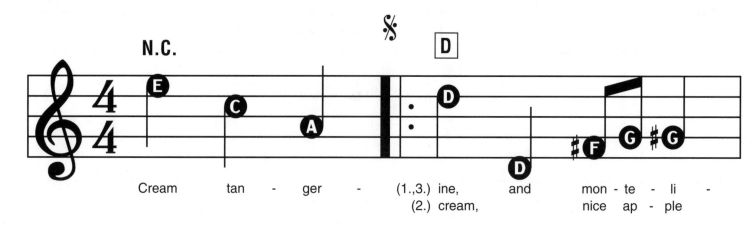

Cream tan - ger - (1.,3.) ine, and mon - te - li -
(2.) cream, nice ap - ple

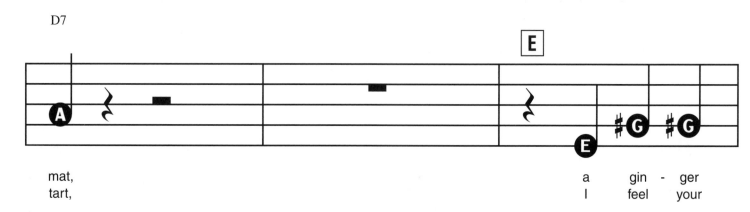

mat, a gin - ger
tart, I feel your

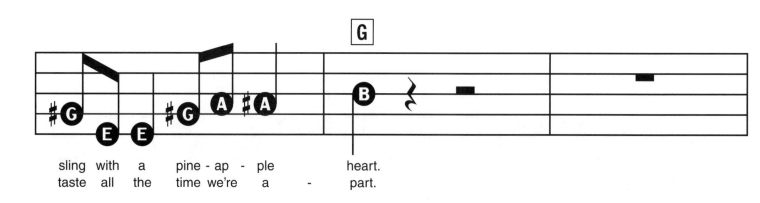

sling with a pine - ap - ple heart.
taste all the time we're a - part.

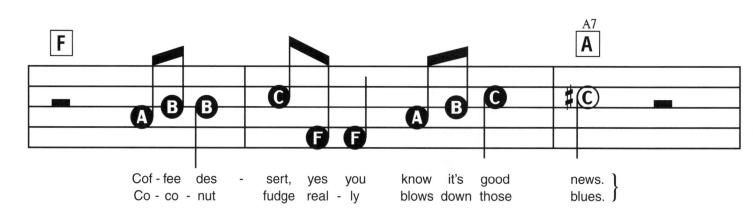

Cof - fee des - sert, yes you know it's good news. }
Co - co - nut fudge real - ly blows down those blues. }

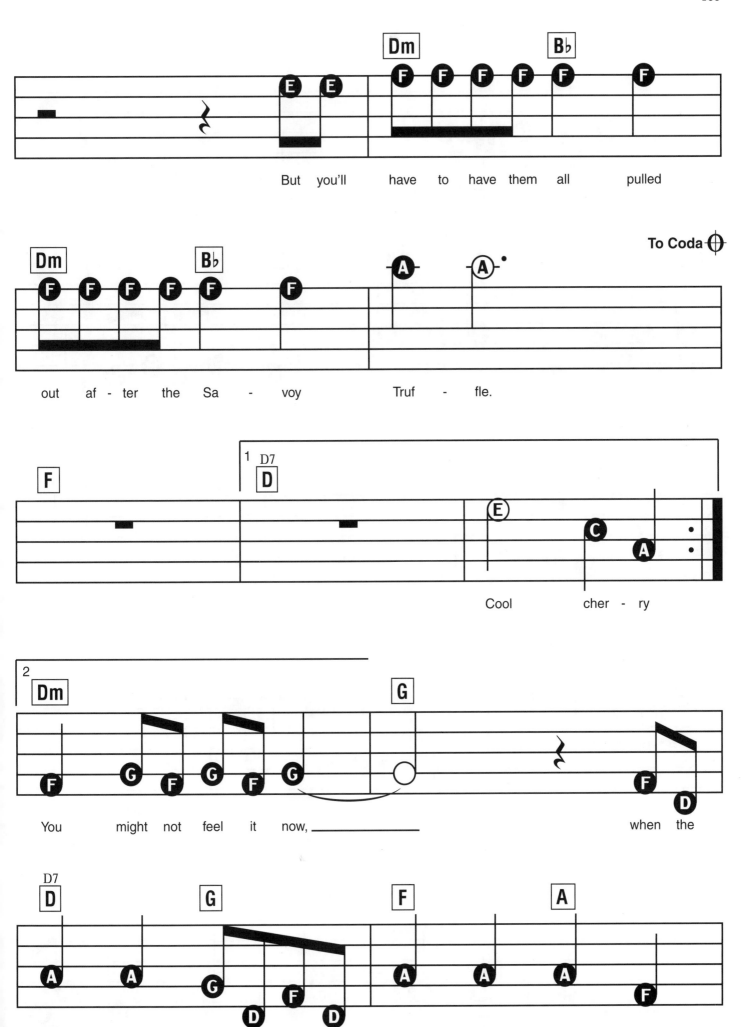

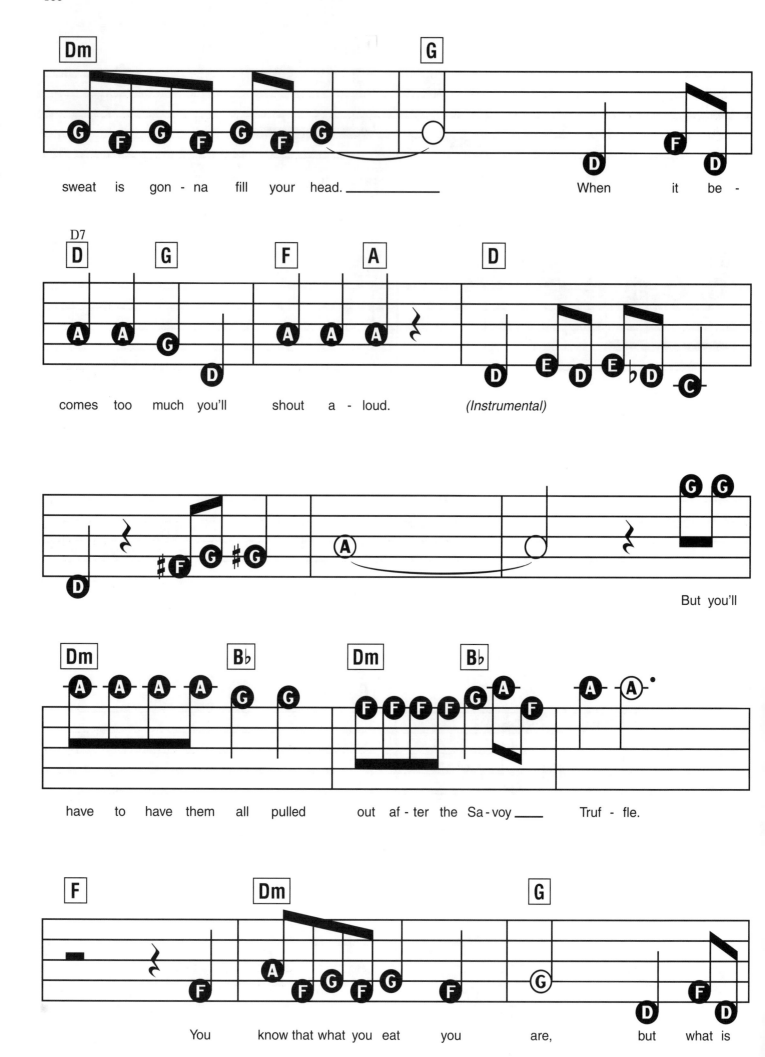

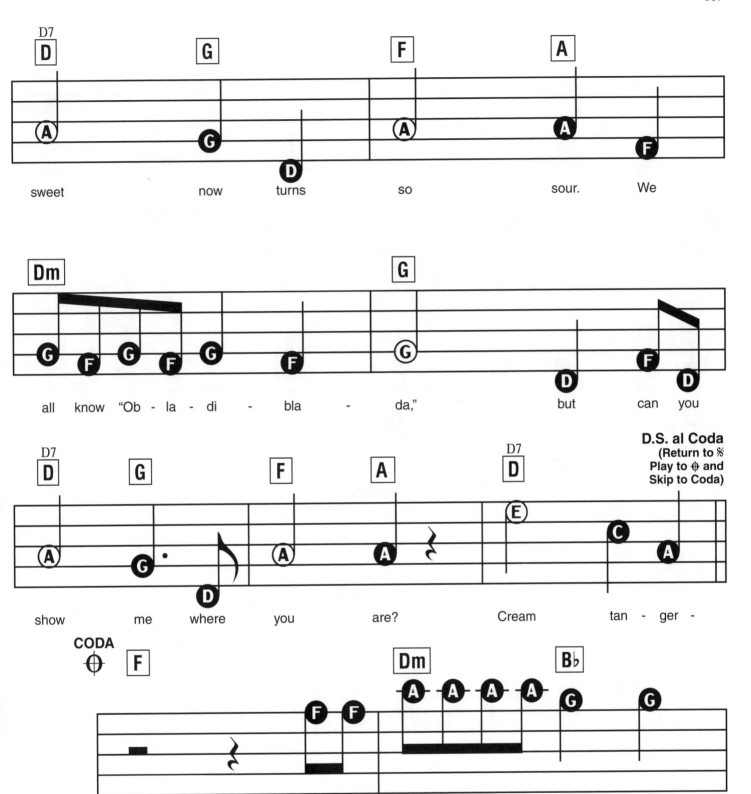

sweet   now   turns   so   sour.   We

all know "Ob - la - di - bla - da,"   but   can   you

D.S. al Coda
(Return to %
Play to ⊕ and
Skip to Coda)

show   me   where   you   are?   Cream   tan - ger -

CODA
⊕

Yes, you'll   have   to   have them   all   pulled

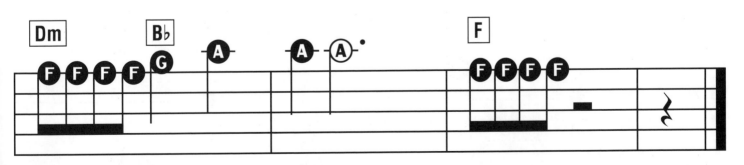

out af - ter the Sa - voy   Truf - fle.   *(Instrumental)*

Sexy Sadie

Registration 7
Rhythm: Rock

Words and Music by John Lennon
and Paul McCartney

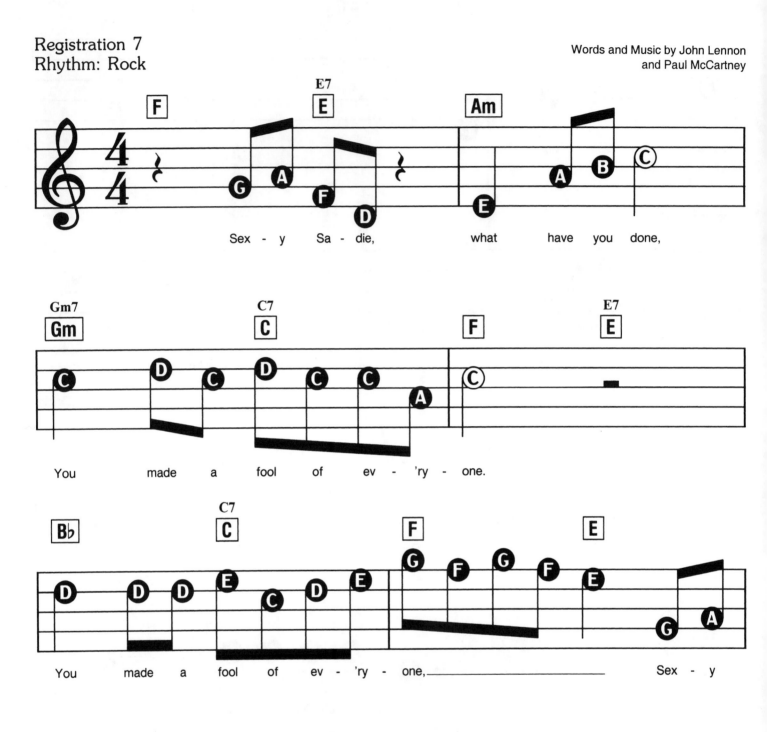

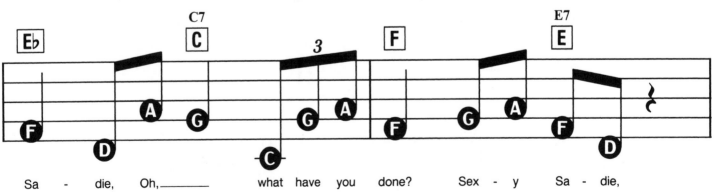

169

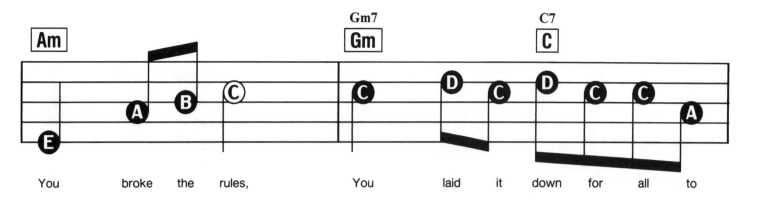

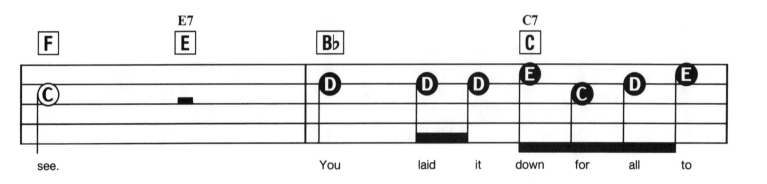

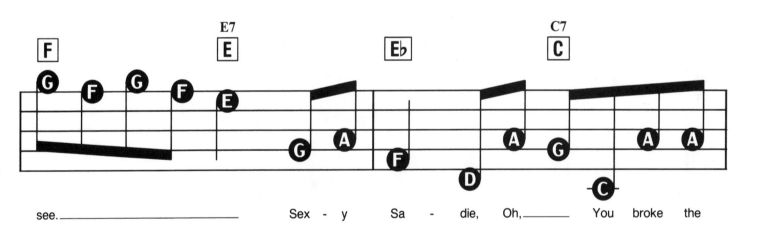

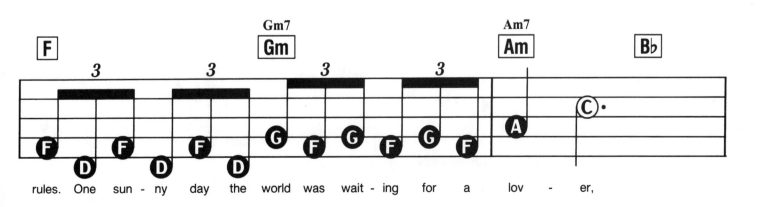

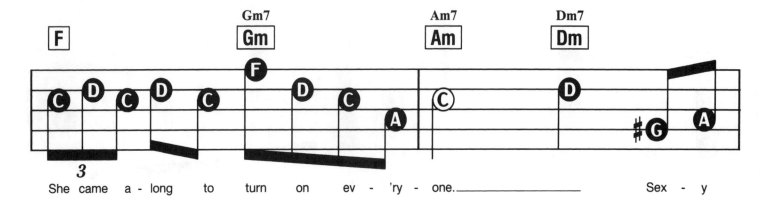

She came a - long to turn on ev - 'ry - one._____ Sex - y

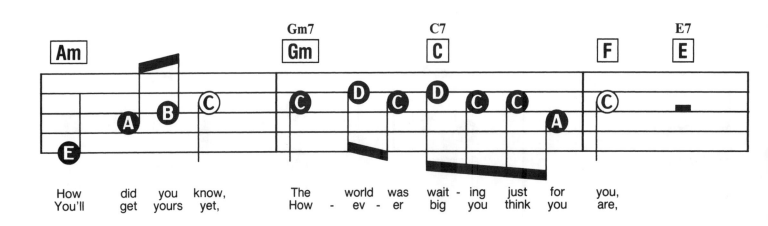

Sa - die, the great - est of them all. Sex - y Sa - die,
know? Sex - y Sa - die,

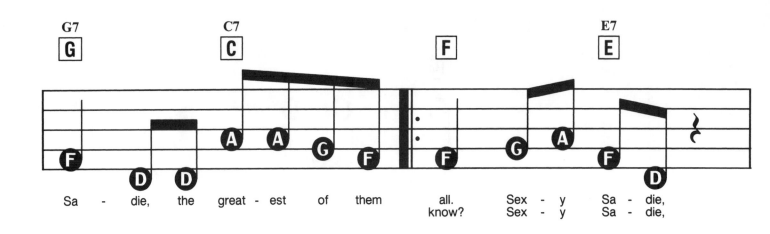

How did you know, The world was wait - ing just for you,
You'll get yours yet, How - ev - er big you think you are,

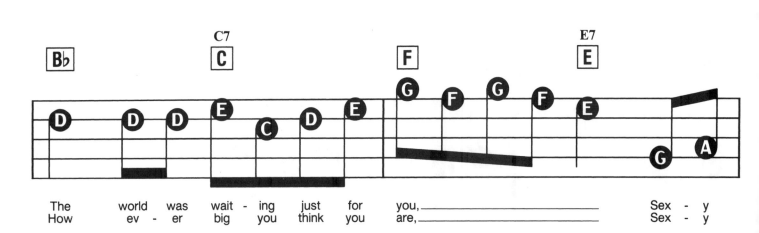

The world was wait - ing just for you,_____ Sex - y
How ev - er big you think you are,_____ Sex - y

171

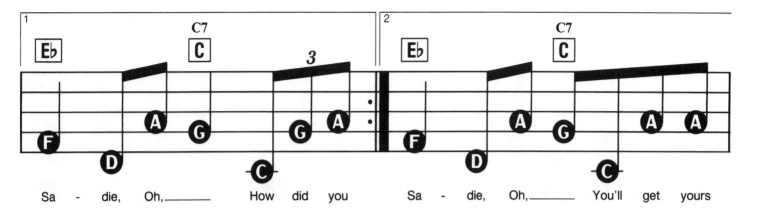

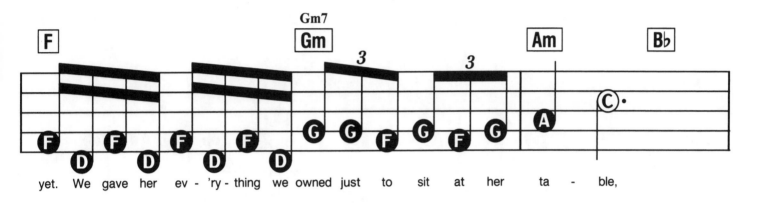

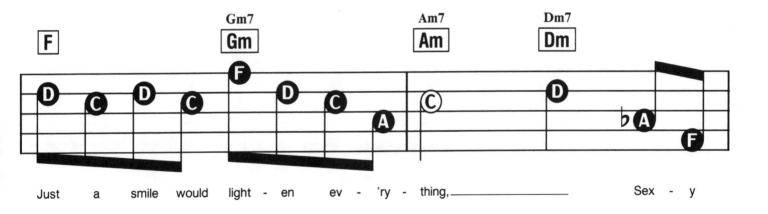

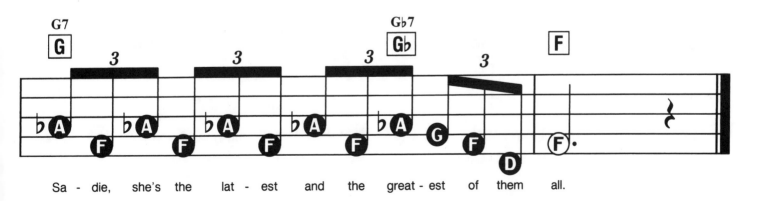

Sgt. Pepper's Lonely Hearts Club Band

Registration 4
Rhythm: Rock

Words and Music by John Lennon
and Paul McCartney

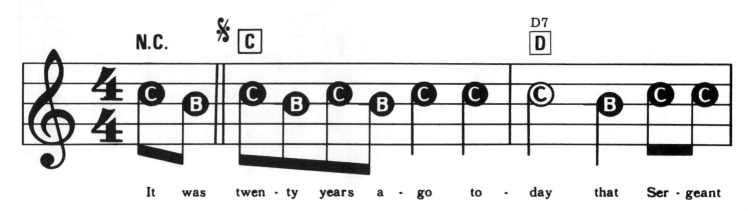

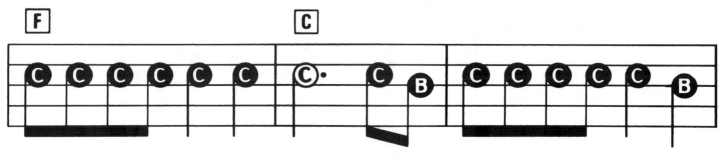

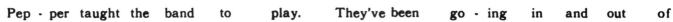

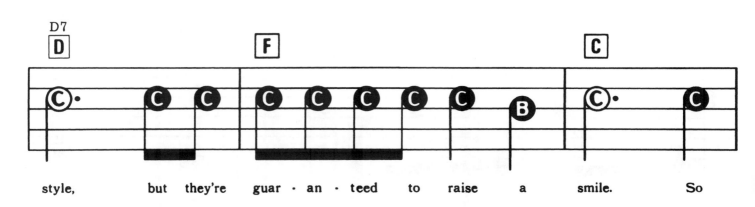

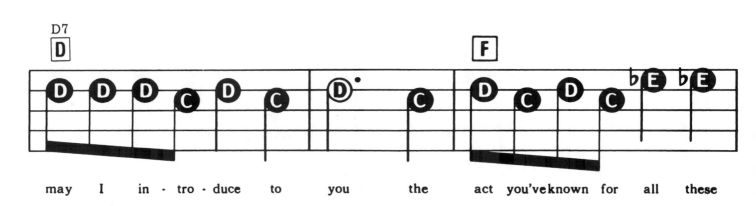

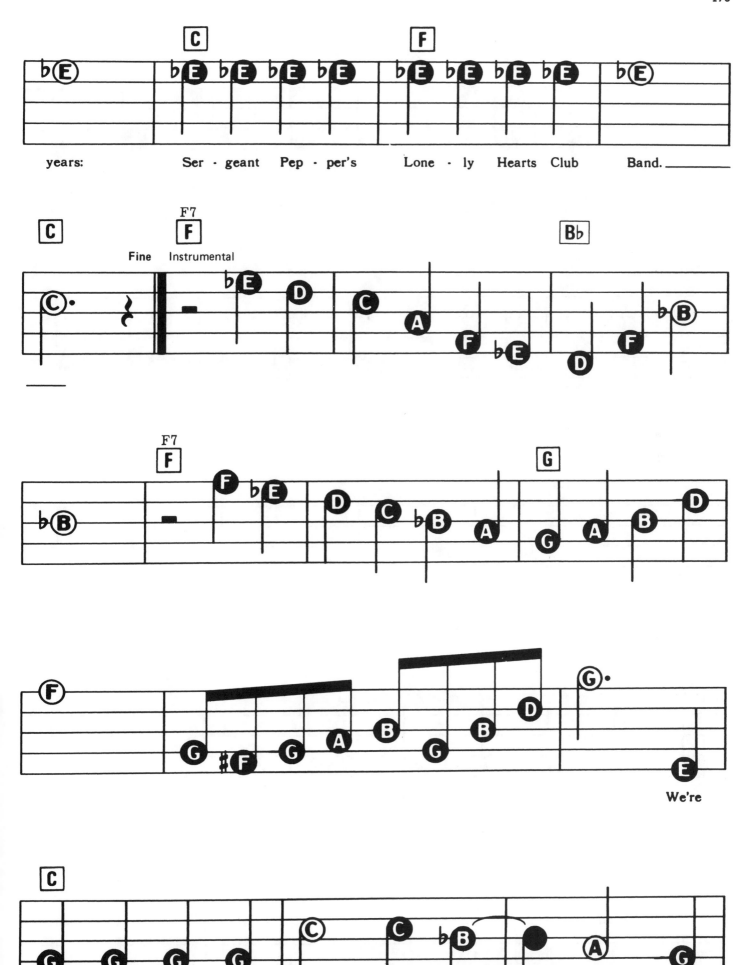

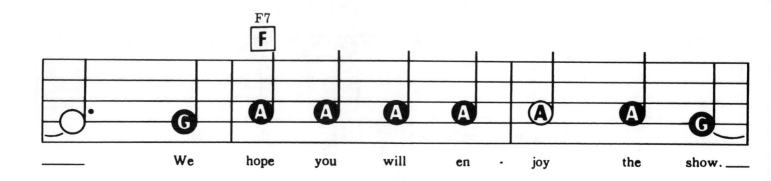

We hope you will en · joy the show. __

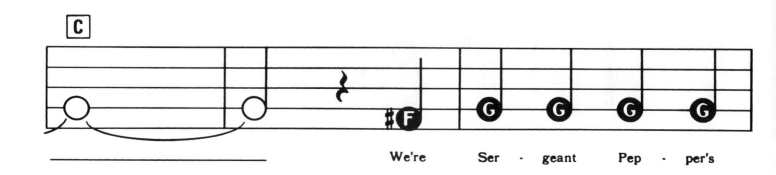

___ We're Ser · geant Pep · per's

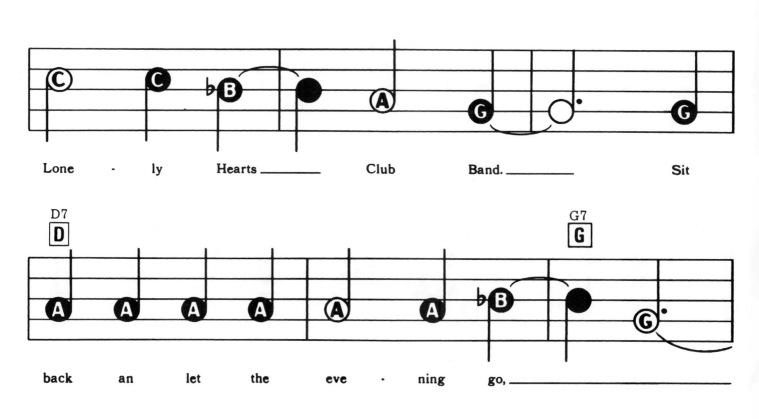

Lone · ly Hearts ___ Club Band. ___ Sit

back an let the eve · ning go, ___

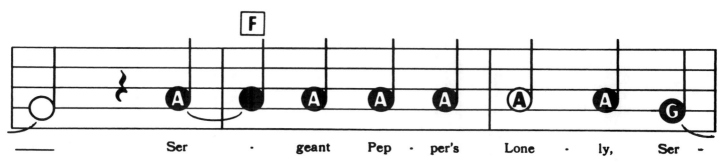

___ Ser · geant Pep · per's Lone · ly, Ser ·

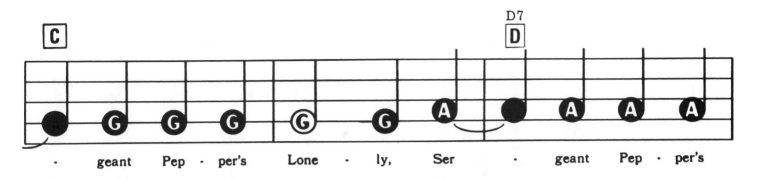

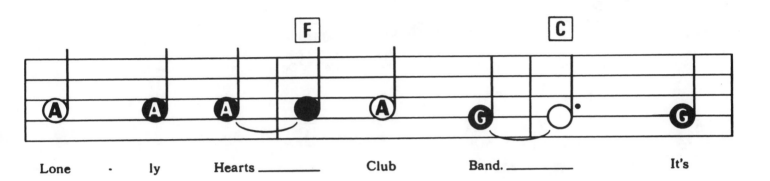

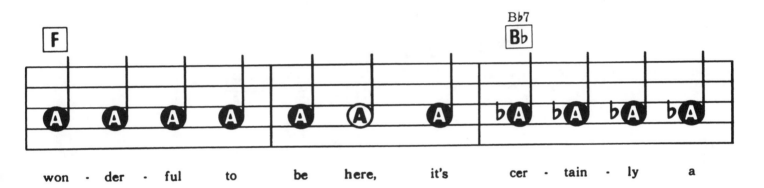

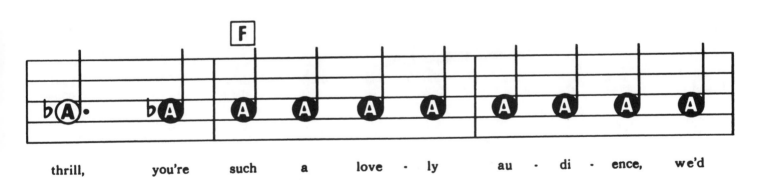

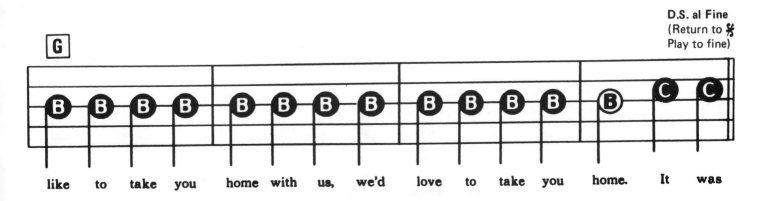

She Came In Through the Bathroom Window

Registration 1
Rhythm: Rock

Words and Music by John Lennon
and Paul McCartney

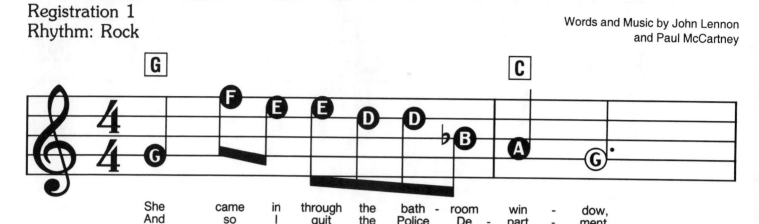

She came in through the bath - room win - dow,
And so I quit the Police De - part - ment,

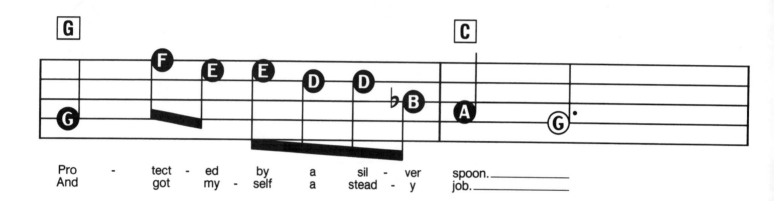

Pro - tect - ed by a sil - ver spoon._____
And got my - self a stead - y job._____

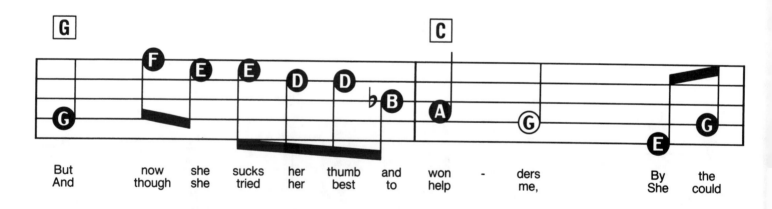

But now she sucks her thumb and won - ders me,   By the
And though she tried her best to help   She could

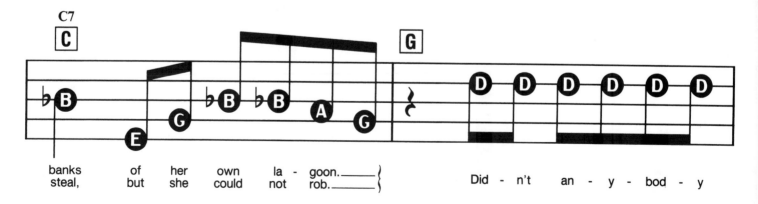

banks of her own la - goon._____   Did - n't an - y - bod - y
steal, but she could not rob._____

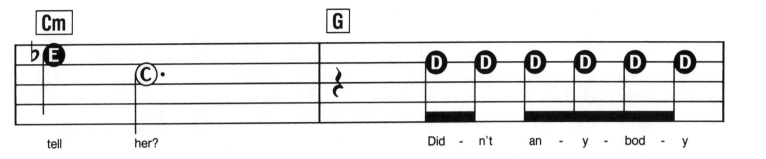

tell her? Did - n't an - y - bod - y

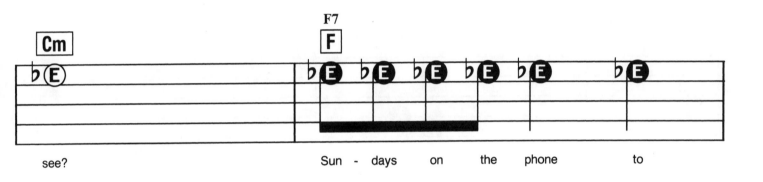

see? Sun - days on the phone to

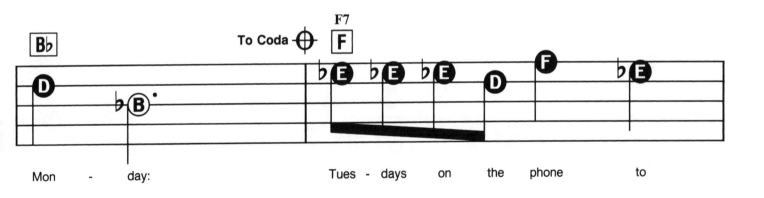

Mon - day: Tues - days on the phone to

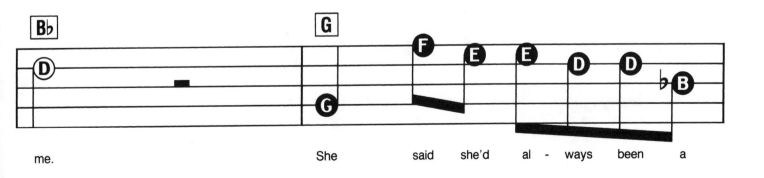

me. She said she'd al - ways been a

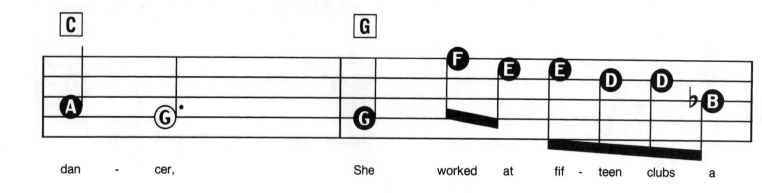

dan - cer, She worked at fif - teen clubs a

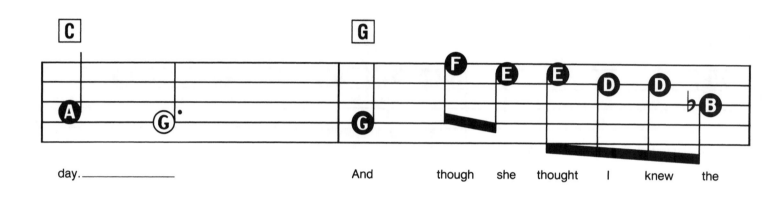

day._____ And though she thought I knew the

C7

D.C. al Coda
(Return to beginning
Play to ⊕ and
skip to Coda)

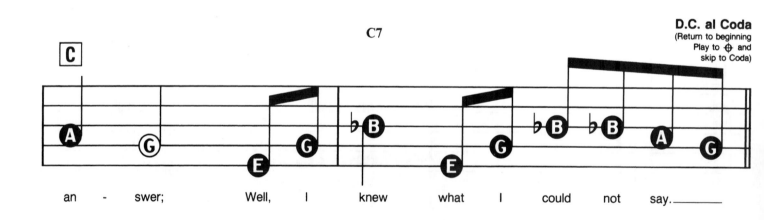

an - swer; Well, I knew what I could not say.____

CODA   **F7**

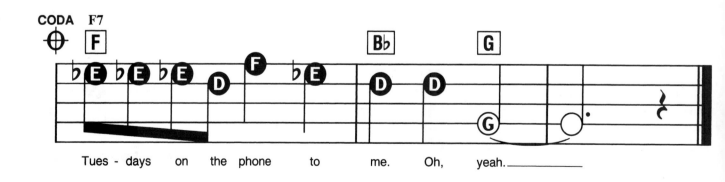

Tues - days on the phone to me. Oh, yeah._____

Strawberry Fields Forever

Registration 2
Rhythm: Rock

Words and Music by John Lennon
and Paul McCartney

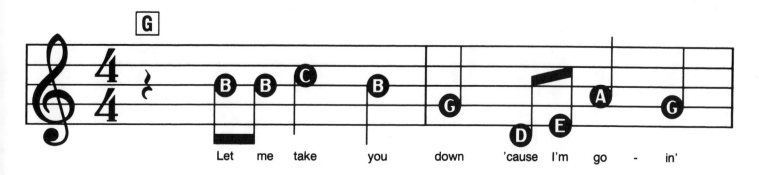

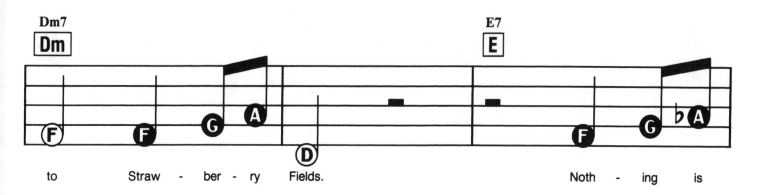

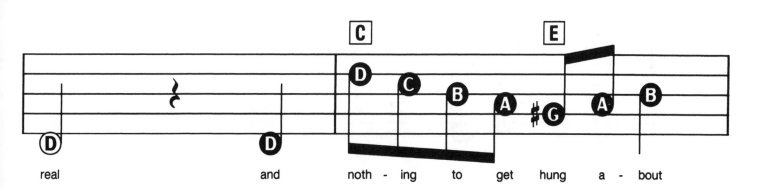

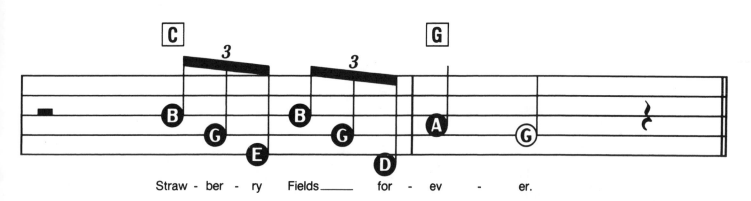

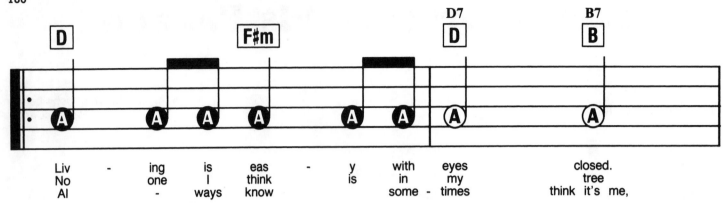

Liv - ing is eas - y with eyes closed.
No one I think is in my tree
Al - ways know some - times think it's me,

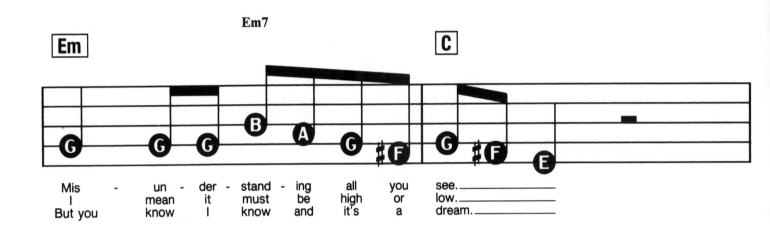

Mis - un - der - stand - ing all you see._____
I mean it must be all high or low._____
But you know I know and it's a dream._____

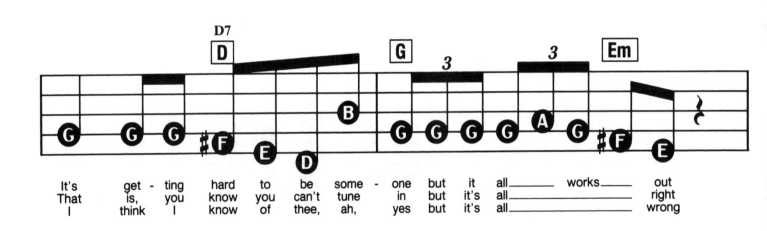

It's get - ting hard to be some - one but it all_____ works_____ out
That is, you know you can't tune in but it's all_____ right
I think I know of thee, ah, yes but it's all_____ wrong

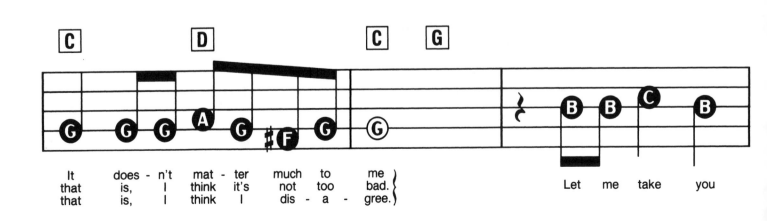

It does - n't mat - ter much to me
that is, I think it's not too bad.
that is, I think I dis - a - gree.

Let me take you

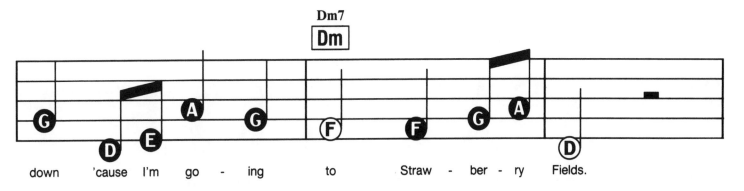

down 'cause I'm go - ing to Straw - ber - ry Fields.

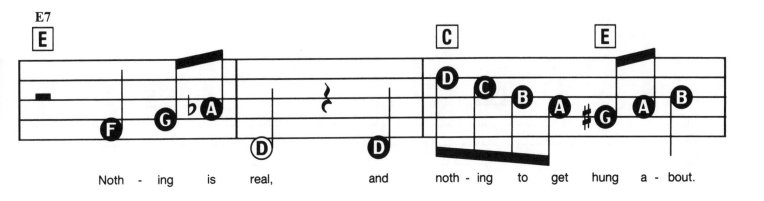

Noth - ing is real, and noth - ing to get hung a - bout.

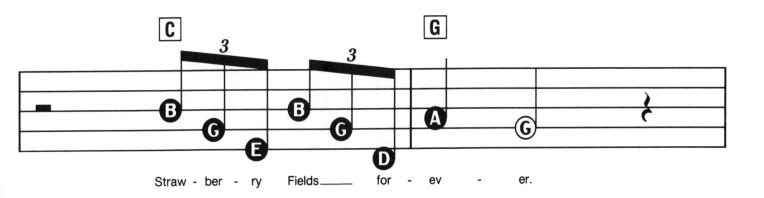

Straw - ber - ry Fields _____ for - ev - er.

Repeat and Fade

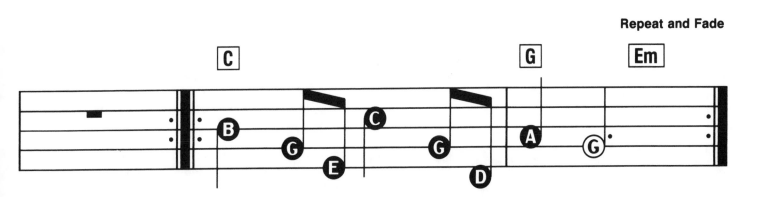

She's Leaving Home

Registration 2
Rhythm: Waltz

Words and Music by John Lennon
and Paul McCartney

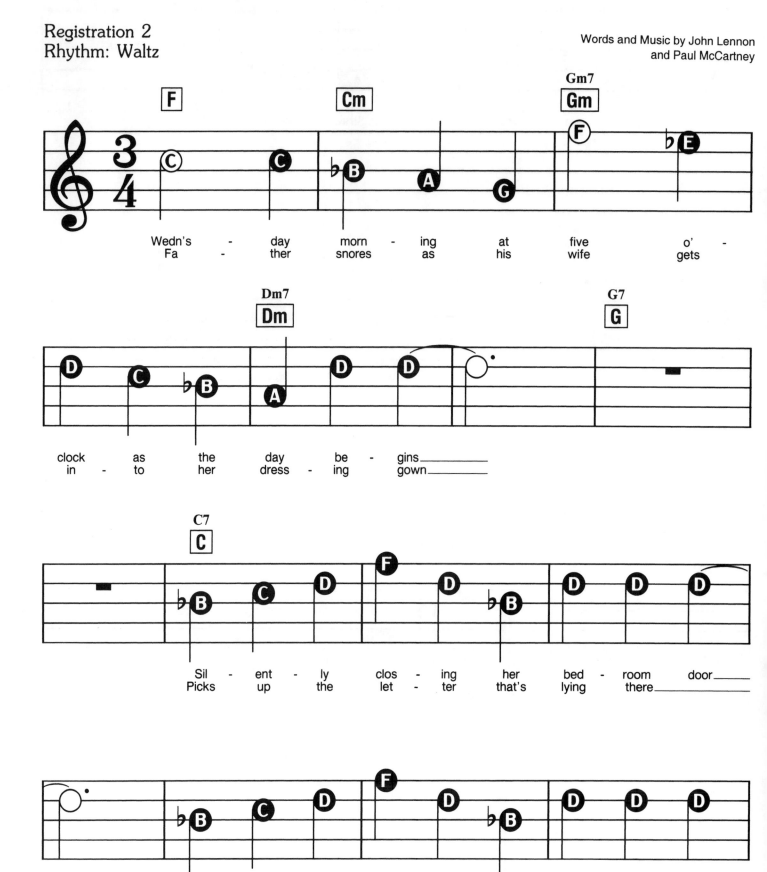

183

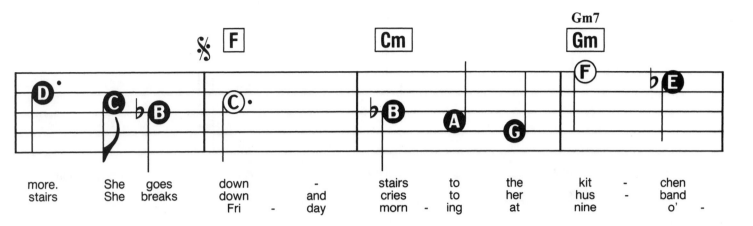

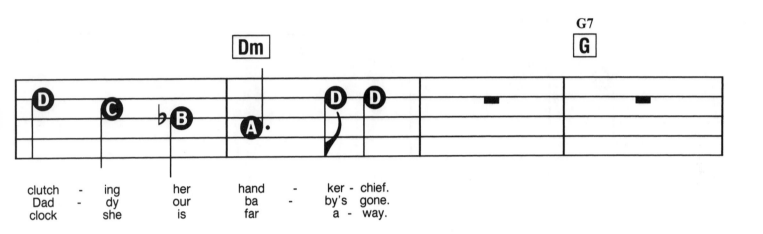

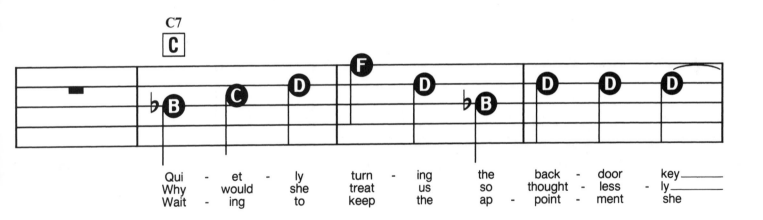

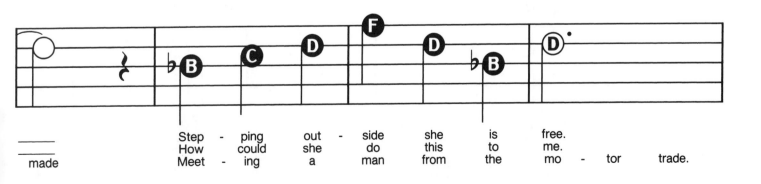

184

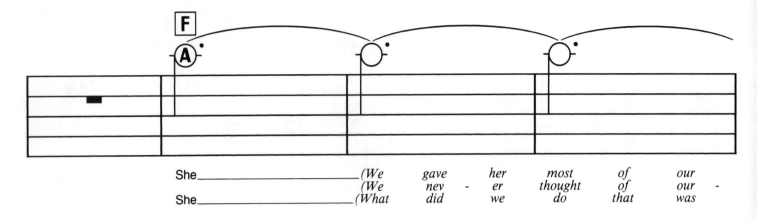

She_____ (We gave her most of our
(We nev - er thought of our -
She_____ (What did we do that was

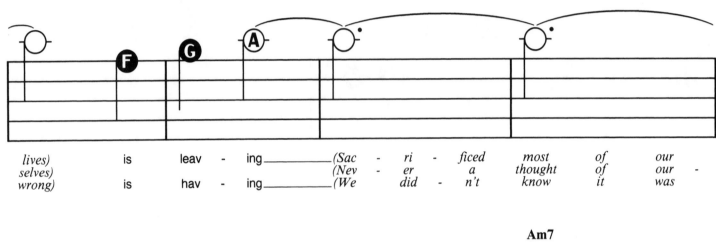

lives) is leav - ing_____ (Sac - ri - ficed most of our
selves) (Nev - er a thought of our -
wrong) is hav - ing_____ (We did - n't know it was

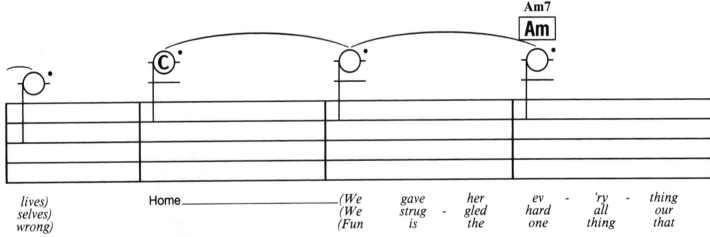

lives) Home_____ (We gave her ev - 'ry - thing
selves) (We strug - gled hard all our
wrong) (Fun is the one thing that

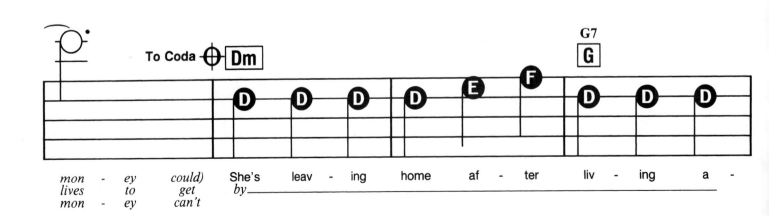

mon - ey could) She's leav - ing home af - ter liv - ing a -
lives to get by_____
mon - ey can't

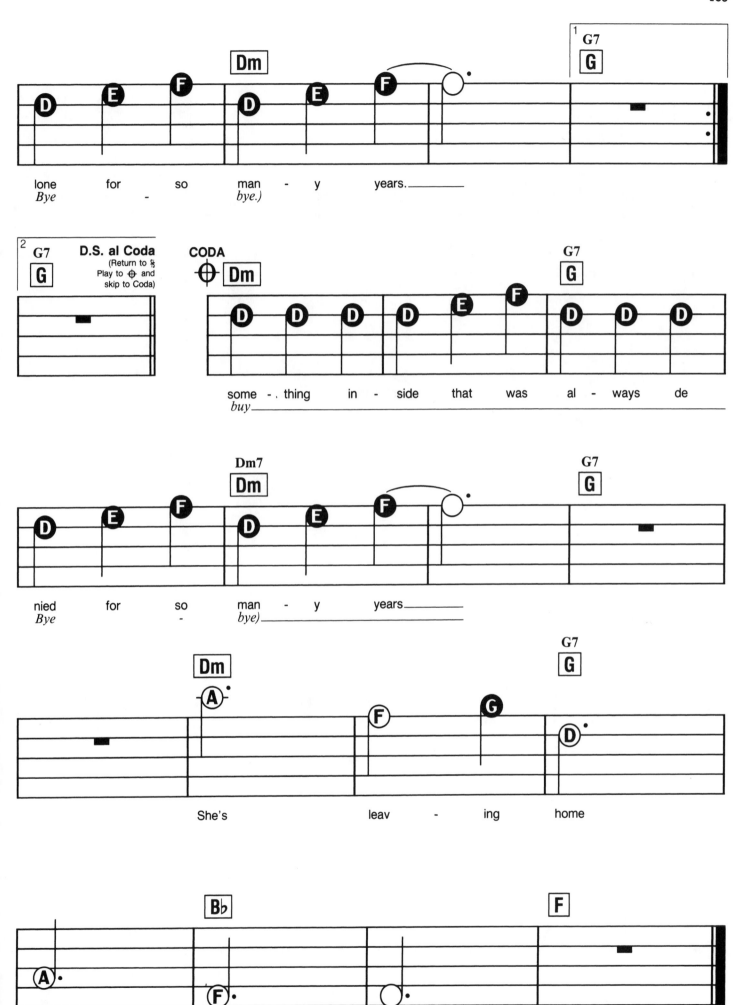

Something

Registration 4
Rhythm: Rock

Words and Music by
George Harrison

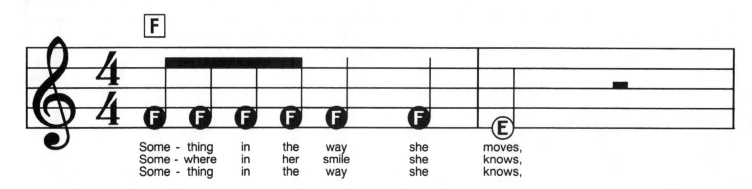

Some - thing in the way she moves,
Some - where in her smile she knows,
Some - thing in the way she knows,

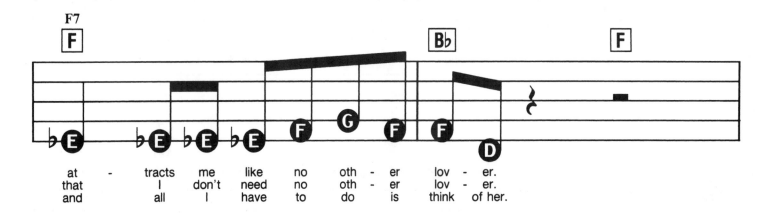

at - tracts me like no oth - er lov - er.
that I don't need no oth - er lov - er.
and all I have to do is think of her.

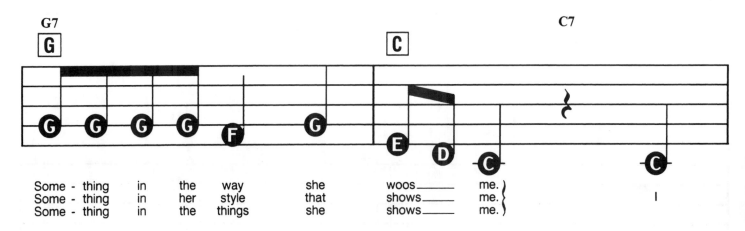

Some - thing in the way she woos_____ me.
Some - thing in her style that shows_____ me.
Some - thing in the style things that she shows_____ me.

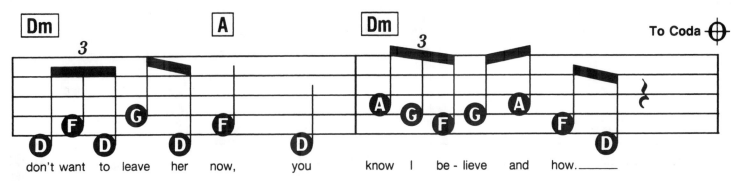

don't want to leave her now, you know I be - lieve and how._____

To Coda ⊕

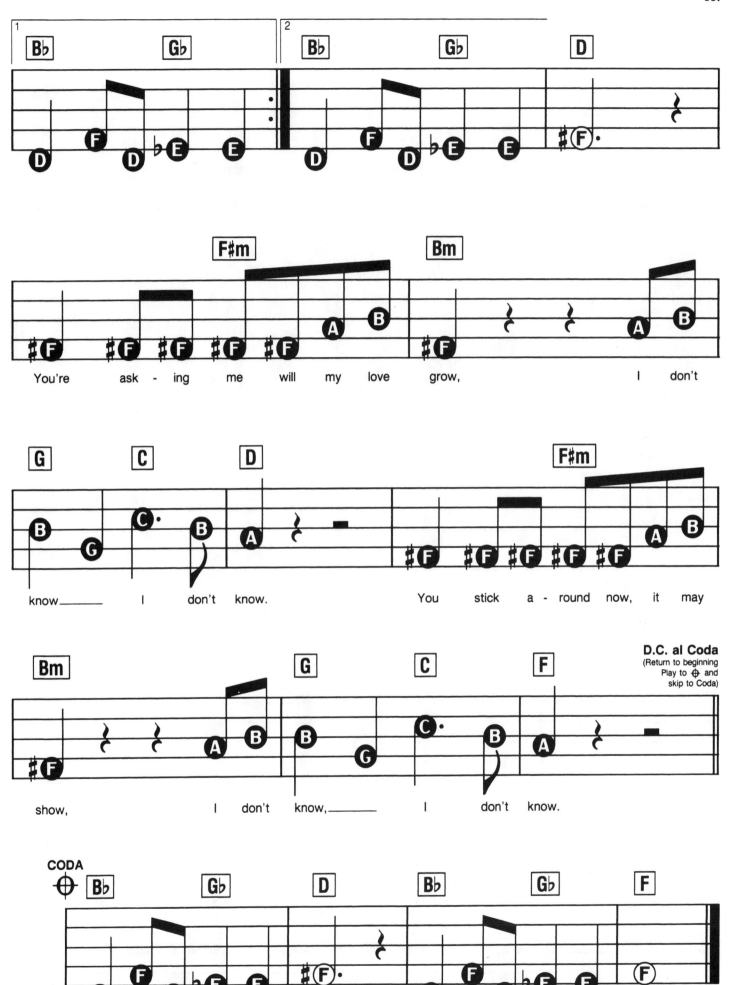

Sun King

Registration 4
Rhythm: Rock or 16 Beat

Words and Music by John Lennon
and Paul McCartney

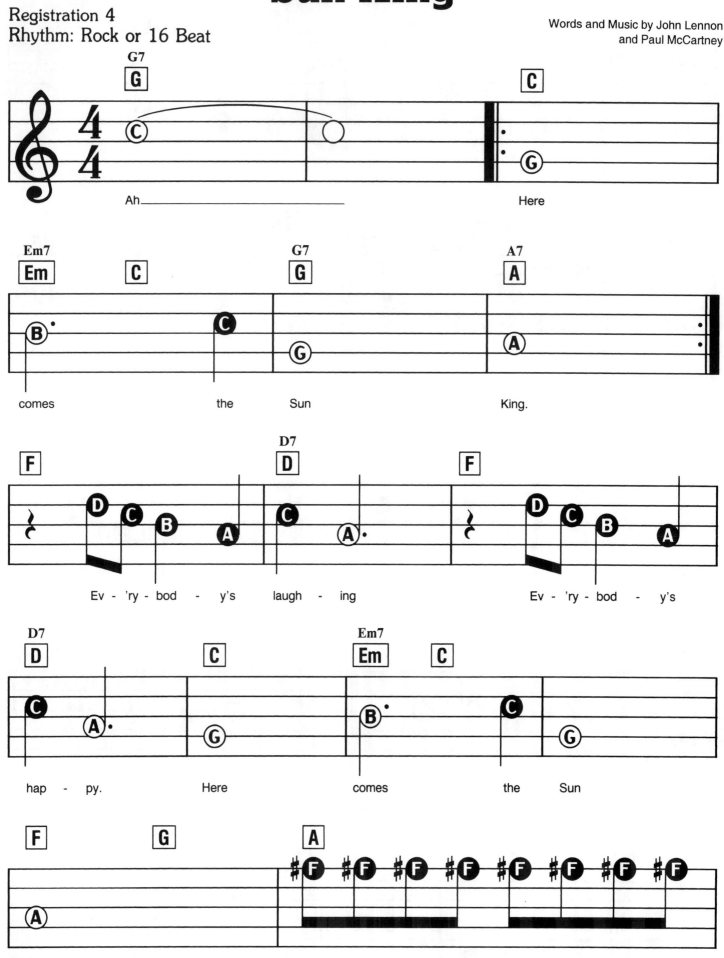

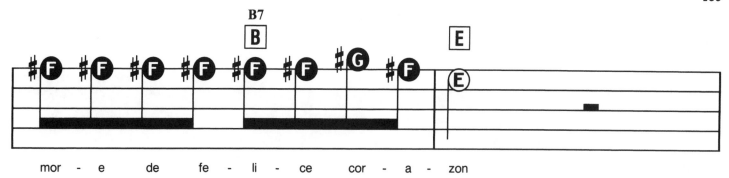

mor - e de fe - li - ce cor - a - zon

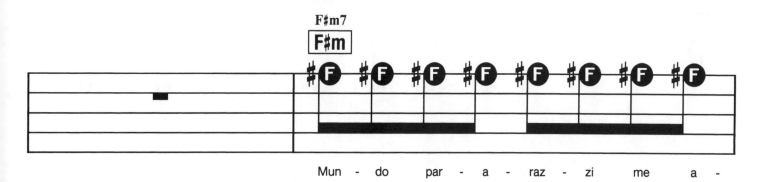

Mun - do par - a - raz - zi me a -

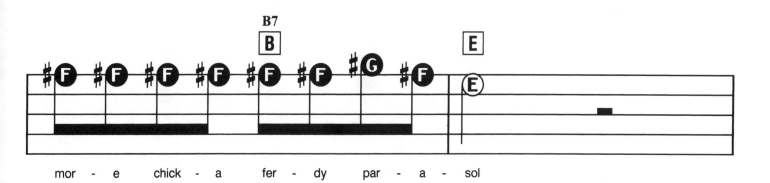

mor - e chick - a fer - dy par - a - sol

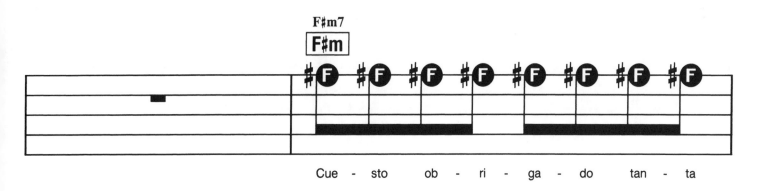

Cue - sto ob - ri - ga - do tan - ta

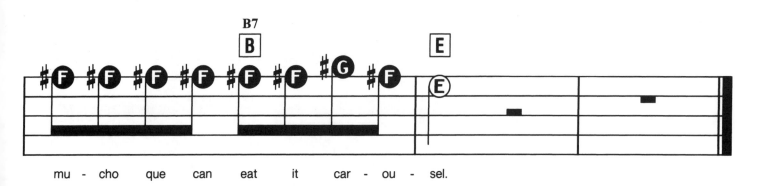

mu - cho que can eat it car - ou - sel.

Taxman

Registration 2
Rhythm: Rock

Words and Music by
George Harrison

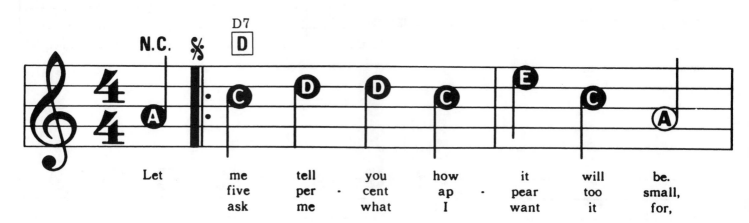

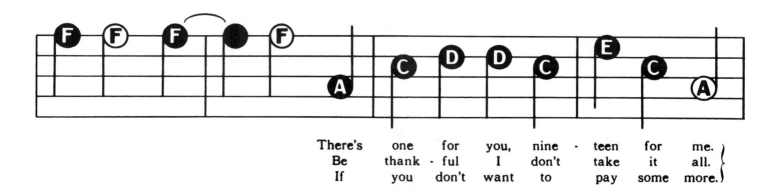

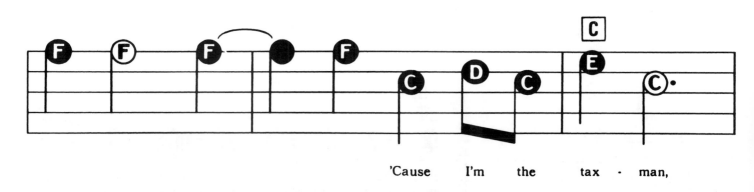

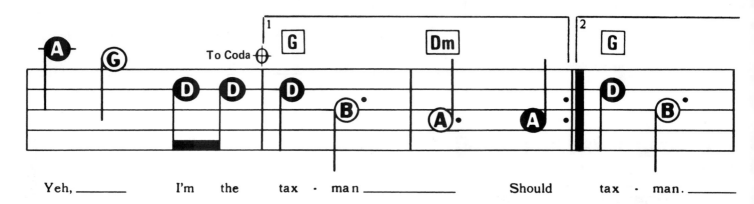

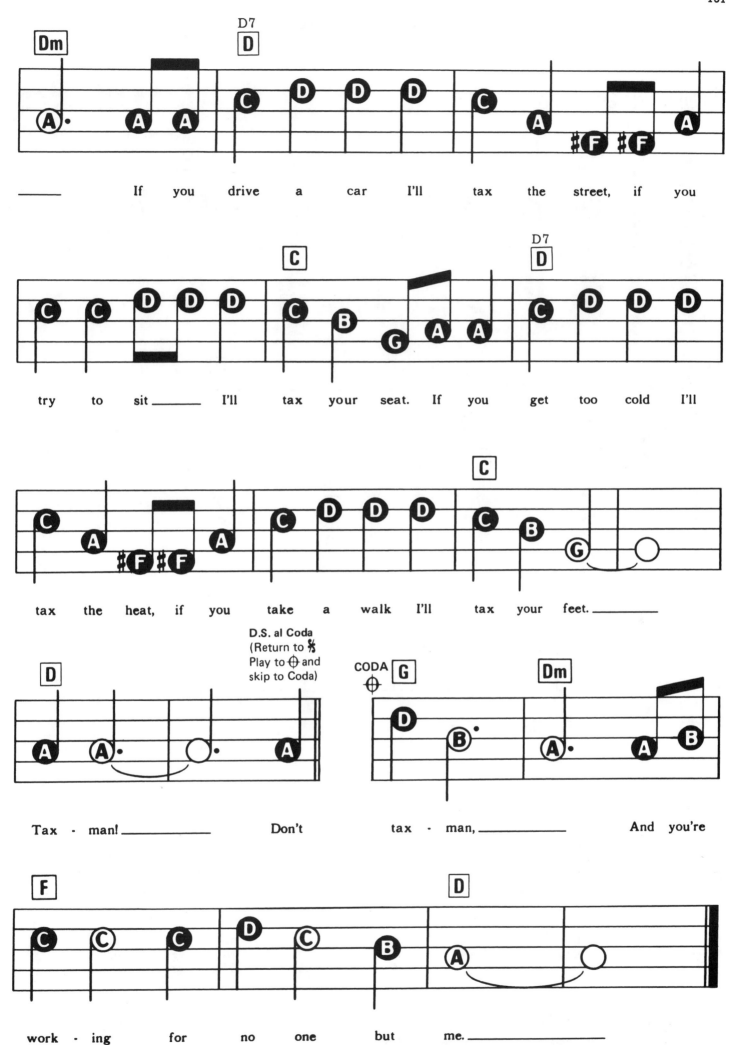

Two of Us

Registration 4
Rhythm: March or Polka

Words and Music by John Lennon
and Paul McCartney

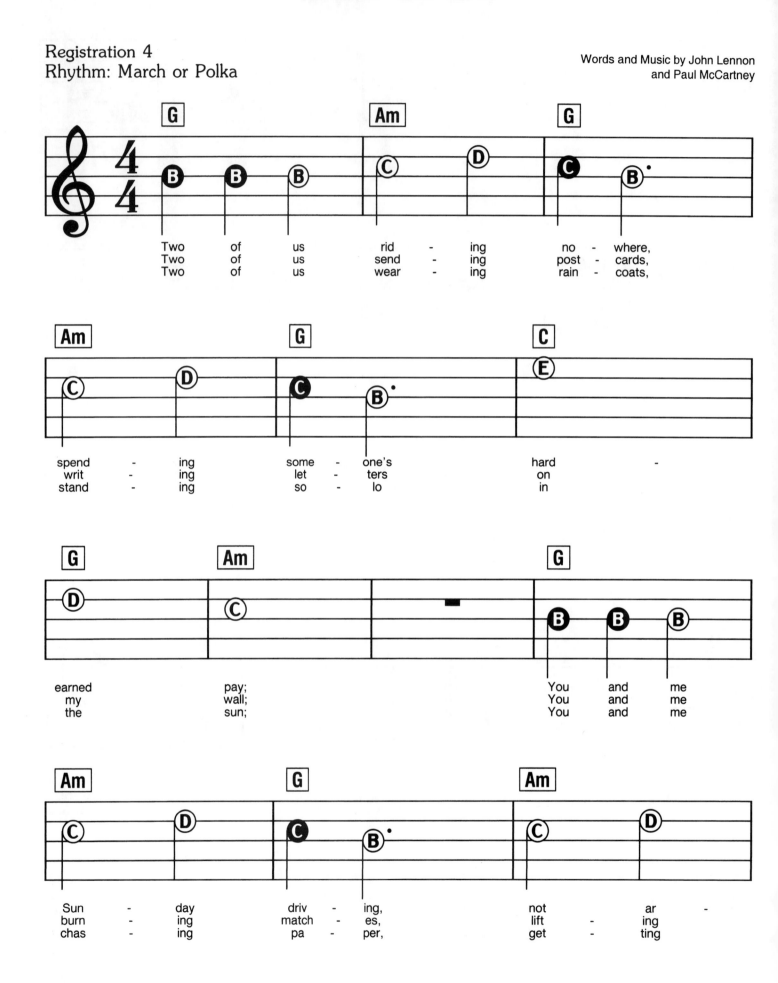

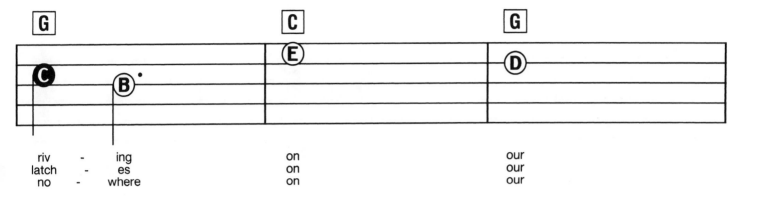

riv - ing   on   our
latch - es   on   our
no - where   on   our

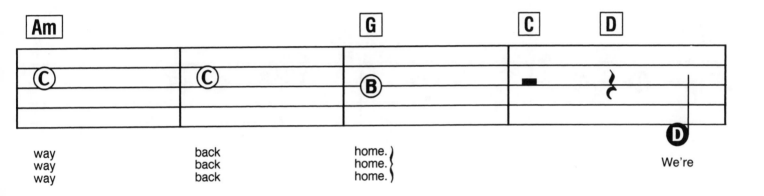

way   back   home.)
way   back   home.{
way   back   home.)   We're

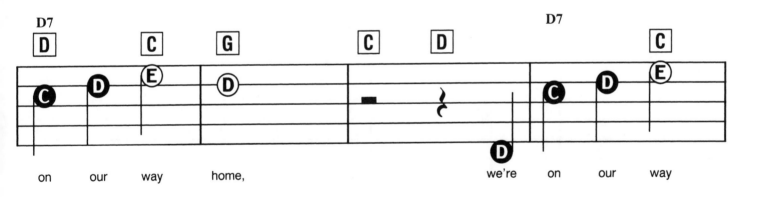

on   our   way   home,   we're   on   our   way

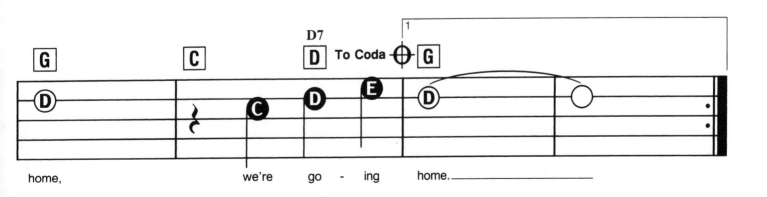

home,   we're   go - ing   home._____

194

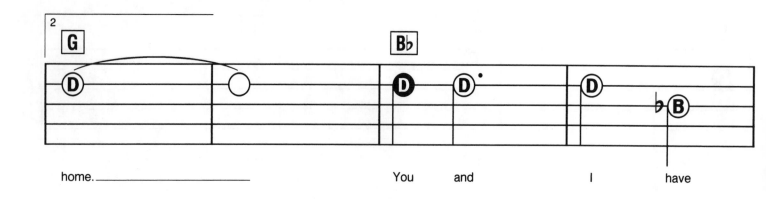

home.   You and I have

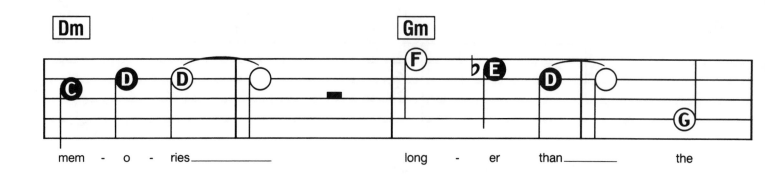

mem - o - ries   long - er than the

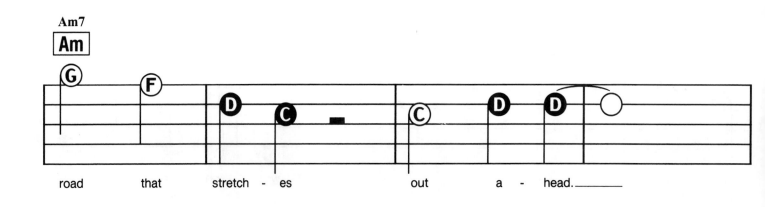

road that stretch - es out a - head.

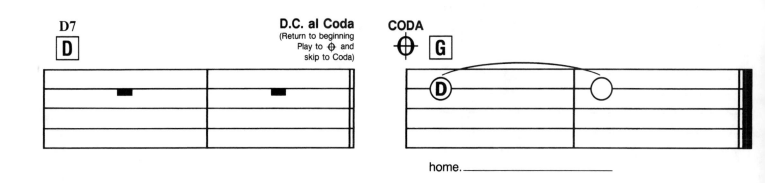

D.C. al Coda
(Return to beginning
Play to ⊕ and
skip to Coda)

CODA

home.

When I'm Sixty-Four

Registration 3
Rhythm: Rock

Words and Music by John Lennon
and Paul McCartney

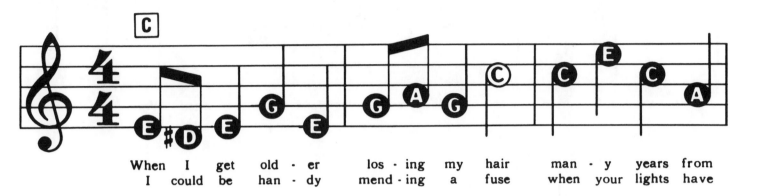

When I get old-er los-ing my hair man-y years from
I could be han-dy mend-ing a fuse when your lights have

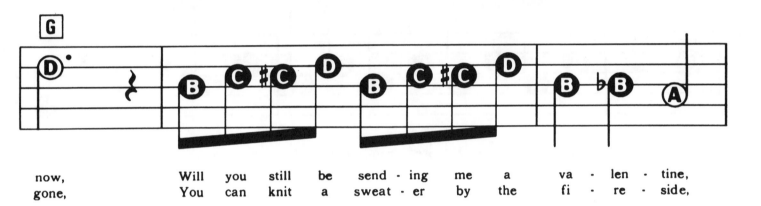

now, Will you still be send-ing me a va-len-tine,
gone, You can knit a sweat-er by the fi-re-side,

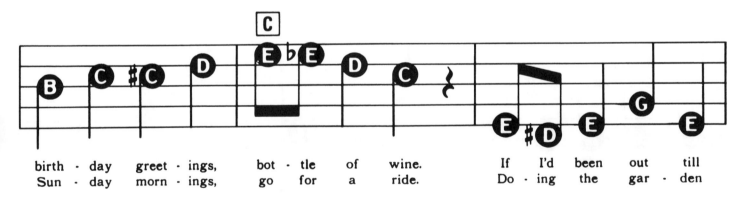

birth-day greet-ings, bot-tle of wine. If I'd been out till
Sun-day morn-ings, go for a ride. Do-ing the gar-den

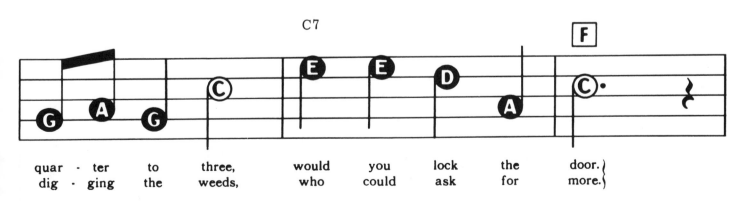

quar-ter to three, would you lock the door.
dig-ging the weeds, who could ask for more.

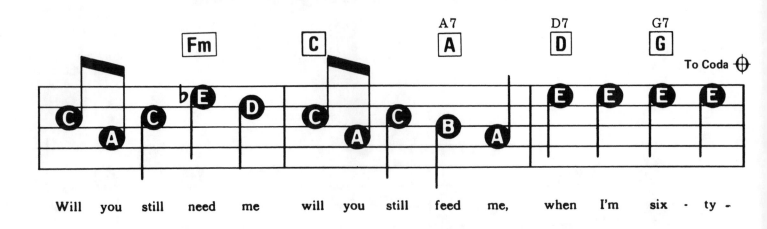

Will you still need me will you still feed me, when I'm six - ty -

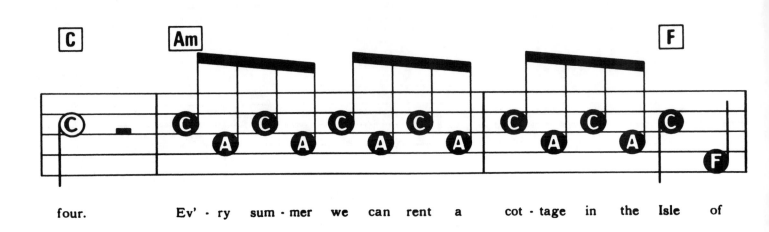

four. Ev' - ry sum - mer we can rent a cot - tage in the Isle of

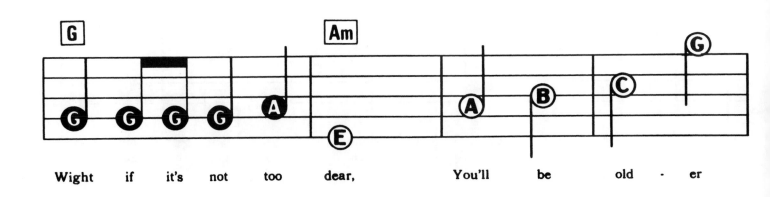

Wight if it's not too dear, You'll be old - er

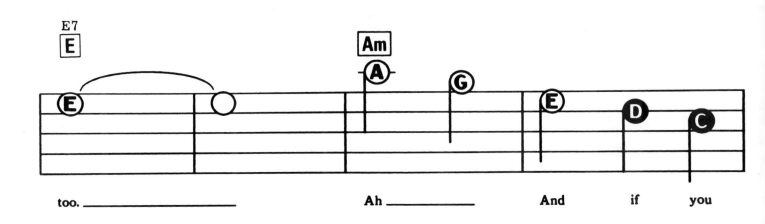

too. _____ Ah _____ And if you

197

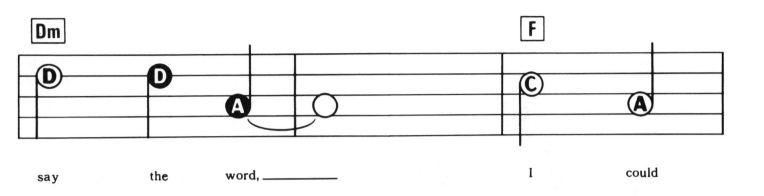

say   the   word, _____   I   could

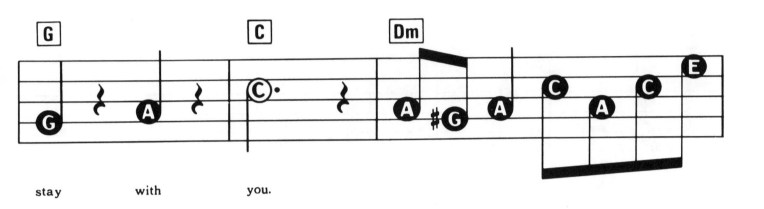

stay   with   you.

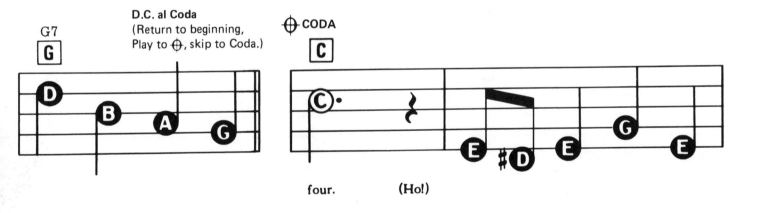

four.   (Ho!)

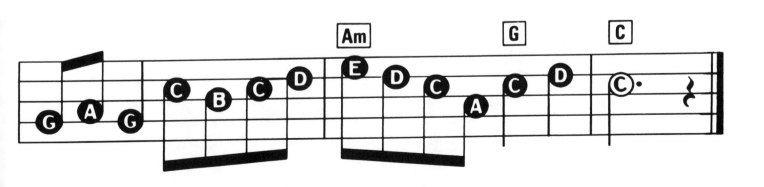

While My Guitar Gently Weeps

198

Registration 7
Rhythm: Rock or Latin

Words and Music by
George Harrison

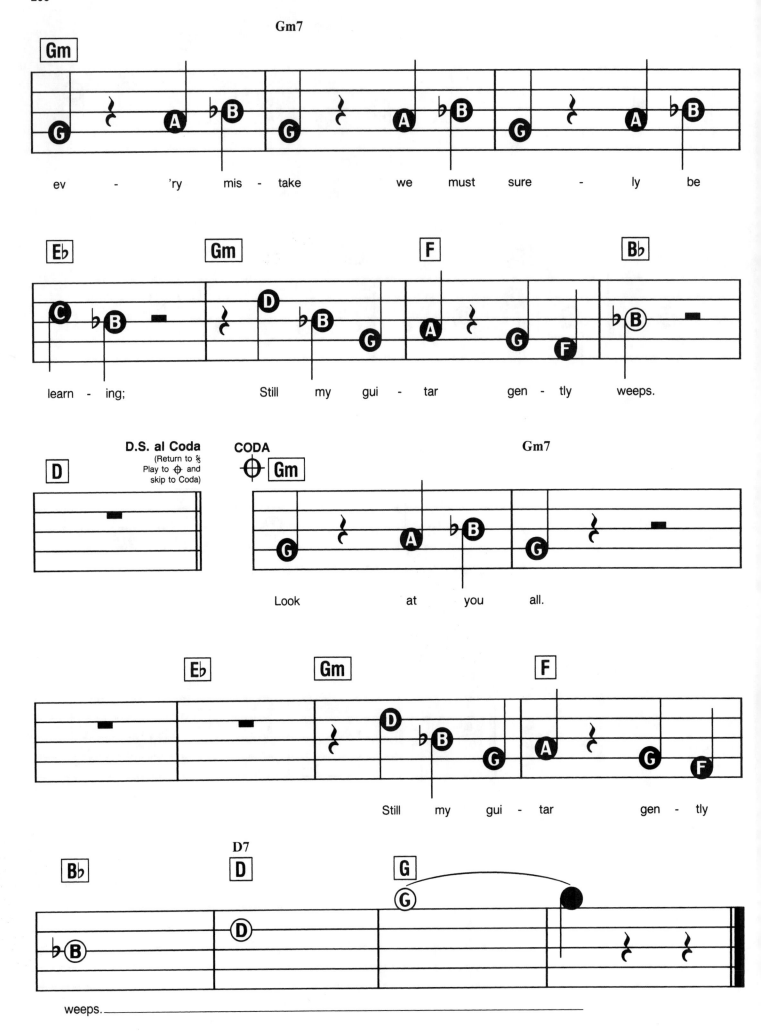

Why Don't We Do It in the Road

Registration 4
Rhythm: Rock

Words and Music by John Lennon
and Paul McCartney

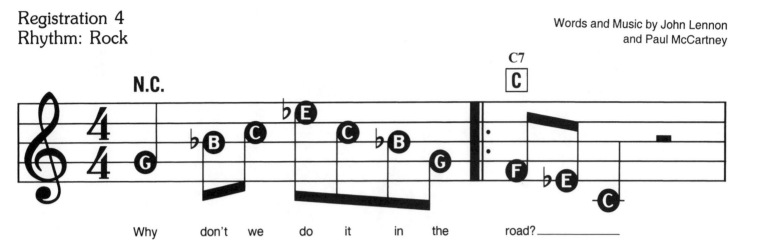

Why don't we do it in the road?_____

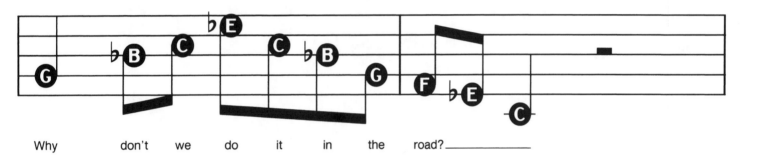

Why don't we do it in the road?_____

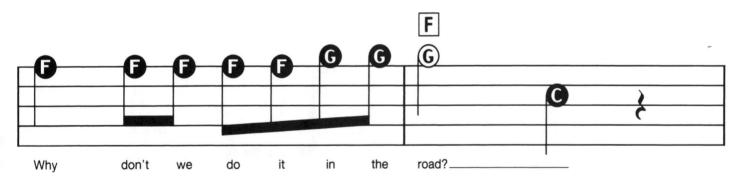

Why don't we do it in the road?_____

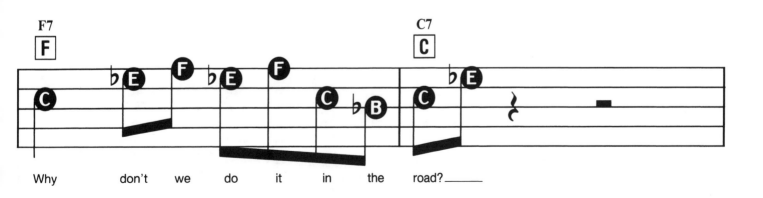

Why don't we do it in the road?_____

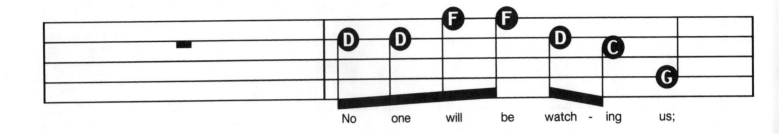

No one will be watch - ing us;

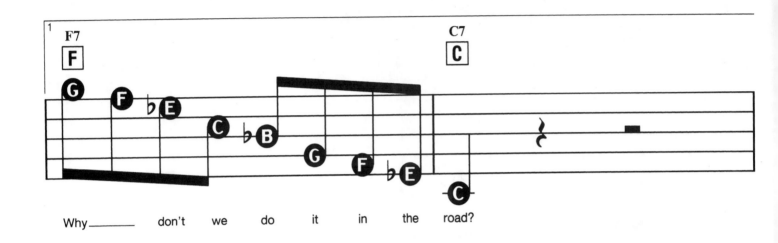

Why____ don't we do it in the road?

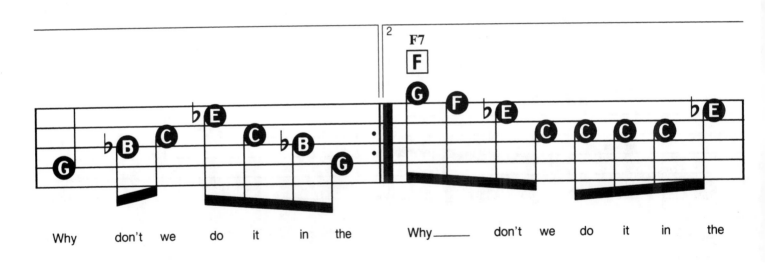

Why don't we do it in the   Why____ don't we do it in the

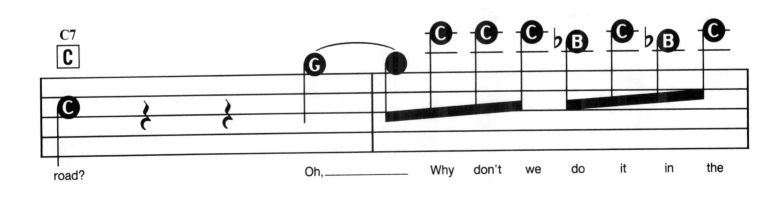

road?   Oh,_____ Why don't we do it in the

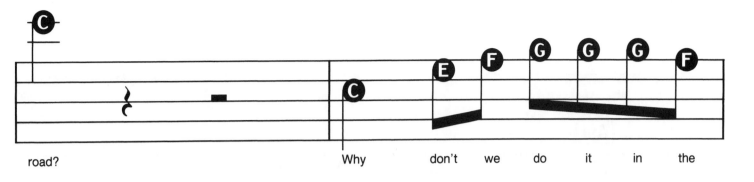

road?

Why don't we do it in the

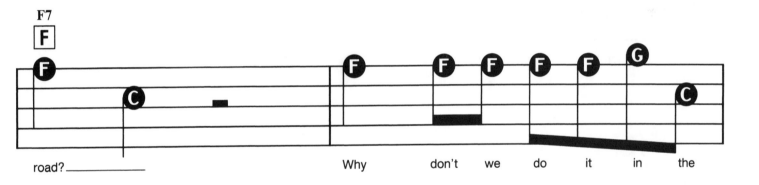

road?_____

Why don't we do it, do it in the

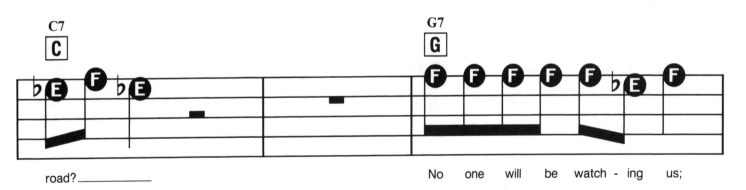

road?_____

Why don't we do it in the

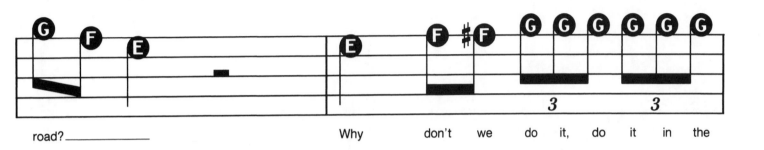

road?_____

No one will be watch-ing us;

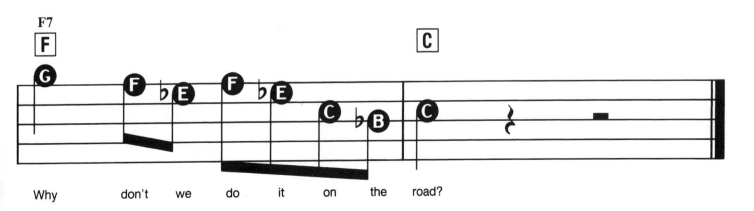

Why don't we do it on the road?

You Never Give Me Your Money

Registration 5
Rhythm: Rock

Words and Music by John Lennon
and Paul McCartney

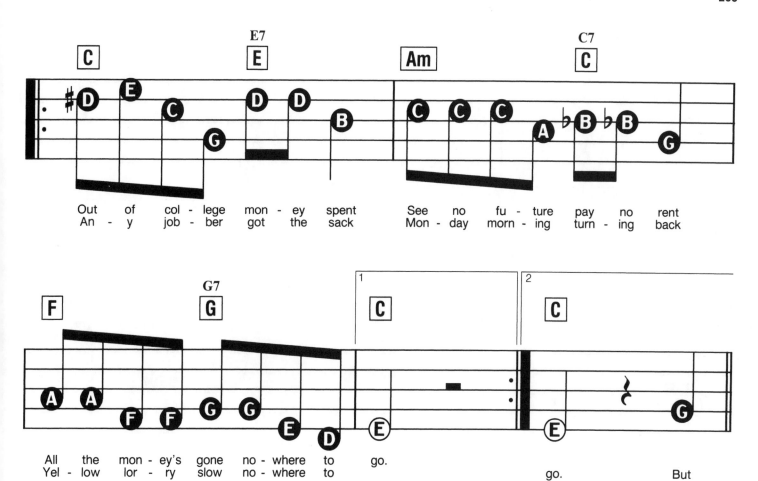

Out of col - lege mon - ey spent
An - y job - ber got the sack
See no fu - ture pay no rent
Mon - day morn - ing turn - ing back

All the mon - ey's gone no - where to go.
Yel - low lor - ry slow no - where to go. But

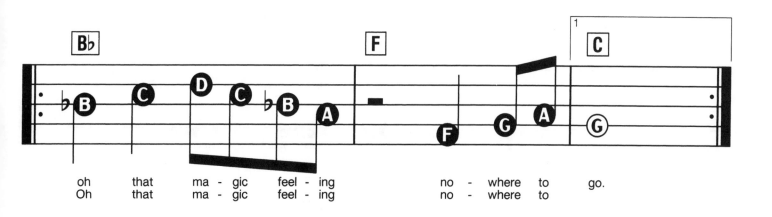

oh that ma - gic feel - ing no - where to go.
Oh that ma - gic feel - ing no - where to

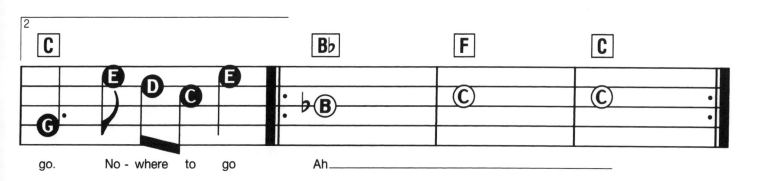

go. No - where to go Ah

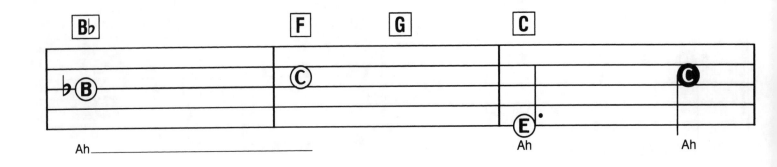

Ah

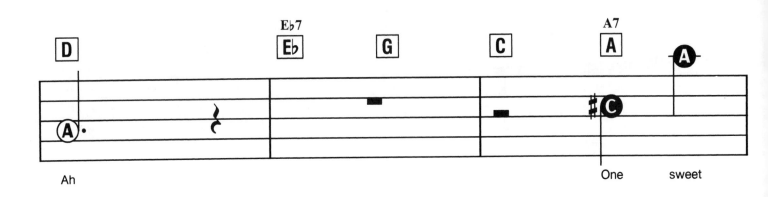

Ah   One   sweet

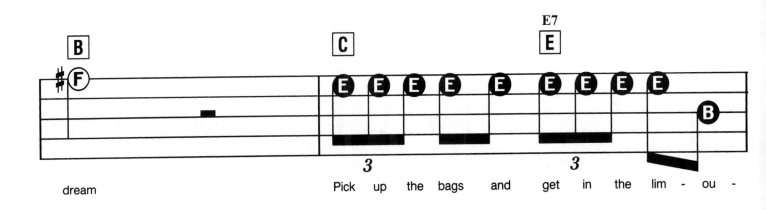

dream   Pick up the bags and   get in the lim - ou -

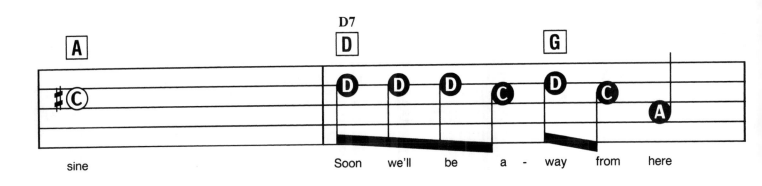

sine   Soon we'll be a - way from here

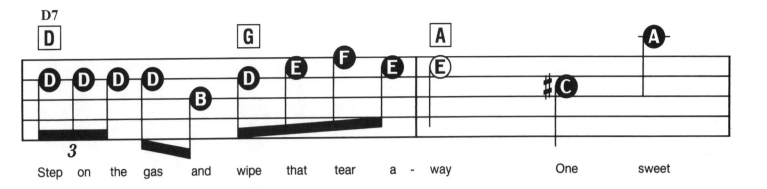

Step on the gas and wipe that tear a - way   One   sweet

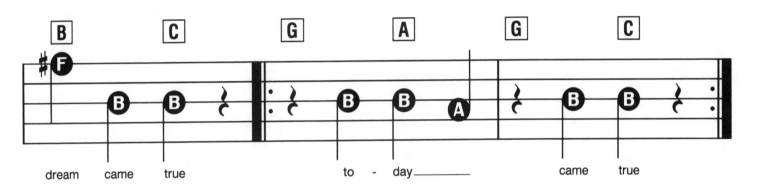

dream   came   true   to - day____   came   true

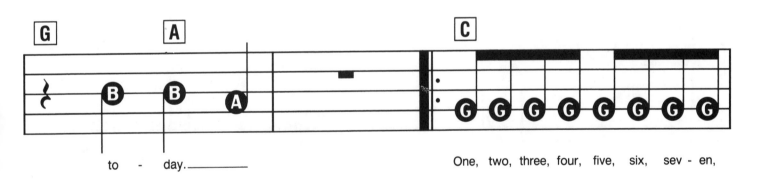

to - day.____   One, two, three, four, five, six, sev - en,

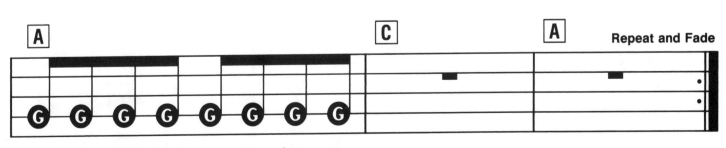

Repeat and Fade

All   good   child - ren   go   to   heav - en.

Your Mother Should Know

Registration 2
Rhythm: Rock or Shuffle

Words and Music by John Lennon
and Paul McCartney

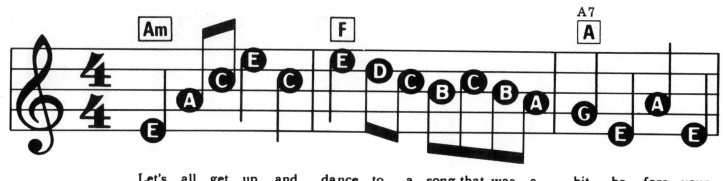

Let's all get up and dance to a song that was a hit be - fore your

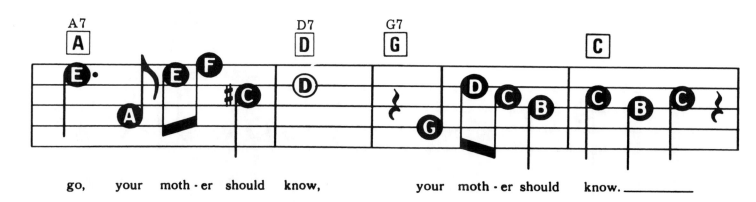

moth - er was born. Though she was born a long, long time a-

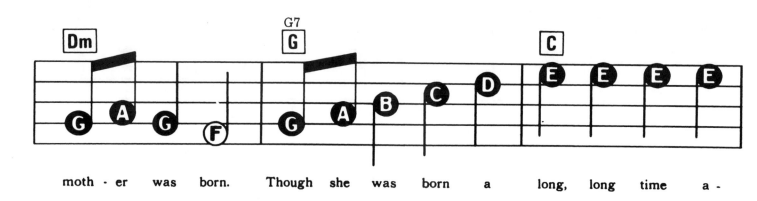

go, your moth - er should know, your moth - er should know._____

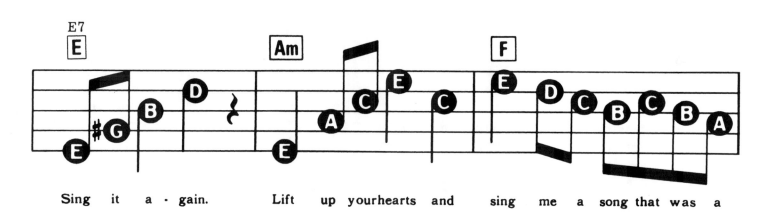

Sing it a - gain. Lift up yourhearts and sing me a song that was a

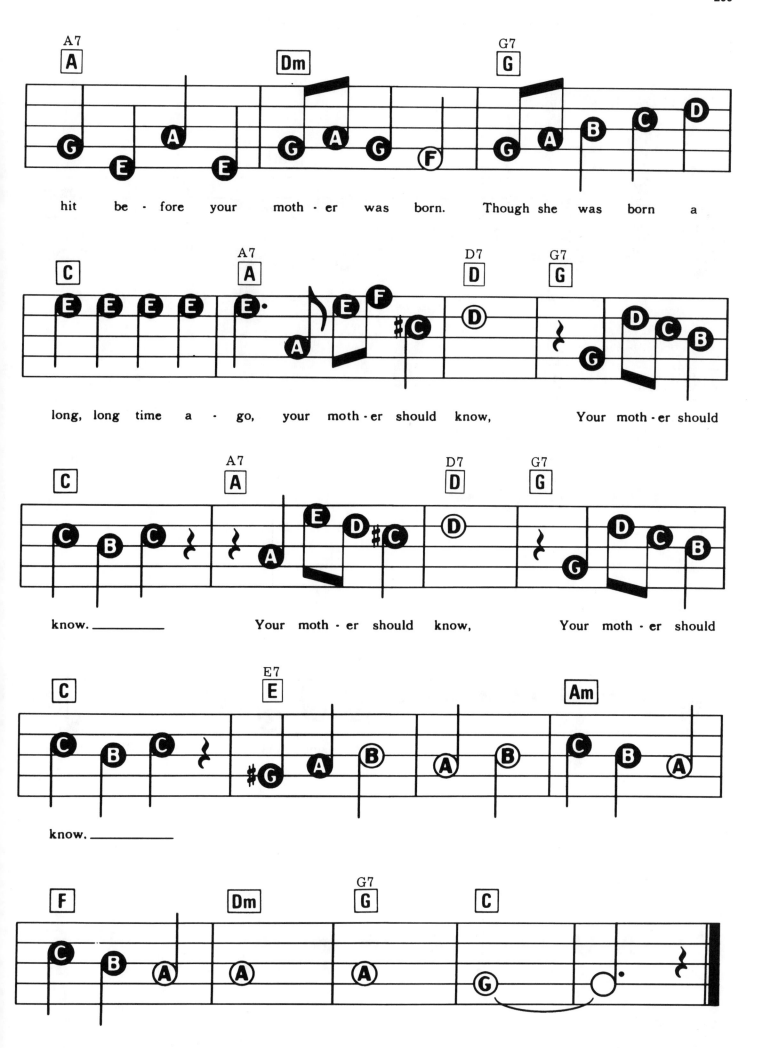

With a Little Help from My Friends

Registration 5
Rhythm: Swing or Shuffle

Words and Music by John Lennon
and Paul McCartney

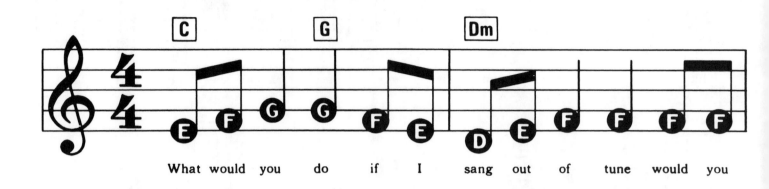

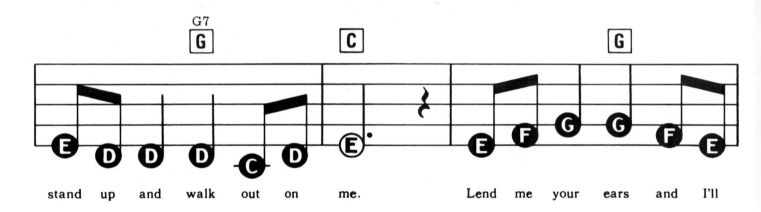

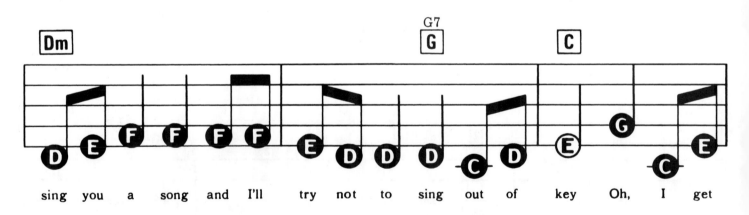

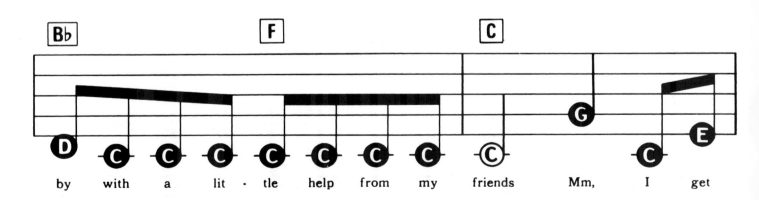

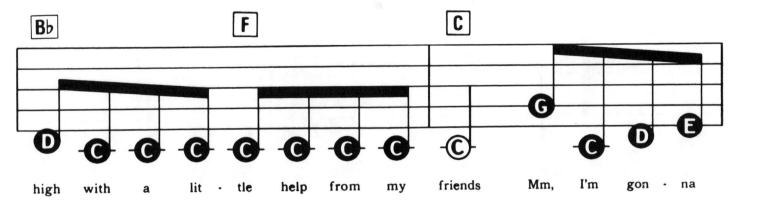

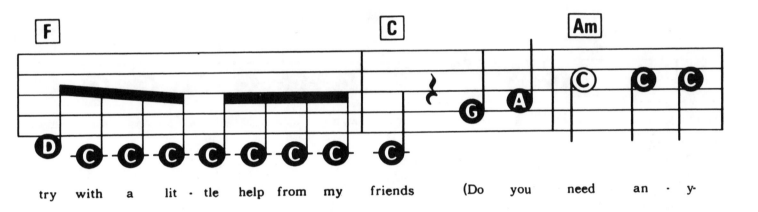

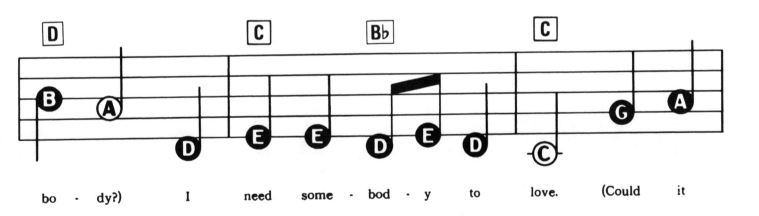

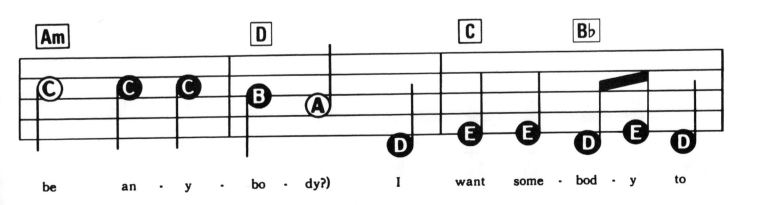